THE FACES OF HONOR

A series of course adoption books on Latin America

SERIES ADVISORY EDITOR: *Lyman L. Johnson,*
University of North Carolina at Charlotte

For a complete list of Diálogos series titles, please visit
unmpress.com

THE FACES OF HONOR

Sex, Shame, and Violence in Colonial Latin America

EDITED BY
LYMAN L. JOHNSON AND SONYA LIPSETT-RIVERA

University of New Mexico Press
Albuquerque

18 17 16 15 14 13   6 7 8 9 10 11

Paperbound ISBN-13: 978-0-8263-1906-7

Library of Congress Cataloging-in-Publication Data

The faces of honor : sex, shame, and violence in Colonial Latin
America / edited by Lyman L. Johnson and Sonya Lipsett-Rivera.
p.   cm. — (Diálogos)
Includes index.
ISBN 0-8263-1924-6 (alk. paper). — ISBN 0-8263-1906-8 (pbk : alk. paper)
1. Honor—Latin America—History.
2. Latin America—Social life and customs.
I. Johnson, Lyman L.
II. Lipsett-Rivera, Sonya, 1961– .
III. Series: Diálogos (Albuquerque, N.M.)
BJ1533.H8F33   1998
306'.098—dc21   98-18974
CIP

For Sue and Sergio

CONTENTS

ILLUSTRATIONS

INTRODUCTION

THE CULTURE OF HONOR

Let us begin our discussion of colonial Latin America's culture of honor with a story from the unsettled and violent period that followed the fall of the Aztec capital of Tenochtitlán in 1521. After defeating the Aztecs, Hernán Cortés led an ambitious new military expedition to the south. When rumors that Cortés and his followers had been killed in battle began to circulate, a violent struggle for power broke out among the men delegated to rule the new colony in the conqueror's absence. According to Francisco López de Gómara, Cortés's secretary, the ambitious and cruel Gonzalo de Salazar proclaimed himself governor and began to imprison his rivals. When Juana de Mansilla, the wife of one of the men who had gone with Cortés, was heard to deny Salazar's claim that Cortés was dead, she was arrested and then publicly whipped like a common criminal. As Gómara makes clear, Salazar's brutal treatment of Juana de Mansilla was intended as a punishment and a public humiliation; he sought to injure both her body and her honor. After Cortés returned and ended the tyranny of Salazar, he attempted to repair Juana de Mansilla's damaged honor, in the words of Gómara, "by carrying her behind him on his horse through Mexico [Mexico City] and addressing her as doña Juana."[1] In the sixteenth century *doña* was the designation for a woman of the nobility, a social status so elevated that the honor of its members was nearly unassailable.

In this incident we see illustrated the public nature of honor. As one modern scholar has defined it, "Honor was more than a set of rules for governing behavior. It was your very being. For in an honor-based culture there was no self-respect independent of the respect of others . . . unless it was confirmed publicly."[2] Salazar had intended to strip Juana de Mansilla of her honor, and the actions of Cortés were intended to repair the injury her honor had received at Salazar's hands. But even these highly public actions by Cortés, the most powerful person in Mexico, could provide no guarantees for the reputation of an individual. Honor was always subject to the court of public opinion. Gómara reminds us of this fact when he ends his discussion of the incident by relating how a humorous rhyme composed after these events deflated Juana de Mansilla's claims to honor by suggesting that, "adding a doña to her name was as absurd as putting a nose on her arm."[3]

The history of colonial Latin America presents us with numerous questions related to understandings of honor. Why, for example, were government officials, Catholic priests, and even university professors in the Spanish and Portuguese colonies so willing to pursue lengthy and expensive law suits and appeals to government authorities in order to gain or protect their right to superior seating arrangements at public festivals? What were the social consequences when members of elite society conceived a child out of wedlock? Could that illegitimate child later enter elite society, gain a favorable marriage, or achieve a successful career? In a culture that defined masculine identity narrowly, could elite status protect the reputation of a man accused of sodomy? Could an artisan or laborer allow himself to be branded a coward or cheat without responding violently? Was it possible for a former slave to assert and defend her honor in court by suing her husband for divorce?

In order to answer these questions about the cultural history of colonial Latin America, we must penetrate the minds of people who lived centuries ago. How did the women and men of these distant societies order their world? What were the rules by which they lived? How was honor defined and defended? Fortunately the answers to these questions are revealed in the documents of the period. By examining lawsuits, criminal cases, and the records of colonial bureaucracies, historians have gained insights into both the formal system of values established by the institutions of church and state and the informal social rules evolved to guide everyday behavior in public and private arenas.

When the Spanish and Portuguese established colonies in the Americas, they brought not only their material culture—technologies, clothes, cuisines, architecture, crops, and animals—but also their affective and intellectual traditions. Among the more important elements of this cultural transfer was the notion of honor. It is impossible to define honor with the precision of a chemical formula or botanical taxonomy; the meaning of honor is and always was situational, located in a specific place and time. Nevertheless the central features of the culture of honor can be confidently asserted. A useful definition of honor has been provided by William Ian Miller:

> Honor is above all the keen sensitivity to the experience of humiliation and shame, a sensitivity manifested by the desire to be envied by others and the propensity to envy the success of others. To simplify greatly, honor is that disposition which makes one act to shame others who have shamed oneself, to humiliate others who have humiliated oneself. The honorable person is one whose self-esteem and social standing is intimately dependent on the esteem or the envy he or she actually elicits in others.[4]

The men and women of colonial Latin America referred to honor constantly in the documents they produced. The culture of honor provided a bedrock set of values that organized their society and their individual lives. Legal codes, social gatherings, seating arrangements at public events, were all imbued with cultural meanings that helped to define status within a system of honor. Men and women, the rich and the humble, had an acute sense of what it meant to live honorably as individuals and families. These claims of honor, however, often provoked challenges, since any claim to individual or family honor was necessarily an attempt to place others in a position of inferiority. As a historian writing about France put it, "[honor] was never secure, required constant reaffirmation, and was always open to challenge."[5]

STATUS AND VIRTUE

In the Iberian world there were two complementary meanings of honor: status and virtue. In fact in Spain and in some Spanish colonies these two distinct, but related, meanings were distinguished by using two different words: *honor*, which refers to the status of an individual, and *honra*, which is synonymous with virtue. The words *honor* and *honra* were present in the Portuguese language as well, but the clear distinction between status and virtue found in Spanish was less clear in everyday Portuguese usage. In Brazil in the colonial era, the word *honra* was the more commonly used, subsuming the concepts of status and virtue; *honor*, when used, was a synonym.

In the Spanish-speaking world, on the other hand, the two words retained some of their representational distinctiveness until the end of the colonial era. A person could be born with or without honor, depending on his or her legitimacy of birth and family status. Those born at the highest levels of society had the greatest honor-status. The inherited attributes of birth conferred both elite status and honor on some while shutting out the great majority of the population. These qualities could seldom be altered, although participation in the Spanish conquest of the Aztec and Inca empires elevated the status of many men from obscure families. Indeed later in the colonial period, great wealth gained through silver mining, the ownership of plantations or large ranches, and commerce often provided access to a status previously monopolized by members of the aristocracy or high functionaries of church and state.

But honra, or honor-virtue, could be won or lost, accumulated or squandered through the actions of an individual or family. Virtue was revealed through conduct; honra was more narrowly reputational than honor. An individual's physical courage, honesty, wealth, occupational skill, and generosity could all confer virtue. Abstaining from activities that stained individual and family honor was also important to a reputation for honra. Any allusion to the promiscuity or immorality of a mother, wife, or daughter was potentially devastating to the reputation of an individual man or a family. Treason, cowardice, homosexuality, or gross criminality were similarly viewed as taints on the reputations of both an individual and his or her family.

Before the establishment of colonies in the Americas, Spanish law, in particular the medieval code Las Siete Partidas, had defined certain occupations and forms of conduct that barred families and individuals from claiming honor. Most artisan occupations and even retail commerce were viewed as dishonorable in early modern Spain and Portugal. In the first essay in this collection, Mark Burkholder demonstrates that these prejudices against manual labor and, to a lesser extent, participation in trade, were transferred to the colonies. Men who joined gangs of robbers, who were strolling minstrels, pimps, or charlatans, men who fought animals or other men for money (bullfighters and pugilists), and usurers were all defined by these ancient codes as lacking honor. Conviction for sodomy, forgery, adultery, theft, bribery, and treason could also strip an individual of honor. For women the code defined certain sexual conduct as dishonoring: adultery and the initiation of a sexual relationship or remarriage within a year after a husband's death, for example, were defined as dishonorable.[6] These and other Iberian legal and customary practices provided the foundation for colonial understandings of honor. Once transferred to the Western Hemisphere, the system of honor rooted in the historical experiences of Spain and Portugal would be modified by the cultural and ethnic diversity of the colonies and the later economic and social transformations of the Atlantic world that followed the development of capitalism.

The kings of Spain and Portugal and their political representatives had the potential to augment the honor of an individual or family by granting titles of nobility and high positions in the government or by providing positions of honor in public gatherings. These forms of public preferment and the privileges they conferred gave weight to an individual's claims to honor. They represented a nearly irrefutable acknowledgment of individual and family honor. But these reputational achievements carried burdens as well. Since honor was achieved competitively, and the elevation of one person or family was viewed as a defeat by others who sought these distinctions, every social advance predictably excited the hostility of rivals, as is well illustrated in the story used by Ann Twinam to begin her essay.

In addition Iberian notions of honor were closely tied to a hierarchical conception of family background expressed through the concept of *limpieza de sangre,* or purity of blood. In the early modern societies of Spain and Portugal, individual reputation was largely inherited from one's ancestors. Any Jewish, New Christian (converted Jewish), or Muslim ancestors were viewed as stains on a family's bloodline. The illegitimacy of an ancestor or any prosecution of an ancestor by the Inquisition also damaged the reputation of a family. Once known these perceived stains severely affected career and social advancement, educational opportunity, and marriage prospects for family members for generations.

The Iberian culture of honor was transferred to the Western Hemisphere with the founding Spanish and Portuguese colonies. With the passage of time, this culture was adapted to New World realities that included the presence of indigenous and, through the slave trade, African cultures. In the colonies the discriminatory racial and cultural exclusions traditionally associated with the concept of limpieza de sangre were expanded to include new groups of presumed social inferiors—Indians, Africans, and later, mixed populations. The uniform enforcement of these discriminations, however, proved difficult. With the passage of time, miscegenation (the mixing of races) and assimilation (the acceptance of Christianity and Spanish and Portuguese languages by non-European populations) blurred cultural and racial boundaries associated with limpieza de sangre. Nevertheless the ideals of "purity of blood" and legitimacy remained fundamental concerns for members of the colonial elite, as is illustrated in the essays by Burkholder, Twinam, and Muriel Nazzari in this collection. The colonial elite never wavered in its public insistence that honor was uniquely associated with European and Christian origins.

In addition to these very useful historical sources, the authors in this collection also rely on the theoretical work of scholars interested in other places and times or grounded in other academic disciplines. The study of honor often overlaps the boundary between the disciplines of history and anthropology; the work of anthropologist Julian Pitt-Rivers on honor in the Mediterranean cultural context remains one of the most influential efforts to define its elusive qualities.[7] It remains today one of the best elaborations of the hues and shades of honor and provides an important conceptual starting point for many of the authors represented in this book. Nevertheless the authors collected here demonstrate clearly that there is no single theory or definition that can be used uncritically when discussing honor in colonial Latin America. As Ann Twinam forcefully argues in her essay, "Different historical sources, at different times and places, will give different definitions and descriptions of honor; these differences need to be acknowledged and clarified." This book begins that difficult but exciting task.

HONOR AND ANONYMITY

The successful installation of Iberian political institutions, architectural forms, and technologies combined with the spread of Christianity and the Spanish (or Portuguese) language to create a cultural medium for the transfer and later adaptation of Iberian values and beliefs, including the culture of honor. But the open spaces of the Americas and the greater physical mobility of both men and women in the colonies loosened the traditional European connection between family status and reputation and the culture of honor. The colonial societies of the Americas were, put simply, more anonymous than the societies of contemporary Spain and Portugal. Therefore, because colonial communities lacked the intense collective memories of older European communities, administrative authorities and the courts often became arbiters of questions related to honor.

As the colonial societies of Latin America matured, the culture of honor spread across a highly heterogeneous colonial social landscape. Unfortunately most academic discussions have failed to acknowledge that definitions of honor may have changed from one colonial region to another or with the passage of time. Were understandings of honor the same in colonial Brazil as in colonial Cuba or Mexico? Were they the same in 1520 as in 1820? The authors collected in this book argue that the values and behaviors associated with the culture of honor not only pierced class boundaries in colonial Latin America, spreading from the elite to the plebeian class, but that the culture of honor was modified over time in response to the development of distinctive regional cultures. It is for this reason that the reader will notice small differences in the definitions and analytical categories used by the authors in this collection.

As the definition of honor provided earlier by William Ian Miller suggests, in an honor culture an individual's value and status are essentially reputational.

Without confirmation by society, an individual's claim to honor is unsustainable. The pursuit of honor, therefore, necessarily leads to disputes and sometimes to violence. Within every class or cultural cohort of colonial Latin America, honor had to be asserted and defended. If a person's claims were rejected by peers, his or her position in society was put at risk.

It is for this reason that claims to honor in colonial Latin America were often acknowledged in highly public and ritualized ways. Invited attendance at public ceremonies, seating arrangements in churches or theaters, the order in which artisan guilds marched in public ceremonies, and invitations to private homes all served as filters for the mediation of claims to honor. Within these and other social contexts, men and women assented to the claims of the more powerful by deferring to their opinions, by taking off their hats or bowing their heads, or by addressing them in an especially respectful and reverent manner. Any alteration in these arrangements and forms could place the reputation of an individual or family at risk.

From their beginnings the societies of colonial Latin America were organized hierarchically. Historians who have studied the conquistadors and early colonial elites have long acknowledged the importance of honor in explaining the behaviors of these powerful groups. Among royal officials and the Catholic clergy, a prickly concern for reputation and advancement led to innumerable conflicts. Diego de Almagro's sense of shame when denied what he believed was his proper share of the booty collected after the defeat and capture of the Inca ruler Atahualpa by his partner Francisco Pizarro eventually led to the violent deaths of both Almagro and Pizarro and a decade of civil war in Peru. As colonial society matured, elite concern with honor would lose this highly sanguinary character. Nevertheless elite passion for honor would continue to be manifested in duels, lawsuits, an enthusiasm for family genealogies, and a scrupulous concern for the selection of appropriate marriage partners for one's children.

HONOR AND FICTION

Members of Latin America's colonial elite were born within honorable families and were educated to take their places at the pinnacle of these societies. If they followed the rules and lived blameless but not necessarily inhibited lives, they could die without any stains upon their reputation or their social status. This traditional Hispanic vision of honor is revealed, indeed celebrated, in many classic works of literature, such as *Don Juan Tenorio, Don Quixote,* or the works of Juan Ruiz de Alarcón. These dramatic works, which glorify the chivalric tradition, highlight the powerful drives of young men who wished to seduce virgins to enhance their reputation and the desperation of fathers who tried to protect the virginity of their daughters and thus the family honor.

Tales of betrayal and redemption dramatically brought to life the daily struggle of remaining true to the ideals of the culture of honor. But did these works of literature have anything to do with reality? In fact, as Melveena McKendrick argues elsewhere and as Richard Boyer demonstrates in his essay in this collection, authors of the period would have their readers believe that honor was a brittle and fragile thing, when in fact it was dynamic and malleable.[8] Honor once compromised could often be repaired or defended after the fact. As the authors in this volume make clear, the Catholic church, Spanish and Portuguese administrative practices, and individuals all contrived convenient fictions to remedy the effects of dishonorable behavior. Both Twinam and Nazzari indicate that illegitimate children could be raised in their parents' households disguised as foster children; the monarch could order the eradication of an illegitimate birth generations after the fact; and an ambitious and successful person of mixed race could purchase a document that created the legal fiction of European racial identity.

These literary representations, therefore, contributed to the creation of a romanticized idea of honor—a flattering fiction that the elites of colonial Latin America found convenient to believe. Despite the relatively humble origins of most immigrants to the Spanish and Portuguese colonies in America, those of their descendants who became the emerging elite claimed that only they were imbued with honor, as the pinnacle of Latin American colonial society. Honor, their myth affirmed, existed only at the highest level of society. Everyone else, from the middle classes of small merchants and artisans to the lowest social ranks inhabited by bound laborers and slaves, regardless of merit, could not claim to have honor. From the perspective of nobles, high-ranked bureaucrats, and other members of the colonial aristocracy, the idea of honor in the lower ranks was unthinkable, if not outrageous. For the wealthy and powerful, the men and women of the lower ranks were unalterably tainted by illegitimacy, racial impurity, and low habits.

HONOR AND CLASS

It was the privileged material basis of elite life that sustained this narrow and self-absorbed social perspective. Wealth allowed the elite to surround itself with the external trappings of honor—rich garments, servants, and carriages. Wealth could purchase privacy as well. In their daily lives, the better off members of colonial society were generally shielded from the physical jostling and verbal challenges of street and marketplace. They lived in large homes with high exterior walls and traveled through the streets in carriages or sedan chairs, sometimes protected by liveried servants. Because legitimacy, marriage, and untainted lineage were generally well documented for members of the elite (and most representatives of colonial middle groups as well), they had an easier time asserting and maintaining claims to honor than did plebeians. Moreover wealthy and powerful men and women were insulated from many of the common threats to honor experienced by the poor. If accused of crimes, members of the *gente decente,* a term used for the elite and middle groups, were seldom incarcerated in prison with common criminals. If found guilty, they were almost never whipped or subjected to other forms of humiliating corporal punishment. As Geoffrey Spurling illustrates in his essay in this collection, the seventeenth-century Peruvian cleric accused of sodomy, Dr. Gaspar González de Sosa, did not suffer as much as did his lower-class lovers. Instead an alliance of elite family members, colleagues, and friends worked to protect his position in the church, even though they disapproved of his lifestyle.

Many attacks upon honor occurred in the public arena. Only the elite could afford the privacy to hide and cover up their shame, but even they had to face gossip and insults when they left the protection of their homes. When honorable women went into the street, they shielded themselves with a cloak of privacy by wearing clothes that hid them in colors that did not attract attention and by moving in a self-effacing manner. If they were particularly wealthy, they only walked out with servants and slaves and thus took the mantle of home and honor with them. Yet even so, they faced potential insults, gossip, and other stains upon their good name. If such elite women were not immune from attacks upon their honor, how much more difficult must it have been for women and men of the lower classes?

While plebeians were forced to deal directly with any insult or challenge to their honor, members of the elite could repair injuries to their honor by successfully petitioning for official redress in documents called *gracias al sacar.* Wealth and high position were generally the key to gaining one of these useful dispensations, since royal officials were more likely to respond to petitioners who could lubricate the legal process with gifts and bribes. Commonly purchased or arranged through powerful connections, these documents smoothed over potentially embarrassing problems that could bar access to high governmental positions, such as the illegitimacy of an applicant or one of his ancestors. Even questions of limpieza de sangre, such as a New Christian, Indian, or African ancestor might be overcome through gracias al sacar. As suggested by the experience of Juana de Mansilla, however, neither the support of a powerful figure like Cortés nor a document of gracias al sacar could always protect the wealthy and powerful from ridicule.

The lives of the rich were certainly different from those of the poor in colonial Latin America, and the wealthiest and most powerful members of these societies believed that only they could have or defend honor. Members of the colonial elite, therefore, were quick to dismiss claims to honor made by a small-town shopkeeper, an immigrant artisan, or a mixed-race woman. Many modern historians have uncritically followed these elite prejudices. However, as the essays collected in this book show, there is strong historical evidence to suggest that members of middle and plebeian classes asserted and defended their claims to honor as well, despite the contemptuous resistance of presumed social betters. These essays, then, represent an effort to broaden and expand the discussion of honor, tracing its values and behaviors across the remarkably diverse social landscape of colonial society.

The historical evidence shows that men and women in the bottom ranks of society were very much concerned with their social positions and commonly differentiated among themselves on the basis of income, gender, race, occupation, and family status. These differences often served as proxies for honor, arranging both individuals and families of the plebeian class in a hierarchy of presumed merit. Members of the colonial nobility and the economic elite usually ignored this complex cultural geography, seeing only an undifferentiated plebeian class.

As Douglas Cope has shown in his study of seventeenth-century Mexico, plebeian visions of racial identity and class were much more subtle and fluid than those formulated by the elite.[9] As a result the sense of individual and collective identities among plebeians could not easily be forced into the tight categories used by the colonial bureaucracy or represented by contemporary social theorists. Plebeians could alter their identities, moving across racial and social categories as circumstances allowed. A good marriage, good fortune in business or employment, an official position within a town council, or a change of towns could all help to transform the way those at the bottom of the social ladder saw themselves and their neighbors.

How could honor have become important to a class defined as lacking the birth, race, and wealth necessary to the workings of the Iberian culture of honor? As is suggested in the essays by Boyer, Lyman Johnson, Sonya Lipsett-Rivera, and Sandra Lauderdale Graham, plebeians especially coveted a reputation for honor, because the economic and political vulnerability of their lives put them in perilously close proximity to squalor, forced labor, prostitution, and illegitimacy. A good reputation, even a reputation for violently defending oneself against insult, helped to create a valuable defense against submersion into the class of desperate beggars and prostitutes that infested colonial cities or the class of bound laborers that peopled the countryside.

As Arlette Farge showed in her study of the Parisian poor, people with limited means depended upon the cooperation of their neighbors, who sometimes provided small amounts of credit to help them through periods of unemployment or high prices.[10] If a plebeian lost his or her claim to honor, he or she could no longer count upon relatives, neighbors, and workmates to grant them credit for food, raw materials for their trades, or housing. In fact Lauderdale Graham argues that Henriqueta, a poor black woman in Rio de Janeiro, underwent an extremely lengthy court case simply to disassociate her reputation from that of her husband, thereby preserving her honor and therefore her credit. For those living at the margins of colonial society, reputation was their capital. Plebeians did not enjoy the reputational insulation provided by great wealth and did not have the capacity to erase transgressions through expensive lawsuits or lengthy appeals to colonial administrators.

The essays by Boyer, Johnson, Lipsett-Rivera, and Lauderdale Graham also demonstrate that blacks, Indians, and people of mixed race eventually came to assert and defend essential elements of the culture of honor in public ways. Even when plebeian men and women avoided the explicit use of the word *honor* in order to escape the ridicule of judges, colonial administrators, and other powerful members of the elite, they made unambiguous references to the values and behaviors traditionally associated with honor. Because they believed that life without honor was unlivable, these men and women of humble circumstances struck out with fists or knives, lawsuits or petitions when a rival or enemy sought to strip them of their honor, despite the dangers of incarceration or worse.

Because the lives of the elite and plebeians were so different, the reactions of these groups to any challenge to personal honor tended to differ as well. Wealthy members of society were trained to value restraint and, as a result, they were likely to act behind the scenes, using the courts or the bureaucracy to try to repair any damage to their reputations or threats to their honor. When members of the elite used violence to defend their honor, this violence commonly occurred within the highly regulated and closely supervised format of the duel. As Boyer, Johnson, and Lipsett-Rivera demonstrate, plebeians were much more spontaneous in their responses to an assault on their honor, often immediately lashing out with fists or weapons when challenged or insulted.

But this generalization should not be pushed too far. Many plebeians also used the courts when they believed their honor had been offended, especially when the author of the offense was a social superior. Or, as Lauderdale Graham illustrates in her essay, the courts were employed when differences in physical strength or social power disarmed the cultural expectation that wounded honor required a blood revenge. Women and older or disabled men were not expected to physically challenge a stronger or younger tormentor who slandered or ridiculed them. Although there were numerous exceptions to this rough outline of elite and plebeian protocols for the protection of honor, the historical record does make clear that the groups located at both ends of the social spectrum found the means to express their anxieties and rage when honor was threatened.

The essays collected here also overturn the notion of a passive feminine participation in the culture of honor. As the traditional literature on honor points out, the behavior of women, particularly in terms of their sexuality, was a central concern to the honor of their fathers, husbands, and brothers. But women valued their own and their family's reputations independently as well. Women did not necessarily wait for their fathers, brothers, or other males to defend their honor. Instead individual women or women acting with kinswomen or friends mobilized to protect their reputations through the legal system or, on occasion, with the use of violence. As Nazzari documents in her essay, elite women in colonial Brazil sometimes conspired to hide unwanted pregnancies and avoid damage to their own, or a relative's, reputation by placing illegitimate children with foster parents. Plebeian women had fewer resources and less privacy and, as Lipsett-Rivera recounts, were more likely to use the desperate act of infanticide to protect individual and family reputations. Both upper- and lower-class women could also be provoked to use violence, physical intimidation, or insults to protect their good names from injury. Although arguing or fighting in a public place might have been generally condemned as unfeminine in colonial society, verbal confrontations and violence often proved an effective means of protecting a woman's honor.

If these essays give us a new way to see the women of colonial Latin America—as active agents in the creation and defense of their own identities—they shed new light upon their male contemporaries as well. Masculine violence is too often dismissed as rooted in biology or as the natural outcome of machismo.[11] Yet the angry masculine confrontations that often led to fist fights or, less often, to the use of more deadly weapons in colonial Latin America were commonly framed by the desire to defend personal honor or the honor of family.

Since masculine culture permitted, even encouraged, the use of insults, taunts, and practical jokes to forge friendships or establish the hierarchies of work and leisure, the potential for violence was nearly always present among plebeian men. Peace was maintained by the careful inculcation of rules that guided the interaction of men across the fault lines of colonial society: wealth, age, skill, occupation, color, and physical strength. When transgressors crossed these nearly invisible boundaries, explosions of violence could occur. In these aggressive contests, men sometimes effectively feminized an enemy or rival by forcing him to accept a passive or subordinate role. Once humiliated in this manner, the defeated male was stripped of his honor among peers. The essays of Spurling and Johnson both illustrate the complex ways in which concepts of masculinity and honor were intermixed. Across class boundaries, men used insults and jokes to express their contempt for men who failed to meet masculine expectations. Homosexuals, as in the case of Dr. González, whom Spurling examines, or cowards, as revealed in the violent confrontations among Buenos Aires artisans described by Johnson, commonly found life difficult indeed. We hope that our readers will agree that the internal logic of colonial Latin America's masculine culture is clarified by our use of the culture of honor as a magnifying lens.

HONOR AND HIERARCHY

The societies of colonial Latin America had inherited from the founding Iberian cultures the belief that honor emanated from the top of the imperial order, a hierarchy that began with God and flowed through the monarch and the nobility to the commoners. Beggars were as much a part of this natural order as were noblemen. Both church and state taught that God had created the colonial social order and that social justice was the maintenance of divine intentions. Colonial Latin American society was certainly much more hierarchical than the society we inhabit. The conquest of indigenous peoples and the African slave trade further elaborated and strengthened the social hierarchy inherited from Europe. In a social universe where whites were presumed the natural rulers of nonwhites and men were legally and culturally expected to rule their households, conceptions of honor were necessarily informed by these hierarchical assumptions. But colonial society only imperfectly imitated these ideals of race, class, and gender.

Social place and identity were slippery questions, but they were central to notions of honor. Although the social categories of class, race, and gender were asserted or assigned as if their meanings were unchangeable, the following essays provide numerous examples where social position was bitterly contested. A person's appearance, such as their race, clothes, jewelry, and even hairstyle, frequently offered reliable clues as to individual status and claims to honor; but even race, the most fixed of these characteristics, sometimes proved alterable.

Clearly an individual's social position could change during his or her life as income, marriage status, occupation, and social networks altered.[12] Individuals, therefore, could ascend or descend a social ladder where the gradations were very subtle and subject to differing interpretations.

Social place also had a local character, with each city and region evolving distinct hierarchies of reputation and prestige. Thus within relatively small groups of people (sometimes numbered only in the hundreds or thousands), the reputation and social status of individuals were established or contested. When people moved from one place to another, as from one class to another, they would commonly have to assert and defend their claim to honor and their social status anew. As a result, the vulnerability and fluidity of personal identities in colonial Latin America required eternal vigilance in the defense of honor. Except for the wealthiest and most powerful members of the nobility, personal honor had to be carefully reconstructed with every entry into a new social environment.

THE FACES OF HONOR

As with other cultural phenomena, the ideas and social codes associated with honor do not easily conform to the chronological categories imposed by political history. The Latin American culture of honor was strongest and most widely embraced during the colonial period, when the ideas of social discrimination based on race, class, and gender were viewed as natural and, indeed, divinely sanctioned. With independence and the emergence of the democratic political values and ideals of citizenship associated with republicanism, the culture of honor was slowly transformed. Initially the more egalitarian political culture of the postcolonial era promoted recognition by the elite of plebeian claims to honor, claims previously frustrated by colonial social prejudice. The constitutional dignity of citizenship was, after all, the political articulation of essential elements of the colonial code of honor. Despite these changes it is striking that the passion for honor that Boyer found motivating the actions of plebeians in seventeenth-century Mexico is so similar in content to that found by Lauderdale Graham in a divorce action brought by a former slave in nineteenth-century Brazil.

The code of honor that played such an important role in organizing the societies of colonial Latin America may seem antiquated to readers who live in a society without an aristocracy, a society that celebrates social mobility and entertains itself with the confessional deluge of daytime TV. But the history of the United States has also been influenced in consequential ways by the culture of honor. The antebellum South provides historians with one of the best examples of the connections between a concern for honor and violence. Bertram Wyatt-Brown's explorations of masculine violence in the American South has clearly shown that a prickly defensiveness in the face of insult was, if anything, more highly developed there than in the Iberian colonies of Latin America. Measured by the thousands of duels that settled questions of honor among elite males and the even more common fights with knives, clubs, and fists that resulted from the offended honor of more humble men, the culture of honor reached its most sanguinary expression in the American South rather than in colonial Latin America.[13]

Honor was not an abstract notion for the people described in these essays. For the men and women of colonial Latin America, honor was their lifeblood, and they were willing to expend enormous quantities of wealth and energy in its defense. Even grave physical risks were accepted to protect honor. Moreover they commonly resorted to subterfuges when their own behavior dishonored their reputations (as in illegitimate pregnancies) or when they were challenged by powerful rivals or enemies. Insults, slights, and other challenges were discovered in apparently innocent jests. A mistake in seating arrangements at a dinner could undermine a friendship and provoke a feud. Although from a modern perspective some of these incidents seem silly or self-indulgent, colonial society was unforgiving of those who would not protect their honor. When individuals crossed the line of acceptable conduct, when they violated social norms or caused shame, it was necessary to react or suffer the consequences to one's honor.

Honor not only helped to order society, it also held the potential to disrupt it. Every claim of honor was asserted in a system of relationships, branding some as inferiors while acknowledging the higher status of others. As a result every conversation, every effort to arrange a marriage or seek an office placed this asserted status at risk, since any rejection or insult would necessarily result in humiliation. The public character of identity, the face that people showed to the world and hoped would be accepted, was therefore inseparable from the idea of self-worth. The real person was the public person.

In colonial Latin America, honor had many faces; that is to say, social context, geography, and chronology all influenced its definition. Honor had very different meanings in a small Andean village and in the exalted circles of the viceregal court of Lima. Yet despite these varied meanings, individual and family honor always reflected public judgment. Honor was not merely a set of rules to govern behavior; it did not mean correct behavior or fairness. Instead the desire for honor was almost always a desire to be envied, to be exalted above others. The desire to gain honor was necessarily associated with a willingness to lose it. We can, therefore, return again to Cortés, the conqueror of the powerful Aztec state, to illustrate the place of honor at the origins of colonial society. Cortés was zealous in his efforts to achieve honor, taking extraordinary risks in the face of enormous odds. When his men feared to advance farther, Gómara tells us, Cortés urged them forward with the words, ". . . we shall win the greatest honor and glory that were ever won up to this time, not only by our own nation, but by any other. The greater the king we seek [Moctezuma], the wider the land, and the more numerous the enemy, so much greater will be our glory. . . ."[14] It is the scale of these risks that suggests to us his insatiable hunger for honor; but this passion would persist across the sweep of colonial history and come to permeate nearly every social class.

NOTES

1. López de Gómara, *Cortés: The Life of the Conqueror by His Secretary,* trans. and ed. Lesley Byrd Simpson (Berkeley: University of California Press, 1964).

2. William Ian Miller, *Humiliation and Other Essays on Honor, Social Discomfort, and Violence* (Ithaca, NY: Cornell University Press, 1993), 116.

3. López de Gómara, *Cortés,* 341.

4. Miller, *Humiliation,* 84.

5. Robert A. Nye, *Masculinity and Male Codes of Honor in Modern France* (New York: Oxford University Press, 1993), 13.

6. Julio Caro Baroja, "Honour and Shame: A Historical Account of Several Conflicts," in *Honour and Shame: The Values of Mediterranean Society,* ed. J. G. Peristiany (London: Weidenfeld and Nicolson, 1965), 86.

7. Julian Pitt-Rivers, "Honour and Social Status," in *Honour and Shame: The Values of Mediterranean Society,* ed. J. G. Peristiany (London: Weidenfeld and Nicolson, 1965), 21.

8. Melveena McKendrick, "Honour/Vengeance in the Spanish 'Comedia': A Case of Mimetic Transference," *Modern Language Review* 79(2) (April 1984): 332.

9. R. Douglas Cope, The Limits of Racial Domination: Plebeian Society in Colonial Mexico City, 1660–1720 (Madison: University of Wisconsin Press, 1994).

10. Arlette Farge, *Fragile Lives: Violence, Power and Solidarity in Eighteenth-Century Paris,* trans. Carol Shelton (Cambridge, MA: Harvard University Press, 1993).

11. There is a large literature devoted to the topic of machismo. Among the many worthwhile studies, see Ray González, ed., *Muy Macho: Latino Men Confront Their Manhood* (New York: Anchor, 1996); Matthew C. Gutmann, *The Meanings of Macho: Being a Man in Mexico City* (Berkeley: University of California Press, 1996); Tina Rosenberg, *Children of Cain: Violence and the Violent in Latin America* (New York: Morrow, 1992).

12. Ramón Gutiérrez, When Jesus Came, the Corn Mothers Went Away: Marriage, Sexuality, and Power in New Mexico, 1500–1846 (Stanford, CA: Stanford University Press, 1991), 205.

13. Bertram Wyatt-Brown, *Southern Honor: Ethics and Behavior in the Old South* (New York: Oxford University Press, 1982). See also his "Community, Class, and Snopesian Crime: Local Justice in the Old South," in *Class Conflict and Consensus: Antebellum Southern Community Studies,* ed. Orville Vernan Burton and Robert C. McMath, Jr. (Westport, CT: Greenwood, 1982), 173–206 for an excellent discussion of how these issues played out across class lines.

14. López de Gómara, *Cortés,* 113–14.

CHAPTER ONE

HONOR AND HONORS IN COLONIAL SPANISH AMERICA

MARK A. BURKHOLDER

"These crazy Spaniards have more regard for a bit of honor than for a thousand lives; they do not know how to relax and enjoy life."[1] So wrote a contemporary of Columbus in one of many testimonies to the Spanish passion for honor. Nobles and commoners alike strove to maintain honor, simply defined as one's self-esteem as well as the public esteem other members of society bestowed on an individual.[2] According to one commentator, Spaniards "value honor so greatly that most will choose death rather than tarnish it".

Honor embodied interrelated concepts of nobility, Catholicism, "pure blood lines" (*limpieza de sangre*), privilege, precedence, title, office, form of address, dress, and the lifestyle that the conquistadors, first settlers, and later Castilian emigrants carried to colonial Spanish America. Added to military and religious conquest, this cluster of ideas justified the hierarchical colonial society and defined Spaniards' (and their Creole descendants') place within it. Since honor required public esteem, the honorable man would defend his honor against charges that impugned it through words, deeds, or litigation. Solidified during the lengthy Reconquest of the Iberian peninsula from the Moors, honor not only survived migration to the Indies but grew stronger in a social and racial environment that was more heterogeneous than that of Spanish society. Although independence modified its components, the concept of honor persisted long afterward.

HONOR IN SPAIN

Honor emerged from the Reconquest as a noble value that commoners endorsed but could not fully emulate.[3] Thus only a small proportion of the Castilian population actually exhibited honor's numerous manifestations. Nobles argued strongly that honor could be attained only through military valor or the display of Christian and civic virtues inherent in their status. Privileges enjoyed by virtue of noble birth thus provided public recognition of the nobility's honor.

At the time Pizarro was leading the conquest of Peru, the Castilian nobility numbered perhaps 2 percent of the population, or some eighty-five thousand people. By the close of the eighteenth century, there were just over four hundred thousand nobles in the whole of Spain, about 4 percent of the population. *Hidalgos,* by far the majority of the nobility, enjoyed all noble privileges including exemption from personal taxes, from imprisonment for debt, and from degrading punishment such as decapitation. While some hidalgos might be wealthy, many were not. An intermediary although not always distinguishable category of nobles was that of *caballero,* which typically involved nobles who were urban dwellers.[4] Above caballeros were titled nobles (*títulos*)—normally dukes, marquises, and counts—and their sons. Grandees, who also held titles, formed the pinnacle of nobility. At the time of their creation in 1520, these magnates of Castile possessed enormous estates and accounted for 20 of the 35 titled nobles of the realm. The number of titled nobles subsequently increased to 99 by the death of Philip II in 1598 and to 528 by 1700. The census of 1797 revealed 1,323 titled nobles throughout the whole of Spain.

The number of nobles in Castile varied enormously according to region. As a consequence of privileges gained during the Reconquest in the north, the entire native-born population of the Basque provinces of Guipúzcoa and Vizcaya claimed nobility as hidalgos, as did half of Santander and Asturias. By the late eighteenth century, these provinces were home to over half of the nobles in Spain. In contrast less than one percent of the population of Andalusia, a common origin of emigrants to the Americas in the sixteenth century, was noble. Unlike the hidalgo landowners in the Basque provinces, titled nobles dominated landholding in Andalusia. After it became Philip II's capital in 1560, Madrid quickly became a magnet for titled nobles. The census of 1797 listed 289 residing there. Economically powerful and socially preeminent, Spain's nobility remained a pillar of Old Regime Spain and a constant reminder to the colonists of the "natural" order of society.

The implications of the conception of honor limited the range of acceptable noble occupations. Already in the thirteenth century, knights could lose their rank for engaging in commerce "or any low manual occupation to earn money without being a prisoner of war." As defined in the mid-fifteenth century, "base occupations" included "carpenter, tailor, furrier, stonemason, smith, barber, grocer, cobbler, etc."[5] A listing of "low and vulgar offices" adopted by the Order of Santiago in 1560 included "silversmith and painter . . . , shopkeeper and moneylender, embroiderer, stone-cutter, inn or tavern keeper, scribe (other than one of the royal scribes), public attorney, or any other pursuits similar or inferior to these."[6] Although after the discovery of the New World neither participation in wholesale trade nor work on the land imperiled a noble's status, the consequence of numerous occupations being considered ignoble was that nobles with estates and rents insufficient for them to live in a manner befitting their station were largely restricted to the pursuit of military and civil offices and thus dependent upon serving the monarch. This generalization needs qualification, however, for in the Basque provinces and Asturias, regions with high proportions of nobles, they engaged in manual occupations without loss of status.

LIMPIEZA DE SANGRE IN CASTILE

The association of honor with aristocracy and the accompanying belief that honor was transmitted through noble inheritance from generation to generation merged into the broader Spanish obsession with limpieza de sangre, or purity of lineage and bloodlines. A series of anti-Jewish riots and the accompanying forced conversion of Jews in the late fourteenth century resulted in the creation of a new and suspect group of *conversos* known as "New Christians." The conversions made the New Christians eligible for state and church positions previously denied them because of their Jewish religious beliefs. Old Christians, however, questioned the sincerity of their conversion, and a growing emphasis on limpieza de sangre brought two responses.

The first reaction to the New Christians, initially enacted in the second decade of the fifteenth century, was the prohibition against admitting males with "impure" blood to the university college (*colegio mayor*) of San Bartolomé at the University of Salamanca. The city of Toledo subsequently prohibited conversos from holding municipal offices. Other cities, educational institutions, cathedral chapters, and the like joined in adopting similar discriminatory provisions. Through this emphasis upon ancestry, Old Christian lineage became an indispensable criterion for access to a wide range of employment. Indeed in 1522 all but one university in Castile was forbidden to confer degrees on conversos.

The second reaction, closely linked to the first, was the establishment of the Tribunal of the Inquisition to examine the genuineness of the New Christians' religious beliefs. Approved by a papal bull of 1478, the first tribunal began functioning soon afterward, and in 1481 the first public *auto de fe* was held in Seville, at which six heretics burned at the stake. By 1492 Castile had eight more tribunals, and perhaps nearly twenty thousand conversos had been punished. Punishment by the Inquisition affected not only the condemned; it meant that their children and grandchildren could hold no public or ecclesiastical offices or honors. Nor could they be "judges, mayors, constables, magistrates, jurors, stewards, officials of weights and measures, merchants, notaries, public scriveners, lawyers, attorneys, secretaries, accountants, treasurers, physicians, surgeons, shopkeepers, brokers, changers, weight inspectors, collectors, tax-farmers, or holders of any other similar public office."[7]

The filters of race and the Inquisition further clarified the bounds of honor; infamy was the unavoidable consequence of New Christian ancestry or an ancestor punished by the Inquisition. The penitential garment (*sanbenito*) worn by a person convicted by the Inquisition was to be hung in the person's parish church, "in order that there may be perpetual memory of the infamy of the heretics and their descendants".[8] In short, honor as well as dishonor was inherited.

Spanish racism and the Inquisition forced Spaniards to verify their limpieza de sangre. In the most rigorous cases, one of the royal councils, the Council of Orders, evaluated and certified claims of blood purity and claims of nobility after the king had awarded membership in one of the noble or military orders established during the Reconquest—Alcántara, Calatrava, and Santiago. When examining the credentials of would-be knights, or caballeros, in the early seventeenth century, this body of experienced jurisconsults, all of whom belonged to a noble order, applied the following criteria: legitimate birth; nobility by birth and not by royal concession; purity of blood; religious orthodoxy, that is, no ancestors condemned by the Inquisition; good name and reputation; having reached a minimum age; and *limpieza de oficios,* that is, no history of father or grandfathers having engaged in "vile" occupations and, in some cases, trade. The council's approval of an *hábito* meant that the recipient had met the requirements that together defined honor. Although the crown sold numerous hábitos, the council still examined the purchasers' credentials, and approval was far from automatic. Lack of nobility in the paternal line, Jewish ancestry, and "vile" occupation were the three chief causes for a candidate's rejection.

Membership in a noble order demonstrated definitively a family's nobility and unblemished lineage. In addition it identified the knight explicitly with the aristocratic values associated with the higher nobility. The Council of

Orders thus defined and validated nobility. "Its function is to conserve the Spanish aristocracy, to keep unsullied the purity of noble families, to give honour to persons who merit it, to distinguish the illustrious from the common herd, the noble from the base." Birth rather than wealth, in short, was the explicit criterion for admission to a noble order. As a contemporary wrote:

> In Spain there are two classes of nobility. One greater, which is *hidalguía,* and another lesser, which is purity of blood, the class which we call Old Christians. And although the possession of *hidalguía* is more prestigious, it is much more disgraceful to lack purity of blood, because in Spain we hold a common peasant of pure ancestry in greater esteem than an *hidalgo* of dubious origins.[9]

THE NOBLE LIFESTYLE IN SPAIN

Ostentatious display characterized the noble lifestyle; commoners followed suit to the best of their ability. Gold bracelets, and chains, silver plate, gold rings set with pearls, diamonds, emeralds, and other precious stones; costly clothing; fine walnut furniture; a slave; and, by the late sixteenth century, horse and carriage—these were the trappings of wealthy nobles. As long as their credit lasted, nobles spent and consumed in pursuit of extravagant display. Repeated government efforts to limit such extravagance through sumptuary legislation, moreover, failed to curb the enthusiasm for pretentiousness. Elaborate housing, servants, and an entourage, too, were central to the desired noble lifestyle, and extramarital affairs conducted by noblemen were both routine and expensive.

By the time Hernán Cortés and Francisco Pizarro led their epic conquests of Mexico and Peru, the centrality of honor and its intimate relationship to nobility, limpieza de sangre, an unwillingness to engage in a variety of manual occupations, and a variety of related concepts were firmly rooted in Castilian society. Explorers, conquistadors, first settlers, later immigrants, and their American-born (creole) descendants endorsed these values and made them central to the Spanish experience in the New World.

HONOR AND NOBILITY IN THE SPANISH COLONIES

Beginning with Christopher Columbus, the crown offered rewards of title and prestige to those who advanced its cause in the lands that became known as the

Indies. Columbus himself received appointments as viceroy, governor, and admiral of the ocean sea before setting sail in 1492. For men who subsequently distinguished themselves, formal patents of nobility might accompany locally bestowed land, tribute, labor, and offices. In its contract with Francisco Pizarro, the crown ennobled his junior partner Diego de Almagro and the thirteen men who had remained with Pizarro on the island of Gallo in 1527. These men received all of the "liberties, exemptions, preeminences" and other privileges of their new ranks.[10] The crown granted both Cortés and Pizarro titles of marquis and knighted a few other conquistadors. Thus from the earliest days of exploration and conquest, the crown validated its responsibility to reward its servants with offices, rank, and income and in so doing encouraged the transfer of Castilian values, including an emphasis on honor, to the colonies.

Conquistadors, of course, expected recognition and reward for their role in expanding the royal domain. The crown responded by allowing the leaders of conquests to make grants of native labor and tribute, or *encomiendas* (the term itself carried connotations of nobility and hence honor), to their men. The requirement that *encomenderos* possess a horse, lance, sword, and other arms further tied them to the traditional concept of the noble as warrior. Having survived repeated threats from fractious nobles in the fifteenth century, however, the Castilian monarchy had no desire to create a powerful New World nobility capable of threatening its rule. This policy explains in large part the royal effort embodied in the New Laws of 1542 to end the inheritance of encomiendas. Encomenderos consciously emulated the consumption and display patterns of the Castilian higher nobility and the crown saw no advantage in confirming their pretensions by formally elevating their social status any further. Royal policy and colonial reality often conflicted, however, and the conquistadors believed their actions constituted a service to the crown analogous to the Reconquest and the more recent successful war against the kingdom of Granada. Thus they believed that conquest in the Americas in itself bestowed nobility on them.

By exempting Spaniards in the New World from the tribute imposed on the native population and on some blacks and free mulattoes, the crown confirmed the distinction between nobles, who were exempt from direct taxation, and commoners (*pecheros*), who were not. In addition the crown specifically granted explorers, conquistadors, and first settlers permission to carry both offensive and defensive arms, the traditional privilege of the nobility, while prohibiting Indians, mestizos, blacks, and mulattoes from doing so. Philip II went further when he explicitly declared the first settlers and their descendants hidalgos, with "all the honors and preeminences" of hidalgos and caballeros in Castile, "according to the *fueros* [privileges], laws, and customs of Spain."[11]

Given this background, when word reached Spain in 1726 that judges of the Audiencia of Mexico had sentenced two peninsulars to service in an *obraje* (textile factory using forced labor), the crown's reaction was outrage at this "scandalous and unheard-of sentence." The king ordered the two men released and decreed that no "true and legitimate" Spaniard was ever to be subjected to this treatment.[12] Similarly natives and descendants of natives of Vizcaya were exempted from degrading sentences (*penas infames*) for they were nobles (*como nobles, notorios hijosdalgo*). As an eighteenth-century observer noted, "the precedent established at the time of the conquest gave all Spanish settlers the right to enjoy the privileges of the nobility. . . [Those who migrate] acquire in the Indies the two things they esteem most but which they cannot enjoy in Spain—wealth and nobility."[13]

Despite the crown's reluctance to acknowledge formally any unproven nobility of Spaniards in the New World, the viceroy of New Spain in 1582 noted that the descendants of conquistadors, by virtue of lineage alone, were considered noble and hence de facto hidalgos. Similarly in 1582 the Viceroy of Peru reported that it would be futile to try to sell grants of nobility (hidalguía), for the Spaniards there believed themselves nobles (caballeros), so that such a purchase was unnecessary. In the same year, the crown acceded to repeated complaints by the city council of Seville against the inflation of honors resulting from the sale of grants of nobility and, in exchange for 50,000 ducats, agreed to cease selling the grants in the city or its district. Thus the crown simultaneously yielded to the colonists' claimed nobility while restricting the growth of the hidalgo ranks within Spain's nobility. Although the crown sought to sell grants of nobility again half a century later, royal policy subsequently changed, resulting in a reduction of such grants. For example when Don Ignacio Francisco de Estrada sought hidalguía in 1786, the Council of the Indies recommended against the petition, despite his status as a legitimate son of Old Christians "always considered as nobles".[14]

The vast majority of the conquistadors and early settlers, of course, were Spanish commoners who made the costly and sometimes perilous voyage to the New World with the intention of improving their lot in life. Despite early attempts by the crown to encourage Spanish emigrants to engage in agricultural pursuits, it became clear immediately that few Spaniards had any intention of planting, tending, and harvesting crops themselves. Those peasants who emigrated, and their number appears to have been very modest, did so to abandon a life of manual labor as farmers or herdsmen. While they wanted a European diet, as conquerors and settlers they expected the native population to produce it for them. A succession of labor institutions ensured that natives and other laborers would in fact do so.

Figure 1. The nobility in colonial Latin America had coats of arms that signified their membership in a very select group. These symbols were proudly displayed on public occasions. (Escudo de Diego de Mendoza Austria y Moctezuma, ramo Tierras, vol. 1586, exp. 1, no. 1125, Archivo General de la Nación, Mexico City.)

Although artisans were among the first Spaniards to settle in the Americas, and some even became aldermen, the noble attitude toward manual labor received reinforcement in the colonies. In 1552 the crown prohibited stone-masons, tailors, potters, and other "low persons" who worked as artisans (*oficios mecánicos*) from serving as provincial officials (*corregidores*). As clarified in 1609, it was well known that many peninsulars as well as creoles in Peru were of "humble stock and poor" (*gente humilde y pobre*) "and not inclined to labor in the fields or mines or other productive enterprises or to work for other Span-iards."[15] A European commentator on customs in Venezuela near the close of the colonial era emphasized that creoles believed that "Decency . . . debars them from agricultural pursuits, and enjoins them to treat the mechanical arts with sovereign contempt. . . . The laborious husbandman is an object of contempt. Every one wishes to be a gentleman, to lead an idle life, addicted to the frightful vices of luxury, gaming, chicane and calumny." In Caracas, "no white Spaniard is a commoner but when he is poor." A creole "would think himself disgraced to owe his subsistence to the sweat of his brow, or the hardness of his hands. . . . Nothing, according to him, degrades a man so much as labour. He believes that it is impossible to preserve one's dignity, and do honour to one's ancestors, except with a pen in hand, a sword by the side, or a breviary under the eyes."[17]

THE VOCABULARY OF RANK, PRESTIGE, AND HONOR

And yet the terminology of nobility only slowly and incompletely came to enshroud the colonists. For the men who conquered Peru, the term *don,* "lord," still retained its meaning, and only those directly related to high-ranking Spanish nobles or in possession of a small number of civil or eccle-siastical positions employed it. Spanish women in Peru at the same time, however, used the term *doña* much more frequently. Over time contemporaries employed both terms more extensively, but as late as 1689 in Mexico City, they were applied to only about 40 percent of Spanish women and under 10 percent of Spanish men. In the early 1790s, the editor of the *Mercurio Peruano* uni-formly listed the nearly four hundred subscribers to the paper as don or doña or by a term of employment such as *oidor* (civil judge on Lima's regional high court, or audiencia) that gave them even more status. In Venezuela in the early nineteenth century, every white with "a tolerably decent appearance" was called don. Nonetheless Spaniards not distinguished by the increasingly hon-orific titles remained numerous at the time of independence, amid the general inflation of honors that had occurred. A 1821 census of Guadalajara, Mexico, indicated that just under half of the Spanish males were dons, while a little more than half of the Spanish females were doñas. Strikingly, ten Indians, two mestizos, and one mulatto were also listed as dons.

Conveying more honor than the terms don or doña was membership in a noble order. Initially, however, the American-born heirs of the immigrants did poorly, with only 17 creoles entering noble orders by 1600. When the penurious crown began to sell hábitos openly and increasingly grant dispensations for failure to meet the statutory requirements for membership, during the reign of Philip IV (1621–65), however, Americans began to enter the orders in unprecedented numbers. The crown conferred 166 hábitos to creoles from 1601 to 1650 and 257 more in the second half of the century. It conferred nearly as many in the eighteenth century, with the new civil order of Charles III (created to recognize distinguished service in the bureaucracy) accounting for 92 of the total of 409. From 1801 to 1825, the crown granted another 91. The crown's need for revenue and desire to reward high-ranking bureaucrats proved major lubricants for facilitating upward social mobility and recognition.

Admission to a military order provided the knight with "honor and luster," and the crown repeatedly conferred hábitos in order to increase the dignity of and respect for officials in the New World. Thus, for example, when don Josef de Uribe Castejón y Medrano was appointed an oidor of the Audiencia of Mexico in the early eighteenth century, the crown acceded to his request for an hábito, as it had earlier with other ministers.

TITLES OF NOBILITY

Families with a title of nobility—typically marquis or count—stood at the pinnacle of colonial society. "The honor that titles conferred" was among the most valuable awards the monarch could make.[17] Such families, however, were exceedingly rare prior to the 1680s, with only 6 titles granted in Mexico and no more than 20 in Peru. Indeed in 1675 the Council of Castile mocked the author of a proposal to sell 150 titles and 1,000 hábitos in the Indies as a person of "little judgment" or knowledge of the Indies, where few persons had the wealth to purchase or maintain either.[18] Soon, however, the door opened. The crown granted 7 titles in Mexico from 1682 to 1692 and 20 in Peru during the same years. During the remainder of the 1690s, it granted 8 more titles in Peru but none in Mexico. From 1700 to 1808, the number of titled nobles increased markedly as the crown created over 70 in Peru and nearly 50 in Mexico.

A majority of the recipients of titles were peninsulars, although at least 19 of the 49 new titles granted from 1700 to 1810 in Mexico went to creoles. In Peru only 15 went to native-born creoles during the entire colonial period. Among the men honored were high-ranking officials, merchants, and miners. Excluding the officials, the common denominator among the recipients was wealth, as on numerous occasions the crown simply sold titles. In 1741, for example, the viceroy of Peru was authorized to sell 3 titles of Castile for 20,000 pesos each, with the proceeds designated to help rebuild the earthquake-damaged cathedral of Concepción, Chile.

In contrast to the original recipients of titles, heirs to titles were typically creoles. Thus in 1721 there were 28 titles in Peru, including one held by the viceroy, and creoles held all but 3 or 4 of them. Strikingly the author of the list considered only five rich, while ten were poor. He described the first one on the list, the Conde del Portillo, as a native of Lima and "very poor." Created in 1640, the title was the oldest present in the city.[19]

By the late eighteenth century, some commoners had obtained titles of nobility, and a number of title holders lacked the resources to maintain them "with decency." One consequence was that such penurious nobles wed spouses who brought wealth but also inferior social status to the marriage. Informed of this situation, the crown in 1790 required an aspirant to a title to document personal hidalguía and family ties through marriage as well as to prove possession of adequate wealth to maintain a lifestyle appropriate for a titled noble.

RANK AND PRECEDENCE

Colonists believed that the natural form of society was hierarchical and, by virtue of conquest and Spanish descent, that they formed its highest level in the New World. While the wealthiest families were almost invariably Spanish, there were also impoverished Spaniards. Regardless of income, however, Spaniards considered their ancestry alone sufficient to warrant high social status in a multiracial society.

While claiming racial homogeneity vis-à-vis Indians, blacks, and persons of mixed racial background, the Spanish segment of colonial society was itself divided not only economically but in regard to place of birth. In the mature colonial society, peninsulars (Spaniards born in Spain) brought to the New World one quality that creoles envied—unquestioned "pure" Spanish ancestry. As the intrepid travelers and peninsulars Jorge Juan and Antonio de Ulloa noted in discussing eighteenth-century creoles,

it is rare to find a family which does not have impure blood or some other equally significant defect. . . . Each one [creole] points up and provides information about his lineage which highlights his family's illustrious background so that he might have more status than the others in the same city. So that there can be no mistake about it, each one brings to light all the deficiencies, stigmas, and flaws which denigrate the pure lineage of the others.[20]

Creoles, the travelers continued, "feel it is an honorable thing to give their daughters in marriage to Europeans, forsaking unions with creoles who lack good family lineage (as is common everywhere) . . ."[21]

The social and religious life of the urban populations, in particular, afforded numerous opportunities for individuals to affirm or reaffirm their place in the social hierarchy. The inhabitants of seventeenth-century Mexico City celebrated ninety or more festivals of European origin, and eighty-five confraternities took part in the annual Corpus Christi procession. Viceregal receptions were among the most elaborate, and the formal entry of the viceroy into the city began with a parade of dignitaries all appropriately dressed in clothing and accessories that identified them.

The bureaucratic nature of Spanish colonial institutions resulted in a pecking order of officials whose rank could be determined by salary, perquisites, and place in public processions. Thus in the major administrative capitals, the chief executive, whether titled viceroy, captain-general or president, enjoyed precedence. The royal appointees who served on the jurisdiction's audiencia—a combination of high court and advisory body to the chief executive—came next and could be easily identified by the distinctive togas or black robes of office they wore. When the viceroy of Peru first met members of the civil and ecclesiastical offices of Lima and other distinguished persons, the audiencia was received first, followed by the tribunal of accounts, the cathedral chapter, local magistrates, members of the merchant guild, the Inquisition, superiors of religious orders, the colleges, and other eminent persons in the city.

Precedence in public events was a tangible recognition of honor. As a result, questions of precedence were hotly and at times lengthily disputed. Nowhere was this more true than in colonial universities, where concern over precedence and ceremony was so great that the University of Guatemala elected and paid a salary to a master of ceremonies, whose chief responsibility "was to see each man in the place to which he was entitled by virtue of his degree, position, and seniority. No one could yield his higher place to another—not even for courtesy."[22] This meant that doctors and masters in the faculties of theology and laws were seated without distinction except for seniority of their degree and ahead of doctors in the faculties of medicine and philosophy. When on one occasion a professor arrived late for an event and discovered that the master of ceremonies had seated him in an inferior position, he "sallied from the room shouting, throwing up his hands, and tearing his hair." Far from being a display of bad manners, the professor's response pointedly reinforced the significance of precedence and the honor and corresponding importance it conveyed within the university.

Bullfights provided another arena for disputes over precedence. The box seats from which the elite enjoyed the spectacle were of different types and locations. In Mexico City, for example, disgruntled recipients immediately protested the assignment of seats they considered inferior to their station. Much worse, however, was to be left out of the assignment, and officials thus offended promptly complained that their honor had been besmirched.

Contemporaries, of course, appreciated the significance of precedence. When the editor listed the initial group of subscribers to Lima's new periodical *Mercurio Peruano*, he placed the name of the viceroy first. He then listed the members of the Audiencia of Lima in order of rank and seniority within rank. Thus the regent came first, the senior civil judge second, and then the remaining civil judges, two honorary civil judges, the criminal judges, the crown attorney for civil affairs, and finally the crown attorney for criminal cases. All preceded the senior ecclesiastical official, the archbishop of Lima. Given the concern for seniority and precedence, it was undoubtedly with considerable chagrin that the second list of subscribers published began with a civil judge of Lima's court, "who was omitted by error of the press in the place that corresponds to him in the first list."[23]

THE NOBLE LIFESTYLE

Extravagant expenditure on clothing, household furnishings, and ultimately carriages and the less pretentious calashes marked the life of the well-to-do who sought to mirror if not exceed the lifestyle of Castilian nobles of comparable means. One observer of Lima in the 1770s described in detail their wedding beds, furnishings, and infant cradles:

> The bed clothes are the most exquisite woven in the best mills in Europe. Draperies at the head and foot are made of scarlet damask no less, decorated with the finest golden braid and fringes made in Milan. The bedspreads, adorned in the same fashion, are of the richest silk stuff woven in Lyons, France. The sheets and pillows are the finest linen made in Cambray, adorned with the widest and most delicate laces and inlay woven in Flanders, to which is added a large cloth, similarly decorated and so

transparent that through it one may perceive the splendor of the pillows, which on the upper part, have scarcely one span of Dutch batiste. The cradle and furnishings of the child are of the same stuff, without mentioning the jewels for adorning the infant, who is usually bedecked with brilliant stones, which I consider a single expense because they also serve for the other children, except those [stones] which are filched by the nurses and servants. So Creoles from houses of average opulence can boast of having been reared in better diapers than the princes of Europe and even those around the Great Turk with all his seraglio."[24]

Generosity and hospitality also characterized the noble lifestyle in the New World and similarly represented honor, for "beneficence transforms economic power into honor." The German traveler Tadeo Haënke who observed Lima in the late eighteenth century underscored the generosity of the creoles who provided "sumptuous" banquets and spent their money so freely that it brought financial ruin to many. The *limeños* also dressed more elegantly and expensively than people anywhere else in the empire and had the finest carriages. Their extreme pride went so far that they even exaggerated the names they called people and events. Thus they called all white men caballeros, any instrumental musical event an opera, and "saint and angel to whoever has some appearance of devotion." Of course they gambled, and many men kept mistresses on whom they exhausted their financial resources.[25]

In the concluding decades of the colonial era, the titled nobility of Mexico included families able to engage in opulent conspicuous consumption. Such expenditures publicly confirmed their wealth and thus gave luster to their honor. Lavish palaces staffed with ten to twenty servants, Chinese porcelain, diamonds, pearls, lace, and imported coaches and matched pairs of horses or mules to convey nobles through muddy streets documented the validity of a claim to preeminence and honor. Religious beneficence, such as funding missionary activities or establishing chantries, also demonstrated a noble's devotion and, implicitly, Old Christian origins.

HONORIFIC OFFICES

Municipal councils in Castile had varying membership requirements. In some only nobles were eligible for membership. Others required that half of the councilors be noble and half be commoners. And some councils drew no distinction between nobles and commoners and granted eligibility to all male citizens. In the Indies, the crown prohibited the division of posts between nobles and commoners in favor of eligibility for "all good men" with pure blood and common esteem.[26] Municipal governments there, nonetheless, provided numerous honorific positions that added or confirmed the luster of their members.

Honorific municipal positions included those of aldermen (*regidores*), who received little or no salary and were prohibited from holding "vile" occupations. While such offices facilitated illegitimate financial gain, men sought them primarily for honorific reasons, at least after the initial establishment of a town. Although their value lay largely in the "local influence, social prestige, and incidental perquisites" they provided as positions of "dignity," a number of aldermen, and certainly many American-born aldermen in Mexico City, used their post as a stepping stone to salaried bureaucratic offices.[27]

Recognizing the demand for the position of alderman, the crown initially awarded appointments as rewards for service, particularly in the conquest or early settlement of a region. The monetary value of such appointments, however, led the crown in 1591 to regularize the sale of the posts. By the end of the century, buyers were paying up to 2,500 pesos in Cuzco, 5,000 pesos in Lima, and 6,000 pesos in Mexico City, although the sales were initially for only the life of the purchaser. The decision in 1606 to allow town councilors to sell their posts or pass them on through inheritance increased the value of the positions to over 10,000 pesos in Mexico City. In the eighteenth century, however, the value of the positions declined, as respect for them dwindled. A majority of the aldermen of Lima in 1721, despite the prestige attached to the position, were described as poor or, in one case, very poor. In Lima, for example, the price paid for the position declined from 11,000 pesos in 1700 to 4,000 pesos in 1777 and to 2,000 pesos by 1790. By 1752 in Cuzco, all the alderman posts were vacant.

Another honorific post was that of the municipal standard-bearer. His role quickly became simply carrying the municipal standard when public ceremonies were held. As with the alderman positions, the crown put this post up for sale in 1591 and made it a piece of heritable property as well in 1606. The 1591 provision that the standard-bearer would also be an ex oficio alderman elevated the value of the post considerably, and it often sold for two or three times more than the post of alderman alone. Since the standard-bearer usually enjoyed precedence over other members of the municipal council, the purchaser was clearly buying honor.

Offices could also provide their incumbents with more concrete special privileges. A 1704 decision, for example, confirmed Lima's city councilors in their immunity from being restrained in the public jail except in case of serious crime, "for the honor and esteem that is due to their positions."[28] This same honor and esteem precluded men whose occupation was "vile" or who had a retail shop or sold goods in a market or tavern from becoming aldermen.[29]

HONORS

The importance of precedence and rank as badges of honor meant that competition was stiff for high-ranking positions that carried substantial salaries and opportunities for financial gain and thus the ability to live nobly. The large number of ambitious office seekers, however, meant that few could attain the higher ranked positions. Given the pressure to reward meritorious service or, in some cases, to provide increased authority to a particular official, the Spanish crown in the eighteenth century frequently granted an individual the "honors" of a higher-ranked office, without actually conferring the office.

By the late eighteenth century, it was commonplace for university professors who had served twenty years with a permanent appointment to receive the honors of an audiencia position upon retirement. Thus senior professors of civil and canon law at the universities of Valladolid and Salamanca in the late 1780s and early 1790s received the honors of a criminal or civil judge of the Chancellery of Valladolid. Citing such Spanish cases as precedents, the Peruvian José Baquíjano y Carrillo successfully gained the honors of criminal judge of the Audiencia of Lima in 1795, soon after his retirement as the senior professor of canon law at Lima's University of San Marcos. This meant not only that he could wear the formal judicial robe but also that he could sit with the criminal judges of the tribunal when they took their seats at public ceremonies. Men serving as criminal judges sought the honors of civil judge, while civil judges and, after 1776, regents of audiencias sought the honors of the Council of the Indies. The councilors, in turn, sought the honors of the Cámara of the Indies, the small and select chamber that made patronage recommendations.

Another category of honors was that of *preeminencias*, or privileges, exemptions, or other advantages granted to an individual. In perhaps its most celebrated form, the grandees of Spain enjoyed the privilege of wearing their hats in the presence of the monarch and addressing him as "cousin." Offices, too, had their privileges. In 1598 the crown extended to lieutenants of treasury officials (*oficiales reales*) the rights of the proprietary incumbents to speak and vote in town council meetings and also to assume their place in public acts. In another case, the rector of the University of San Marcos in Lima received the right to be accompanied by two black swordbearers in the same manner as civil and criminal judges of the Audiencia of Lima and inquisitors. At times the opportunity to extend privileges appealed to an impoverished crown. In 1682, for example, it gave the public notaries (*escribanos*) of Lima the opportunity to purchase the right to wear their hats while conducting business with the local judges.

SWORD FIGHTS AND DUELS

The noble privilege of carrying arms resulted in Spanish colonists occasionally resorting to sword fights or duels to settle points of honor, although the practice was legally banned. Following an exchange of words in Lima in March 1630, for example, don Francisco Flores and don Juan de Sandoval drew swords. Both were quickly placed under house arrest, and the chronicler who recorded the event mentioned no personal harm. Seven months later, Flores again drew his sword, this time against a notary not described as a don, but no fighting followed. In May of the next year Flores's wife filed for divorce to escape his abuse (*malos tratamientos*). Three days later Flores had words with his brother-in-law over the matter and both drew swords. Aside from the seemingly irrepressible and prickly Flores, however, few men fought with swords in Lima, at least in the 1630s.[30] In the mining town of Potosí, dueling was more common; at one time "eight fencing schools were opened to teach men how to kill each other."[31] Enough dueling took place that in 1722 Philip V extended to the Indies the prohibition against duels originally issued for Castile in 1716. By the early nineteenth century, however, an observer in Venezuela was able to state without qualification that "the duel is never employed among the Spaniards to atone for injuries." Rather, they turned to litigation.[32]

RACE AND LEGITIMACY

Corresponding to the emphasis upon a pure, "Old Christian" lineage in Spain, Spaniards in the Americas considered themselves at the apex of a multiracial social structure in which all persons without pure Spanish blood were inferior. Race and birth directly affected honor and family status. While the many racial combinations implied more complexity than was actually the case, and a number of nonwhites changed their racial status as adults, members of the *castas* long suffered on account of their color and presumed illegitimate background. Denied access to many official posts, they found their economic op-

D. Luis Moreno de Monroy

Dª Catharina López de la Paz.

D. Luis Moreno de Monroy casó con Dª Catarina López de la Paz y fundaron los dos mayoras gos y Obra pia de que se trata: dicha Dª Catarina fue Prima Hermana de Dª Maria Lopez Estrada como consta de la Estampa Siguente =

Figure 2. Members of the elite used their genealogies to prove their limpieza de sangre, *or purity of bloodlines. The documents traced the heritage of candidates for official positions back to founding ancestors such as this couple, pictured at the beginning of the genealogy. (Genealogía de Luis Moreno Monroy y Catarina López de la Paz, ramo Vínculos, vol. 42, exp. 8, fol. 5, no. 2852.) Archivo General de la Nación, Mexico City*

portunities severely limited. Even for the most economically successful, crossing the barrier into "white" society was long almost impossible, for race was the principal obstacle to "passing."

In 1549 Charles V barred all mulattoes, mestizos, and anyone else of illegitimate birth from holding royal or municipal office or being served by Indians through *repartimiento* or any other means without a special license. The crown originally excluded mestizos from public positions, on the grounds that they were "neophytes, vicious, of bad customs, of illegitimate birth (*espurios ilegítimos*), and incapable to serve them." Beginning with the first and second councils of Lima, in 1551–52 and 1567, mestizos began to receive ordination as parish priests to alleviate a shortage in the ministry, but they did not advance to cathedral chapters or "other distinguished ecclesiastical benefices." Subsequently bishops could ordain mestizos following examination, provided they met a number of qualifications, including legitimate birth.[33]

For mestizos of illegitimate birth, not even legitimization guaranteed full rights. For example one of the first Spanish settlers in Peru and Chile fathered an illegitimate son with an Indian woman. When his subsequent marriage to a woman of a prominent Spanish family produced no children, he sought legitimation for his mestizo son. The Council of the Indies recommended legitimation in 1596, with the stipulation that the son could hold office and honors and inherit property but could not inherit an encomienda. On hearing that mestizos held a number of public offices, including those of corregidor, alcalde mayor, regidor, notary, and others, Philip III in 1600 called for an investigation of the matter in Peru that would ascertain whether the persons involved had permission to hold them. The implication was clear: without specific permission, the mestizos would lose their posts.

In contrast to its treatment of mestizos of legitimate birth, royal legislation regarding persons of mixed ancestry and illegitimate birth, especially those with African ancestry, considered them stained from birth and of corrupt customs. The crown banned mulattoes from serving as escribanos in 1621, a sure sign that some had become literate and obtained the posts. *Pardos,* according to the Council of the Indies in the early nineteenth century, were descendants of "infected, vitiated mixtures." These and others of "stained birth" constituted "a species very inferior" to that of the commoners of Spain, and the Council rejected the very idea that they could sit in the positions of or replace descendants "of the first conquistadors or of families that were noble, legitimate, white, and devoid of any ugly stain." Only rare dispensations of *calidad,* based on notable service and demonstrated loyalty to king and country, were acceptable unless *morenos* (blacks) or pardos (mulattoes) could document legitimate ancestry for four generations. In such cases they were eligible for posi-

tions held by commoners in Spain.[34] Lawyers (*abogados*), too, were to be of
legitimate birth, although the crown recognized that some lacking this heritage
practiced in Peru, a consequence of the "notorious propagation of illegitimates" there and the shortage of qualified persons of legitimate birth to practice law in the district of Charcas.[35]

The pragmatic perspective of the late eighteenth century modified the significance of illegitimacy. In 1784 Charles III ordered that illegitimacy should
no longer stand in the way of persons who wanted to "exercise the arts and
oficios".[36] Even limpieza de sangre was not demanded to become an alderman
of San Salvador in 1795. A candidate had purchased the position at auction, but
the city council opposed his entering the post by alleging that his maternal
great grandmother was descended from mulattoes. Charles IV, however, accepted the recommendation of the Council of the Indies that he be allowed to
enter the position, agreeing that "the distance," that is the time, between the
"doubtful defect" and the present and his documented good qualities war-
ranted his service.

By the late eighteenth century, the crown was willing to dispense with racial
impediments for a price. It did so, for example, in the case of Julián Valenzuela,
a person of mixed ancestry (pardo) in Antioquia, New Granada, who was of
"white color" and had the customs, education, and style of life of a Spaniard.
While the number of persons who benefited from such gracias al sacar (royal
licenses changing an individual's racial or civil status) for dispensation of the
calidad of pardo or *quinterón,* illegitimate birth, the concession of the right to
use *don,* or the acquisition of privileges of hidalguía is unknown, the use of the
gracias as a means of confirming upward social mobility and the attendant
honor indicated the crown's willingness to disregard on an individual basis old
social barriers based on race and legitimacy.

EDUCATION AND OCCUPATION

Education was an important means of social advancement, for it qualified
youth for subsequent employment by the crown or church. Recognizing this,
colonists in New Spain and Peru sought and secured the establishment of
universities in Mexico City and Lima within decades of the conquest. Graduation alone brought benefits. Graduates of Spain's renowned University of Salamanca were exempt from direct taxation in Spain, a long-standing privilege of
the nobility. This privilege and all others enjoyed by alumni of Salamanca were
extended to graduates of the University of Mexico in 1562, thus freeing any
who went to Spain from direct taxation (*pechos*). In 1568 Philip II ordered that

Figure 3. Military service as an officer confirmed the status of the elite. Lavish uniforms were an obvious sign of status within colonial society. This militia officer is from Argentina. (Archivo General de la Nación, Buenos Aires.)

Figure 4. This militia officer is from Mexico. (Uniformes del Regimiento de Dragones del Príncipe, ramo Correspondencia de Virreyes, ser. 1, vol. 18, fol. 184, no. 77, Archivo General de la Nación, Mexico City.)

the sons of the conquistadors and first settlers of Peru who studied at the university in Lima be favored for high positions in the church (*dignidades de las iglesias catedrales*).

University statutes for admission and graduation were more restrictive than actual practice. Typically persons or descendants of persons sentenced by the Inquisition, having a "note of infamy," or descended from slaves or former slaves were excluded.[37] The constitution of the University of San Marcos excluded those with some "note of infamy," a provision that some used to justify denying admission to the castas. Nonetheless some castas had obviously secured admission, for a 1678 provision instructed the university to abide by the provision in regard to mestizos, zambos, mulattoes, and quadroons. At least in medicine, however, the university was lenient; consequently Viceroy Monclova in 1701 expressly forbade it to educate blacks, mulattoes, and quadroons. The need to reaffirm the provision and its expansion to include mestizos in 1750 confirms that enforcement remained lax, as those castas fortunate enough to learn Latin as youths continued to pursue a profession.[38]

Late in the colonial era, the crown reinforced noble birth as a requirement for those who aspired to high office. Statutes issued for the Royal College for American Nobles to be established in Granada spelled out the admissions policy. Applicants could be "sons and descendants of pure Spanish nobles, born in the Indies, and of ministers *togados,* intendants, and military officials . . . without excluding the sons of caciques and noble Indians, nor those of noble mestizos, who were of a noble Indian and a Spanish woman or of a noble Spaniard and a noble Indian woman." Applicants also had to document their limpieza de sangre and that of their parents and grandparents.

HONOR ON THE EVE OF INDEPENDENCE

In the eighteenth century, the Spanish crown sought to elevate the image of commerce through ennobling a small and select group of merchants. While aristocrats had engaged in wholesale trade for centuries, and successful manufacturers and traders had gained noble status earlier, the crown's willingness to improve the Spanish economy and trade through grants of nobility underscored the continued desirability of such status and honor to those who had made fortunes through commerce or manufacturing. Although their social position benefited from ennoblement, they remained incompletely integrated at the top of the traditional hierarchical society. Noble birth still outweighed wealth.

Enlightened reformers also focused on the traditional "opinion of dishonor with respect to the manual trades." In 1779 some merchants of Cádiz informed Charles III that in their city "there were entire families . . . who did not engage in any trade because they considered it more honorable to live . . . in absolute misery . . . rather than suffer the mark of contempt with which our provinces consider every manual occupation."[39] The problem, then, was to bestow the mechanical arts with honor, "the principal motive of all civic actions," rather than to consider them legally dishonorable or infamous. The crown responded by granting artisans an exemption from consideration by the militia lottery, prohibiting the seizure of their tools for debt, and making them eligible for municipal office. Charles III issued the most significant piece of legislation in 1783. This *cédula* (royal decree) stated:

> not only the trade of tanner but also the other trades and crafts of smith, tailor, shoemaker, carpenter and others of this kind are honest and honorable; the exercise of them does not degrade a family nor the person who exercises them, nor does it prevent obtaining the municipal offices of the republic; . . . nor are the arts and crafts to prejudice the enjoyment and prerogatives of *hidalguía* . . . [40]

While this celebrated proclamation did not represent civic equality for artisans, it did grant them honor and assert that hidalgos already practicing manual occupations would retain their status.

Legislation, of course, did not in itself change attitudes. Ennobling and granting privileges to merchants and elevating the mechanical arts and their practitioners, moreover, took place within a hierarchical social order. In short the redefinition of honor occurred very much within a traditional framework.

The 1783 legislation did not immediately reach the Indies, at least not officially, however. In 1804 the viceroy of New Spain reported that a regional tax collector had discovered the proclamation in a collection of royal declarations and urged that it be circulated in an effort to uproot the idea that living in "idleness and misery" was preferable to working in "occupations commonly considered dishonorable." The viceroy noted that no efforts had been taken to implement it and inquired whether the crown wanted him to do so.[41] He received no answer. The result can be best understood by examining the response of the *fiscal* of the Council of the Indies in January 1807 after another request that the 1783 cédula be circulated throughout the Americas.

Subsequent to the appearance of the 1783 document, a Spanish publication entitled *Febrero reformado* set forth the idea that the declaration that the mechanical arts were honorable eliminated an impediment preventing their practitioners from entering military orders. This "erroneous doctrine," a royal order of 1803 noted, totally misrepresented the 1783 cédula, which had simply stated that every honest occupation was good and the mechanical arts were honorable; this did not imply equality among occupations, even among the mechanical arts. The 1783 declaration certainly had not derogated the membership requirements for the military orders, orders "established and founded on the solid principles of the necessity of conserving the luster of the nobility." If some inhabitants of Spain had so misunderstood the 1783 cédula, it would be much worse in America, "with the multitude of castas, pardos, zambos, mulattoes, *zambaigos,* mestizos, cuarterones, *octavones.*" Since these castas worked as artisans, communicating the 1783 cédula to them would have enormously prejudicial consequences, as they believed that "the vice they have in their origin" had received dispensation. As a result the fiscal counseled treating the matter confidentially and not even acknowledging receipt of the request to circulate the cédula.[42]

This episode reveals graphically both the continued centrality of honor as an organizing principle in Spain and the colonies and its ongoing relationship to blood purity and legitimacy. The occupations of numerous commoners in Spain after 1783 were classified as honorable and, since they were at least theoretically filled by Old Christians of legitimate birth, the government could clarify any misunderstanding concerning their true limitations without grave concern. In contrast castas filled many of the same occupations in the New World. But precisely because they were castas and thus believed to be indelibly stained from birth and carrying defects that only the crown could void through special dispensations, their occupations could not be considered noble in the Indies.

Thus on the eve of the wars of independence, the centuries' old distinction between Spanish honor and the dishonor or infamy associated with persons of mixed racial background persisted. Although the concern with blood purity was less than in the sixteenth and seventeenth centuries, legitimacy continued to form a major social boundary for nearly everyone born outside of the elite. Honor in its many manifestations, in short, remained in good health as the colonial era drew to a close and would profoundly influence the social structure of the newly independent countries.

NOTES

I thank Dr. Suzanne Hiles Burkholder for her careful editorial assistance and comments on an earlier version of this essay.

1. This and the final quotation in the paragraph are cited in Bartolomé Bennassar, *The*

Spanish Character: Attitudes and Mentalities from the Sixteenth to the Nineteenth Century, trans. Benjamin Keen (Berkeley and Los Angeles: University of California Press, 1979), 214.

2. Virtuous behavior and, in the case of women, maintenance of chastity until marriage and fidelity thereafter were other manifestations of honor, as was the adult male's response in protecting female relatives from verbal or physical assaults that impugned their honor. The stress on moral rectitude so common in today's conception of honor did not go much beyond lip service and was not central to honor as developed in this essay. An introduction to types and characteristics of honor is found in Patricia Seed, *To Love, Honor, and Obey in Colonial Mexico: Conflicts over Marriage Choice, 1574–1821* (Stanford, CA: Stanford University Press, 1988), 61–64. For insights into honor among the lower classes, see Steve J. Stern, *The Secret History of Gender: Women, Men, and Power in Late Colonial Mexico* (Chapel Hill: University of North Carolina Press, 1995).

3. Spain as a political entity did not exist until after the War of the Spanish Succession, but I will use it as a shorthand term instead of specifying the various kingdoms belonging to the monarchs of Castile and Aragon.

4. The distinction between hidalgos and caballeros disappeared during the course of the colonial period, and both were subsumed under the term hidalgos.

5. Elena Lourie, "A Society Organized for War: Medieval Spain," *Past and Present* 35 (1966): 75.

6. L. P. Wright, "The Military Orders in Sixteenth- and Seventeenth-Century Spanish Society: The Institutional Embodiment of a Historical Tradition," *Past and Present* 43 (May 1969): 65.

7. Henry Kamen, *The Spanish Inquisition* (New York: New American Library, 1965), 124. The list of prohibited occupations was first promulgated in 1484.

8. Ibid., 130.

9. Wright, "The Military Orders," 40, 50. The first quotation Wright cites is from *Difiniciones de la Orden y Cavalleria de Calatrava, conforme al Capítulo General celebrado en Madrid ano 1652* (Madrid: 1661), 128. The second is from a document in Spain's National Library, Ms. 13043, f. 177v.

10. Richard Konetzke, *Colección de documentos para la historia de la formación social de Hispanoamérica 1493–1810,* 3 vols. in 5 tomos(Madrid: Consejo Superior de Investigaciones Científicas, 1953–62), 1:126–27.

11. *Recopilación de leyes de los reynos de las Indias* (Madrid: Julian de Paredes, 1681), repr. ed. 1943, libro 4, título 6.

12. Konetzke, *Colección de documentos,* vol. 3, tomo 1, 189–91.

13. Jorge Juan and Antonio de Ulloa, *Discourse and Political Reflections on the Kingdoms of Peru,* ed. John J. TePaske, trans. John J. TePaske and Besse A. Clement (Norman: University of Oklahoma Press, 1978), 224.

14. Konetzke, *Colección de documentos,* vol. 3, tomo 2, 591–93.

15. Ibid., vol. 2, tomo 1, 153.

16. F. Depons, Travels in South America, during the years 1801, 1802, 1803, and 1804 . . . , 2 vols. (London: Longman, Hurst, Rees, and Orme, 1807; reprint ed. New York: AMS, 1970), 1:117–18, 2:182–83.

17. Konetzke, *Colección de documentos,* vol. 3, tomo 2, 688.

18. Ibid., vol. 2, tomo 2, 616–19.

19. Conde Bertrando del Balzo, "Familias nobles y destacadas del Perú en los informes secretos de un virrey napolitano (1715–1725)," *Revista del Instituto Peruano de Investigaciones Genealógicas* (Lima, 1965), 14:108–10.

20. Juan and Ulloa, Discourse and Political Reflections, 219.

21. Ibid., 226.

22. John Tate Lanning, *The University in the Kingdom of Guatemala* (Ithaca, NY: Cornell University Press, 1956), 122 and 135 for this and the following quotation.

23. *Mercurio Peruano,* "Lista de señores subscriptores al Mercurio Peruano" and "Continuación de la lista de señores subscriptores . . . ," vol. 1 (1791).

24. Concolorcorvo, El Lazarillo, *A Guide for Inexperienced Travelers between Buenos Aires and Lima, 1773,* trans. Walter D. Kline (Bloomington: Indiana University Press, 1965), 296.

25. Tadeo Haënke, *Descripción del Perú* (Lima: Impr. de "El Lucero," 1901), 21–24.

26. Konetzke, *Colección de documentos,* vol. 3, tomo 2, 550–51.

27. J. H. Parry, *The Sale of Public Office in the Spanish Indies under the Hapsburgs* (Berkeley: University of California Press, 1953), 33; Dominic Azikiwe Nwasike, "Mexico-City Town Government 1590–1650: Study in Aldermanic Background and Performance" (Ph.D. diss., University of Wisconsin, 1972), 52, 68.

28. Konetzke, *Colección de documentos,* vol. 3, tomo 1, 95, vol. 2, tomo 1, 318.

29. *Recopilación,* libro 4, título 10, ley 12.

30. Juan Antonio Suardo, *Diario de Lima,* 2 vols. (Lima: Universidad Católica del Perú, Instituto de Investigaciones Históricas, 1936), 1:59, 103–4, 162.

31. Bartolomé Arzáns de Orsúa y Vela, *Tales of Potosí,* ed. R. C. Padden, trans. Frances M. López-Morillas (Providence, RI: Brown University Press, 1975), xxix.

32. Depons, *Travels,* 1:140–41.

33. Konetzke, *Colección de documentos,* vol. 3, tomo 2, 822–24; mestizos of illegitimate descent were also ordained on occasion, provided they had the qualities, instruction, and ability for the priesthood. See ibid., 1:595–96.

34. Ibid., vol. 3, tomo 2, 821–29.

35. Ibid., vol. 3, tomo 2, 486–88.

36. Ibid., vol. 3, tomo 2, 539–40.

37. Lanning, *University,* 192–96.

38. See "Documents. The Case of José Ponseano de Ayarza: A Document on the Negro in Higher Education," *Hispanic American Historical Review* 24(2) (May 1944): 432–35.

39. Quoted in William O. Callahan, *Honor, Commerce, and Industry in Eighteenth-Century Spain* (Boston: Baker Library, 1972), 45.

40. Quoted in ibid., 52.

41. Konetzke, *Colección de documentos,* vol. 3, tomo 2, 813–14.

42. Ibid., 832–34.

CHAPTER TWO

HONOR, SEXUALITY, AND THE COLONIAL CHURCH
The Sins of Dr. González, Cathedral Canon

GEOFFREY SPURLING

In colonial Latin America, personal honor depended on attitudes and actions strictly defined in gender terms. For men honor was exemplified by assertiveness, courage, authority, and the domination of women; for women it lay in their possession of shame, retained through discretion and sexual control. Though not static through time, nor identically shared by all groups and members of colonial society, the core ideas and concepts of honor nevertheless centered on the unequal (but often contested) ties between men and women, with marriage and the family as key concerns. The values linked to honor, then, were predicated on a set of assumptions regarding appropriate masculine and feminine behavior, within the context of what today we would term heterosexual relations.[1]

Here I examine behavior that broke dramatically with these core assumptions of the honor code, analyzing the honor and dishonor associated with sexual relations between men. I focus specifically on two interrelated court cases involving sodomy, regarded in colonial Latin America as the single most important—and disturbing—same-sex act. How did the accusation of having committed sodomy affect the personal honor of an individual? How did it affect the honor deriving from his social status (his honor-status), the honor of his family, or the collective honor of colonial religious and political institutions with which he was closely tied?[2]

Initially the answers to these questions might seem obvious. In medieval and early modern Europe, as in colonial Latin America, sodomy was considered the most serious of the sins of lust. Its very names conjured up infamy and aberration: sodomy was the *pecado nefando*, or abominable/unmentionable sin; it

Fray Gregorio Carmelite.
Carme déchaussé un des Chefs de l'insurrection.
Vénération des femmes pour les moines.

Figure 5. Members of religious orders inspired respect among the general population that could transcend their moral and ethical lapses in many cases. In addition to the prestige of their religious calling, they enjoyed elite status because of social origins and wealth. (Claudio Linati, Costumes civils, militaires et religieux de Mexique *. . . [Brussels: Ch. Sattanino, 1828].)*

was *contra natura* (against nature), a condemned sexual act that would not lead to procreation. Sodomy was a capital crime (which alone would bring infamy); while those convicted might receive lighter—though generally still harsh—penalties, many were executed. Long linked with heresy, both in law and in popular association, the pecado nefando served as a useful political tool in both the Old World and the New; a well-timed allegation could irrevocably stain the reputation of an adversary.[3]

But a sodomy accusation did not necessarily bring immediate or complete dishonor (or criminal conviction). Much depended on the particularities of the individuals involved, their actions, and the perceptions and values of peasant, plebeian, and elite members of colonial society.

In examining the honor/dishonor associated with sodomy, I focus specifically on the transcripts from two trials in which Dr. Gaspar González de Sosa,[4] cathedral canon in La Plata (capital of the Audiencia of Charcas),[5] stood accused of having committed the pecado nefando. The first trial began in 1595, while the second effectively ended in 1614. Together the two trials span the decades in which the colonial world felt the full effects of the Council of Trent's reforms, directed at regularizing the church's practices and sacraments, at strengthening the institution of the family, and at asserting increased control over both the priesthood and the laity, especially in matters of sexual conduct.[6]

In both civil and ecclesiastical courts, trial prosecutors sought conviction for sodomy either through confession or the eyewitness observation of sexual acts. In the absence of such testimony, or to strengthen their case overall, prosecutors generally called on a variety of witnesses to testify about the actions of the accused, drawing on behavioral "clues" (*indicios*) that would suggest his guilt. Thus while the cases of interest here focus on Dr. González, a single, highly idiosyncratic member of the colonial elite, the recorded testimony cuts across ethnic, status, and wealth distinctions, incorporating the views and perceptions of a wide range of individuals, from household retainers to family members and the doctor's colleagues. The trial transcripts, then, capture a number of commentaries—whether direct or indirect—on sexuality, honor, and dishonor.[7]

THE TRIALS OF DR. GONZÁLEZ

Before his troubles with the law, Dr. Gaspar González had a very promising ecclesiastical career. He had been a priest in the Andes since the late 1570s; he had served as vicar general, as a vicar judge in Potosí, and as visitor general of the entire bishopric of La Plata; he was recognized as an expert in an indigenous language (probably Quechua), and he was a priest in Copacabana during the time when the fame of the cult of the virgin there was spreading.[8] Ambitious, he was granted the post of precentor (the person in charge of music and the third-highest ranked dignitary within the cathedral chapter), but as it was not yet vacant, he applied to be bishop of Paraguay or, failing that, dean of the cathedral in La Plata.[9] In 1587 the Potosí town council wrote a letter on his behalf, noting that he had served there for six years and was "a theologian preacher, so honest and modest, of such a good reputation, leading a good, exemplary life."[10]

Then in 1595 a number of men were arrested in Potosí and charged with having committed the pecado nefando.[11] In the course of the legal investigation, one of the accused said that he had heard that Dr. González had had sex with Juan González, a twenty-year-old man who worked in an apothecary shop. Although he at first denied it, Juan González later testified that he and Dr. González had had sex five or six times in Copacabana the previous year, with Dr. González always taking the active role. As Juan González's testimony had implicated a priest, the case was immediately moved from the civil to the ecclesiastical court for prosecution.

Pedro de Valencia, the vicar judge, then interviewed Juan González a number of times, questioning him about how he had met Dr. González, about who had seen them, and about details of their intimate relationship. He also repeatedly "exhorted" him to tell the truth, saying that if he died having given false testimony about a priest he would go to hell. Juan González was brought face to face with Dr. González, who by this time had been arrested and charged. Juan González swore once again that his statements were true; Dr. González countered that he was lying like a "perjuring heretic." While in the Potosí hospital, where he was imprisoned, the doctor took a deadly poison in an unsuccessful attempt to commit suicide. Juan González's final opportunity to recant his testimony came at his place of execution; he stated for the last time that what he had said about Dr. González was all true, after which he was garroted and his body burned at the stake.

The court then interviewed a number of witnesses about the events in Copacabana, and on October 2, 1595, the judge sentenced Dr. González to torture; he immediately appealed to the dean and cathedral chapter. More witnesses were questioned, revealing other incidents involving the doctor. The dean, however, decided to overturn the earlier judgment and freed Dr. González; the ecclesiastical prosecutor then appealed, and in 1597 the bishop of La Plata reversed the decision of the dean. Dr. González then appealed to the ecclesiastical court in Lima, where he was eventually successful in gaining his release.

In 1608 Dr. González again faced the charge of having committed the pecado nefando. On March 11 of that year, the dean and cathedral chapter of

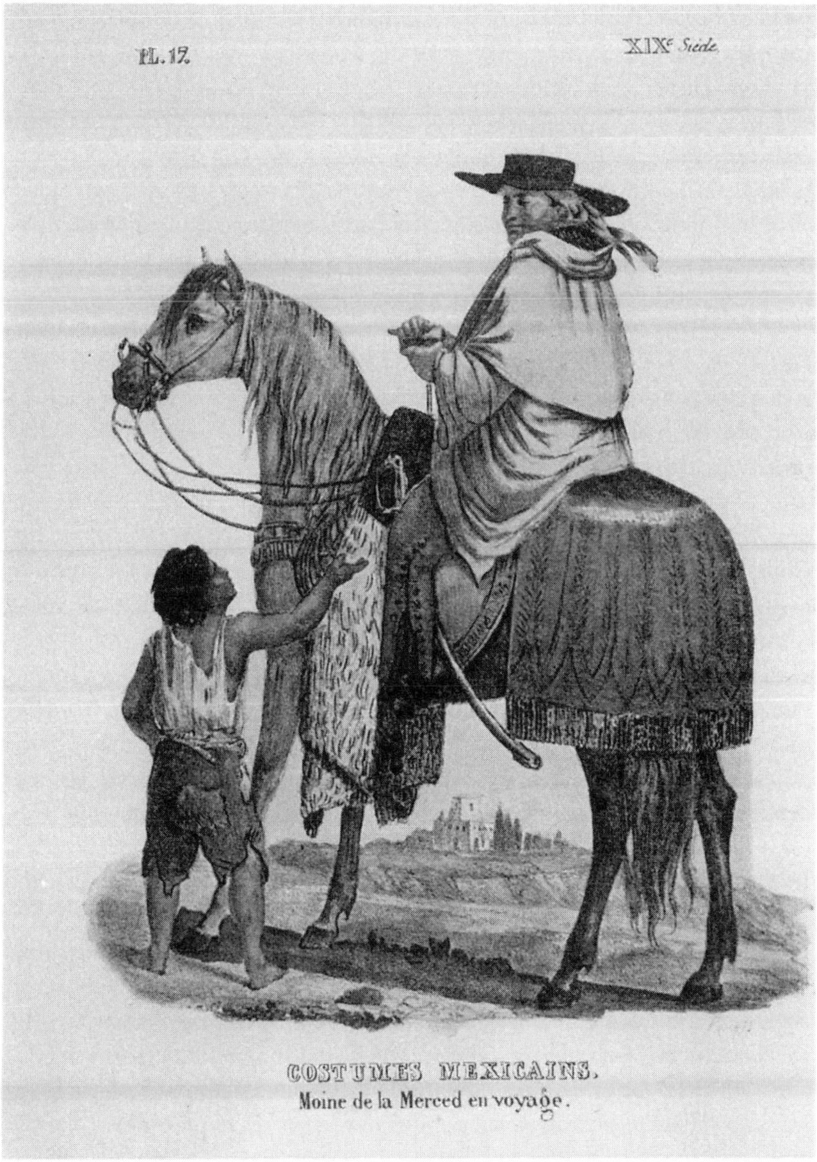
PL. 17.
XIXe Siècle.
COSTUMES MEXICAINS.
Moine de la Merced en voyage.

Figure 6. The richly dressed monk seated on a lavishly saddled horse proudly displays his wealth and status as a member of a religious order. Note the respect conveyed by the young beggar who approaches to ask for alms. (Claudio Linati, Costumes civils, militaires et religieux de Mexique . . . *[Brussels: Ch. Sattanino, 1828].)*

La Plata began an investigation; they noted that the doctor should have lived with discretion, given his past. Instead the doctor had created a huge scandal, as people of all classes and social positions gossiped that he had committed sodomy with don Diego Mexía while carrying out another *visita general* (general inspection). Worse, the scandal was not just limited to the Audiencia of Charcas; it had, in fact, spread throughout the viceroyalty and even to Spain. The dean went on to note that not only had the doctor ignored his advice as well as that of others, but he had also subverted an order from the audiencia to expel don Diego Mexía from the city of La Plata.

Over the next two months, the ecclesiastical court interviewed a large number of witnesses, including the notary, the attorney, and the interpreter who had accompanied Dr. González on the visita, the servants and other retainers who worked in his household in La Plata and at his farm, as well as a variety of others associated with the events and places involved in the case. Their testimonies provide unusual detail on the relationship between Dr. González and don Diego Mexía, particularly with respect to their affective behavior.[12] But while the doctor and Mexía were remarkably open about their affection for each other, for obvious reasons they were extremely circumspect in their sexual relations.

According to the witnesses interviewed, Potosí was the first stop on the visita, which had begun two years before the trial, in 1606. There Dr. González met Diego Poblete, an impoverished young man who was incarcerated in the public jail. They became close friends, and when the *visitadores* (inspectors) departed from Potosí, Poblete accompanied them. Dr. González paid off Poblete's debts and gave him substantial sums of money to buy new clothes. In Porco, Dr. González bestowed on Poblete the honorary title of *don* and changed his surname, announcing to all that henceforth Diego Poblete was to be called don Diego Mexía. Sometime later, González reordered the formal seating arrangement at dinner, moving Mexía so he sat at the head of the table, right next to the doctor. Everywhere they went on the visita, the two slept in the same room, without any servants (which was regarded as highly unusual) and with the door locked from the inside. Everyone associated with the visita was scandalized, especially given public knowledge of Dr. González's previous arrest; gossip spread among and between both servants and the visita officials and quickly extended to those in the towns they visited.

People were particularly offended by their intimacies, which the court regarded as indications of their guilt. They ate from the same plate and drank from the same cup, and a number of witnesses said that Dr. González even took pieces of food that he had already bitten into and offered them to Mexía, at times placing the morsels directly into don Diego's mouth. They shared a toothpick and a small cigar, and they were seen, in more private moments, embracing each other and kissing. While traveling between towns, they always rode side by side, an harquebus shot away from the rest of the company, even remaining together when one of them had to defecate. All of this behavior was closely watched, commented on, and joked about.

When they returned to La Plata, their relationship continued. Don Diego Mexía lived in Dr. González's house, which he shared with his nephew, Miguel González, and Miguel's wife, María de Guzmán. While Mexía had a separate bedroom, he and the doctor frequently slept together. The doctor gave don Diego a number of expensive gifts, including horses and gold jewelry; he purchased for him the position of *regidor* (alderman), and bought him a farm in Zocta, three leagues from the city. The case prosecutor estimated that over two years Dr. González had spent close to 50,000 pesos (an enormous sum) on gifts for don Diego Mexía. When the audiencia expelled don Diego from the city, he merely moved to the farm, from where they exchanged letters and visits (a number of witnesses reported seeing Mexía slip into the city at night).

In both the countryside and the city, their relationship was observed by the retainers who served them. At the farm, Bartolomé Quispe, the sixteen-year-old son of the local *kuraka* (Andean ruler), stated that one moonlit night, after saying prayers, he and the other boys began playing bulls, when he accidentally dislodged a window cover, providing a view of Dr. González and don Diego Mexía in bed together, illuminated by a candle on a side table, hugging and kissing. Catalina de Gálvez, a twenty-year-old mestiza, worked for three months in Dr. González's house in the city. María de Guzmán suggested that Gálvez spy on the two men by hiding under the bed one night, but as the young servant had begun to have sexual relations with don Diego, which made the doctor very jealous, she was particularly fearful of being caught. However, she did resort to peering through the keyhole.

The court regarded Dr. González's jealousy of Mexía's relations with Gálvez and other women as yet another indication of his guilt. One incident in particular received attention. One night don Diego Mexía returned home late, having accompanied a woman to a play; González was so incensed he refused to open the door. María de Guzmán's son, Gasparito, finally tossed the key down from an open window, but for a couple of days Mexía and Dr. González did not talk, and the doctor berated him, saying that he had spent his earnings on gifts, reminding him that he had purchased for him the position of regidor. At dinner Mexía would not look the doctor in the eyes. After two days don Diego finally requested his pardon and they made amends.

With the scandal growing, there came two signs from God, signaling divine disapproval. As don Diego Mexía left the performance of a play late one afternoon, witnesses reported seeing a spark, about the size of the end of a finger, fall from the folds of his cape down to the ground, where it smoked like burning cotton but left no trace. Don Juan de Mendoza, a cathedral canon, saw the event and told his servants to say nothing, but in his house, ashen-faced, he remarked that it was a sign that the doctor and Mexía had to be punished. Later a similar incident happened with Dr. González. As the doctor was descending the stairs of the choir in the church, several witnesses said they saw a ball of flame suddenly fall from his robes.[13]

Faced with these signs from God, with a scandal that had gotten out of control, and with the recalcitrant doctor not responding to the serious entreaties of the dean and others, the church and the audiencia finally acted, arresting both men. Mexía had to face the much sterner justice of the civil courts; he was so severely tortured that he was left crippled in both arms, but he refused to confess. The court found him guilty, sentencing him to ten years exile from the viceroyalty, six years to be spent in the galleys without pay. He was also fined 3,000 pesos, to be paid in part from the sale of the office of regidor. The dean and cathedral chapter of La Plata found Dr. González guilty as well. They ordered that he be defrocked, stripped of all his ecclesiastical privileges, and handed over to the secular authorities for justice; all of his goods were seized.[14] González immediately appealed to the metropolitan judge in Lima, arguing his case largely on technical grounds. On January 19, 1612, the archbishop of Lima communicated the court's decision: he found that it was not proved that Dr. González had committed the pecado nefando, but as it was an obligation of all priests to avoid scandal, the archbishop ordered that Dr. González never again communicate with don Diego Mexía and sentenced him to a prison term equal to (not in addition to) what he had already served, as well as one year of seclusion in a monastery in La Plata, all without pay. Seeking a conviction, the court in La Plata launched an appeal, and in 1613 the archbishop of La Plata wrote to the king saying that the public scandal continued, because Dr. González was saying mass in the church of Santo Domingo, where he was in seclusion. The following year, 1614, the king responded, ordering that Dr. González be removed from the jurisdiction of the church of La Plata, but that he retain his prebend.[15]

These, then, are the major events and details surrounding the trials of Dr. González. We can now turn to the analytical issues, examining how honor and dishonor figured in—and were defined by—the actions and perceptions of the individuals and institutions involved.

Figure 7. A wealthy woman would not leave her house without covering her head. She is accompanied by her child, who is dressed in the habit of a Franciscan monk to satisfy his mother's vow to the Virgin Mary. (Claudio Linati, Costumes civils, militaires et religieux de Mexique . . . [Brussels: Ch. Sattanino, 1828].)

MASCULINITY, FEMINIZATION, AND THE
RELATIVE DISHONOR OF ACTIVES AND PASSIVES

From at least Greco-Roman times to the early modern period, Europeans made both a popular and a legal distinction between passives and actives, between those who were said to take the female role in sodomy and those who took the male role. Assuming the passive position brought infamy and hence dishonor; passives were scorned and reviled, denigrated for having submitted to domination, for being dependent, defeated, violated, and effeminate. In contrast actives apparently did not receive the same ridicule nor suffer an equivalent stigma; the active was masculine, the one who dominated, conquered, penetrated.[16] But the legal and theological emphasis differed from the popular; as the aggressor and initiator, and given the usual age and power differences between the individuals involved (and at times the use of force), actives typically received much harsher sentences and were the focus of ecclesiastical concern.[17]

Can we discern the use, whether implicitly or explicitly, of the active/passive categories in the Dr. González cases? If so, what effect did they have in defining personal honor or dishonor?

While we do know from the 1595 trial that Dr. González always took the active role in his relationship with the apothecary Juan González, we do not have similar information on the sexual behavior of the doctor and Diego Mexía; neither of them confessed, and no eyewitnesses reported seeing them in flagrante delicto. However, the trial transcripts do record in detail many indicios, or clues, as to the nature of their sexual relations; collectively these testimonies construct a rough active/passive dichotomy, though the question of stigma and dishonor seems far less clear-cut than that outlined above.

The marked differences in power, wealth, and status between the two men placed Mexía in a dependent, and hence metaphorically passive, position. Dr. González got him out of jail, gave him gifts and honors, and maintained him at first in a house in the city and then later at his farm. When they quarreled over Mexía's relations with women, Dr. González pointedly reminded don Diego of what he owed him, of his dependency; Mexía responded with submission, casting his eyes down, eventually seeking forgiveness.

Witnesses interviewed during the trial proceedings portrayed don Diego Mexía as the passive, feminizing him in the process. They noted how Dr. González treated him with love and affection, using terms of endearment and referring to him with the diminutive Dieguito, embracing him and kissing him behind the ear, praising his attractive appearance.[18] People drew a direct comparison between their relationship and that of a man and a woman. At dinner, Dr. González would speak to don Diego in "words so tender and loving that no husband to his wife could say more"; he gave him gifts "of a type that couldn't be given except from a man to a woman because male friends would not do so." Some of those testifying referred to Mexía as Dr. González's woman. Others complained that Mexía had subverted the sexual division of labor, noting that at the farm he would go into the kitchen, sit down "as if he were a woman," and prepare food for the two of them with his own hands, even though there were female Andean cooks present.

The testimony of Francisco García, a resident of La Plata, reflects the kind of deprecatory joking behavior that was no doubt prevalent, placing Mexía in the passive role. He said that he was once in the slaughterhouse haggling over calf guts with don Diego; recognizing that the food was destined for the doctor's table, he turned to a black man (*un negro*) who had accompanied Mexía and said that the "doctor shouldn't screw me the way he does don Diego."[19] García went on to claim that those who saw Mexía riding his horse in the countryside would remark that "the doctor's woman rides well," but that they hoped he did not hurt himself so that "the doctor does not find his [Mexía's] ass injured."

While Mexía suffered the stigma and dishonor directly associated with his categorization as the passive, did Dr. González escape a similar invective in his putative role as active? After all, his authority and power commanded a necessary level of respect, and when the scandal had become widespread, he was feared. One witness stated that when he went to visit Dr. González on business, he made a note of the available windows and doors, just in case he had to make a quick exit. But the distinction between active and passive was not always clear. When witnesses compared their relationship to that between a man and a woman, they at times did not distinguish between who fulfilled which role, indicating that both Mexía and Dr. González shared the same category. Francisca, a young *chiriguana* servant of Dr. González, reported that the doctor's nephew, Miguel González, once stole a collection of letters written by both the doctor and Mexía. He read them out to his wife, both of them commenting that "they did not have any shame to have written such things . . . because they said such delicate and tender things as when a man writes to a woman, calling each other my soul, my life, and other complimentary things." Furthermore Dr. González's well-attested intense jealousy of Mexía's relations with women and the excesses of the doctor's intimacies and emotional attachment made him clearly vulnerable and, in a sense, dependent on Mexía and thus "passive."[20] Hernando Romero, a witness at the farm in Zocta, told how Dr. González had offered cheese dipped in honey directly into the mouth of don

Figure 8. The status and authority of the Catholic clergy was derived in part from the enormous power of the church itself. Cathedrals and the buildings of the religious orders dominated public spaces. This is the Franciscan convent of Quito, Ecuador. (Photograph by Sue Johnson.)

Diego, commenting that he was scandalized and that he said to his wife "not a father to his son, nor a *wife* to her husband, nor a brother to a brother would do that" (emphasis added). Both men were referred to as *putos* and *bujarrones*, words one might normally associate with passives;[21] one witness stated that Dr. González "smelled like a puto." And both were considered equally guilty before God, if we can judge by the reported incidents involving the fireballs.

Dr. González was not feminized to the same degree as Mexía, nor was he the recipient of a similarly intense public invective, but he was the subject of ridicule and disdain. In this case at least, the active/passive distinction seems muddy; though differently, both men shared in the social stigma, the dishonor, and the infamy associated with their actions. This case should make us question any neat dichotomy between passive and active that might portray only the former as dishonoring. The two men went beyond sexual relations to a developed relationship (though one clearly not between equals). Their openly expressed affection and long-term association meant that popular disdain and the dishonor of sodomy fell on them both.[22]

HONOR-STATUS AND POWER

Pitt-Rivers notes that a man "may not be thought privately to be honourable, but while no one is prepared to question the matter, he is treated as though he were and granted the precedence which he claims"; he then concludes that "[o]n the field of honour might is right."[23] Dr. González's honor served in the manner described by Pitt-Rivers; in effect his honor-status protected his personal honor, his reputation, wealth, and power at least initially limiting the spread of malicious gossip and in the end saving him from the garrote and the stake. As well, he used his honor-status to grant honors to others, in so doing undermining the honor system itself.

In the first court case, a number of witnesses stated that they did not divulge what they knew of Dr. González because he was an honorable man. Vicente Franco de la Vega, a resident of Potosí, said that he kept quiet because "he [the doctor] was taken for an honorable man and a good Christian." Similarly Cristóbal de la Chica, who was sexually approached by Dr. González when studying with him to be a priest, said that because he was "a priest and an esteemed person he didn't dare tell anyone" except his mother and his closest friend. Honor, and the power behind it, might prevent disclosure, keeping what some knew secret from the general public.

Once the arrests were made, the doctor's allies attempted to keep potential witnesses silent. In the first court case, his friends and relatives tried to convince individuals not to tell what they had seen or experienced. In the second case, the persuasion was more forceful. The servants on the farm, for example, were warned not to speak to the investigators for fear that Mexía and González would be released and would return to beat them; the warning proved accurate, as during the appeal process two friends of Dr. González, both priests, apparently went out to the farm and tried to force a number of individuals to recant their testimony. Such tactics, though, were only partly successful and were obvious to judicial authorities (the prosecutor condemned such witness tampering).

Dr. González's standing and reputation as an honorable member of the church, and juridical ideas concerning the incompetent status and questionable word of many of the witnesses, were certainly key factors in the decisions that saved the doctor from being defrocked and handed over to the harsh justice of the secular court. In the appeal process, the prosecutor argued that it was critically important to allow the testimony of *inauiles* (incompetents; *inhábiles* in modern spelling), the Andeans, mestizos, mulattoes, and blacks who normally were not granted equivalent standing in court. He maintained that such testimony was admissible in cases of the pecado nefando, just as it was in cases of heresy and treason. However, the metropolitan court found differently; the archbishop of Lima noted that "the majority of the witnesses who condemned him [the doctor] were vile and low people," who presented conflicting testimony, as opposed to Dr. González, who was "such a highly qualified preacher."

As a wealthy member of the colonial elite, Dr. González repeatedly used his honorable position and power to promote his own ends. Virtually all of his reported relationships were with men of lesser social standing,[24] and the doctor wielded his wealth and influence like a patron. In the earlier case of the apothecary, the doctor was instrumental in convincing the shop owner to hire him, recommending Juan González as an "honorable and competent man." In one incident Dr. González manipulated the language of honor in an attempted seduction. When González was serving as a priest in Copacabana, he invited a poor student and native of the Canaries, Juan Ruiz, to spend the night after they and others had whiled away the afternoon and evening partying and dancing. Once in bed the doctor expressed his affection for Ruiz and said that he would give him clothes and money. A short time later he began to fondle Ruiz, who immediately responded that the doctor should think about what he was doing, "being such an honorable man with his qualities," and that by neither heaven nor earth should he commit such a sin. Seldom responsive to arguments based on the honor code, Dr. González quickly countered that "many honorable men do it, especially students."

In the case of Mexía, Dr. González more profoundly manipulated the social hierarchy and its associated set of honors. While on the visita, González gave Mexía his new name and commanded that henceforth all were to address him with the honorific *don*; he also reordered the seating, moving Mexía to his side. This change in protocol not only affected hierarchically ordered notions of respect, but it also meant that Mexía would be served (and would eat) second, immediately after the doctor. Out of recognition for González's authority and his position as visitor general, everyone begrudgingly followed his orders, but with a bitterness evident in their respective testimonies. Back in La Plata, Dr. González sought to further elevate don Diego's social standing (now within the urban setting of the audiencia capital), showering him with expensive, visibly high-status gifts and purchasing for him the office of regidor.

González thus demonstrated his ability and his willingness to turn honor and the colonial order to his advantage, but in so doing—especially with the growing scandal and public knowledge of Mexía's humble origins—his actions simultaneously demeaned and undermined the basis of both.

THE DISHONOR OF INDISCRETION

As honor was public, discretion was critically important. Studies of honor have repeatedly emphasized the frequent gulf between the public face and the private act.[25] To maintain that necessary distance, individuals could rely to a degree on the reticence to gossip that might come either from the respect they commanded and/or from the coercive powers they exercised (as we have seen above); more common, though, was to behave with discretion, maintaining secrecy where possible or using sanctioned legal and social remedies to retain one's honor. In his relations with don Diego Mexía, Dr. González failed in the former and rather spectacularly ignored the rules governing the latter.

González's behavior and indiscretion did not just have an impact on his own honor and reputation; others were clearly affected. Individuals reported feeling shame if, for example, they witnessed the two embracing or kissing. With the spread of Dr. González's notoriety, anyone connected to him had to worry about being somehow implicated by association. One day in the plaza in La Plata, the doctor passed by some men, reminding one that they had business to conduct; when González left, the others confronted the man, asking, in a pointed jest, just what sort of business he had with the good doctor.

González's actions affected the family honor of his nearest relatives, his nephew Miguel González and Miguel's wife, María de Guzmán. All of them lived in the same house in La Plata, together with don Diego. Miguel and María were placed in a difficult position: on the one hand, Miguel had close business dealings with his powerful, wealthy uncle, while on the other both he and María had to contend with the scandal carried out under their shared roof. Miguel González went to the dean, asking him to compel the doctor to end his relationship with Mexía. He also attempted to retain his personal honor by issuing a number of threats against Mexía, made publicly enough that they were commented on by a series of witnesses. In a fury one night, Miguel apparently decided to end it all with sword in hand, but he could not get beyond the locked door to the room where the doctor and don Diego were together. This masculine posturing was a necessary response to the challenge to his honor, but the locked door no doubt served as a convenient barrier preventing him from carrying out such a dangerous act.[26]

With the arrests of Dr. González and Mexía, the situation changed. On hearing that the doctor had been taken into custody, Miguel and María immediately entered the doctor's room and removed some silver bars and other money that he had stored; they also began dismantling his desk, taking out jewels and any other objects of value, obviously aware that under the law the doctor's goods would be confiscated. They threatened all of their servants, telling them to say nothing of what they had seen if they were called to testify. The two thus acted to limit the financial damage and to support the doctor's case, recognizing that a guilty verdict for Dr. González would have a disastrous economic effect on the family and would only further stain their honor.

Dr. González's sins also threatened the collective honor of the cathedral chapter, and by extension the church itself, as well as that of the audiencia. A number of entries in the trial transcript reflect the intense and no doubt angry frustration felt by the ecclesiastical elite, as Dr. González repeatedly rebuffed their attempts to persuade him to cease his relationship with Mexía. Their efforts indicate both the extent of González's indiscretion and the degree to which they were prepared to go in order to try to solve the problem among themselves first, before having recourse to the courts. In opening the second trial, the dean condemned Dr. González's behavior and his obstinate refusal to abide by their advice and orders. The dean noted that as Dr. González had already been implicated in having committed the pecado nefando with Juan González, he subsequently should have lived with "the discretion, honesty, and modesty that he owed to the office he held, avoiding all occasions that might cause suspicion"; he pointed out that the cathedral chapter had actually granted González the post of visitor general "to honor him," yet it was on the visita that the scandal began. Further not only did González ignore the dean's advice to cease his relationship, but he also paid little heed to the signs from God or to the expulsion order from the audiencia. In his summary of the court case, the appeals prosecutor reviewed the pressure unsuccessfully placed on González, the "pleas, persuasions, and threats from the audiencia, the dean, his capitular colleagues, and the provincials from the orders," noting that these were delivered clearly and to his face; he argued that for men of such rank and dignity to so confront a person of Dr. González's quality and character, they must have believed the evidence and presumed his guilt.

The central concern, then, was not to punish him judicially for the sins they believed he had committed (as it was in the secular court's treatment of both Juan González and don Diego Mexía), but rather to convince him to end the scandal, to act with appropriate caution and discretion. Only when he refused, when he proved "incorrigible," and when the scandal grew unmanageable, did the church finally act judicially. The dean's reluctance to press charges was overcome by the extent of the gossip and the damage it was doing; he noted that the scandal was general "throughout the province and among all classes and types of people" and that "the infamy extended over all these kingdoms and to Spain." The church was faced with a very serious problem. Though typically lenient in its treatment of clergy, the church could no longer overlook

Dr. González's brazen behavior and the challenge that it posed to the institution's moral authority. The ironies of the situation would not have been lost on the dean or other church dignitaries. As part of his post as visitor general, Dr. González would have questioned and assessed the character and moral life of local parish priests, at the same time that he was quite openly beginning a relationship with don Diego. As a highly trained priest with a doctorate, and as a cathedral canon, González served as a very senior, influential member of the clergy at precisely the time that the Counter-Reformation church was attempting to monitor the actions of priests and institute sexual discipline in the laity.

The ecclesiastical and secular elite could no longer contain the gossip; a solution among nobles could not be crafted, as it had become public knowledge and hence a scandal. Dr. González's sins thus brought into question the respectability, power, authority, and collective honor of the church and the audiencia.

The final sentence issued by the metropolitan court in Lima confirmed that a key concern of the church was public perception and reputation. As mentioned earlier, Dr. González was cleared of the central charge, the competence of many of the witnesses having been called into question because of their socioeconomic and ethnic background, but he was found guilty of acting scandalously. Those who "preach the word of God are obliged not only to be good and perfect but to appear to be, avoiding any occasion that might create scandal."

Colonial institutions and the nobility, then, were particularly concerned with minimizing the damage caused by dishonorable behavior, indiscretion, and scandal. There was a common interest in retaining their honor-status and in defending it when threatened. In his sentence, the archbishop implied that false accusations and calumny were characteristic of colonial society; he stated that "in the Indies, there are born many fanciful remarks, hearsay, and insults, without any fundamental truth, made in passion, hate, and bad faith in order to take revenge." This was clearly meant to further weaken the credibility of the testimonies made against Dr. González, but the statement also implicitly recognized the defamatory potential of pecado nefando accusations, used for political purposes in both Iberia and the Americas.[27] Perhaps, though, we can also read into this both an acknowledgment that the reputation and honor-status of the nobility was vulnerable to the murmurings of the general public, as well as a frustration with the elite's inability to better control the spread of scandal and the damage it caused.

The metropolitan court's verdict did not itself end the censure and infamy; the doctor's reputation in the broader community had been severely injured, and the general public would not stand for a judicial solution that let him retain his position and even continue to say mass. The king was forced to respond, eventually ordering the doctor's relocation. Thus there seems to have been a distinction in conceptions of justice, appropriate punishment, and honor/dishonor, between a scandalized lay public and a somewhat more forgiving church.

CONCLUSION

Each of the cases involving Dr. González centered on the accusation that he had committed the abominable sin of sodomy. Sodomy defied not only the procreative function of sex, but also the gendered division between appropriate male and female behavior. It therefore directly challenged the basis of the family—the fundamental social unit—and in so doing the colonial hierarchy. Sodomy was an offense against God and the "natural order of things"; a reviled act, it could bring infamy.

But work on late medieval and early modern Europe has revealed the differential treatment of "sodomites," with actives generally receiving a more severe sentence, passives the public's ridicule. The case of González and Mexía raises questions about the active/passive dichotomy, with its associated implications of dishonor and shame. While the witnesses interviewed feminized Mexía, defining him as a passive, the position of González was far less clear. Though in many ways he was obviously the dominant partner in the relationship, he did not escape public censure. From the recorded testimony it appears that the important factor in determining popular perception was the longevity and openness of his relationship with Mexía. Though there were inequities, the clearly expressed affection González held for don Diego, indicating his emotional vulnerability, meant that he was not perceived as a dominant, assertive, and to a degree necessarily disinterested active. The stigma of sodomy fell on both of them; they were shamed, dishonored, categorized as putos.

Yet to a surprising degree Dr. González retained his honor-status, which proved to be both powerful and protective. While those with whom he was intimate were tortured, severely punished, and in one case at least publicly executed, he survived, passing years in custody but in an "honorable jail" and eventually winning acquittals. Throughout he was accorded a great deal of respect, even by those who indicted him; his status as a wealthy, well-educated theologian, with years of service to the church, survived the assault on his personal honor. Ultimately he benefited from the relative leniency of the church's metropolitan court and its willingness to forgive, though Dr. González hardly seemed penitent.

And there were limits to the degree to which the church—and civic offi-cials—were willing to overlook the doctor's actions. After all it was not so much what the doctor and Mexía did behind closed doors that was of central con-cern; rather it was their public behavior and their lack of discretion. In using his wealth and power to manipulate the social hierarchy, elevating don Diego's status by conferring on him the symbols and accouterments associated with honor, Dr. González effectively demeaned the honor system itself. Their be-havior displaced and displeased both the wealthy and the poor, challenging the colonial order from the sexual division of labor to the honor of González's immediate family to social divisions symbolized and enforced in protocol and even to the relationship with the divine, incurring God's anger. Rather than behave with the caution and modesty appropriate to his noble status and clerical office, Dr. González behaved with excess. His involvement with Mexía forced reluctant individuals to act, whether in the case of his nephew's armed assault on a locked door and his petitions to authorities or the dean's forthright conversation with the doctor, which the dean felt as an infringement on his personal integrity. To exemplify and uphold the social order, the nobility were always to maintain the appearance of proper, socially (and divinely) sanctioned behavior; the doctor's deeds flew in the face of these most basic hierarchically ordering principles.

In fact what in part makes the case of Dr. González so extraordinary is his adamant refusal to bend to the social pressures placed on him. Most studies of colonial honor stress the unusual and often inventive lengths to which individ-uals would go in order to preserve the appearance of virtue and hence their personal honor. Dr. González made no such efforts, other than to closely guard his sexual behavior from prying eyes. Why did he act as he did, seemingly impervious to the damage he was inflicting on his honor, on the honor of his immediate family, and on the collective honor of the nobility, the church, and the audiencia?

With his wealth, status, and occupation, González had the resources to confront the colonial order, and to withstand social and judicial pressure. His power gave him leeway. But the possibility to act does not explain the actions themselves. Here I think we have to look at the nature of Dr. González's relationship with Mexía and its considerable difference from his earlier ties with the apothecary, Juan González (and with the others who testified regard-ing his attempted seductions). The doctor's relationship with Juan González was short-term and discrete; he responded angrily when faced in court with the apothecary and his accusation. And soon after charges were laid, Dr. González attempted suicide, probably an initial response to the shame and dishonor that he faced. In so doing, the doctor acted according to the honor code. But all that changed with Mexía. As so many witnesses noted, Dr. González was clearly smitten with him; the depth and extent of his affection led him to foster their relationship openly, regardless of the cost to his honor and to the honor of all who were associated with him.[28]

NOTES

Acknowledgments: Work on this project was supported by a Simon Fraser University President's Research Grant and a Social Sciences and Humanities Research Council of Canada Small Research Grant. My thanks to the staff of the Archivo General de Indias in Seville, and Falia González Díaz in particular. Special thanks also to Joanna Spurling, Berta Ares, Christian Büschges (and all the Las Meninas friends and colleagues), Tom Abercrombie, and Tommaso Astarita for comments on a very early version of this paper.

1. On "heterosexuality" as a constructed category with a nineteenth-century origin, see Jonathan Katz, *The Invention of Heterosexuality* (New York: Dutton, 1995).

2. Works on honor generally distinguish between personal honor (or honor-virtue), defined above, and honor-status (or honor-precedence), which was derived from an individual's power, family, social position, wealth, occupation, and ethnicity. Julian Pitt-Rivers first introduced this distinction in the analytical literature on honor; see his "Honour and Social Status," in *Honour and Shame: The Values of Mediterranean Society*, ed. J. G. Peristiany (Chicago: University of Chicago Press, 1966), 21–77, and "Honor," in *International Encyclopedia of the Social Sciences,* vol. 6 (New York: Macmillan/Free Press, 1968), 503–11. For a slightly different view, categorizing honor as vertical and horizontal, see Frank Henderson Stewart, *Honor* (Chicago: University of Chicago Press, 1994).

3. In the medieval and early modern periods, the term *pecado nefando* was used to describe a wide range of sexual behaviors, extending, in its broadest definition, to include all nonreproductive sex. Sodomy as well was often broadly defined. In the sources I examine here, however, the terms *pecado nefando* and *sodomy* refer to anal intercourse, though other forms of sexual activity were of interest to the judges, attorneys, defendants, and witnesses involved in the cases. For studies of sexuality in medieval and early modern Europe, see John Boswell, *Christianity, Social Tolerance, and Homosexuality: Gay People in Western Europe from the Beginning of the Christian Era to the Fourteenth-Century* (Chicago: University of Chicago Press, 1980); Vern L. Bullough, "The Sin against Nature and Homosexuality," in *Sexual Practices and the Medieval Church*, ed. Vern L. Bullough and James A. Brundage (Buffalo, NY: Prometheus Books, 1982), 55–71; Michael Goodich, *The Unmentionable Vice: Homosexuality in the Later Medieval Period* (Santa Barbara, CA: ABC-Clio, 1979); Pierre J. Payer, *The Bridling of Desire: Views of Sex in the Later Middle Ages* (Toronto: University of Toronto Press, 1993); and Guido Ruggiero, *The Boundaries of Eros: Sex Crime and Sexuality in Renaissance Venice* (Oxford: Oxford University Press, 1985), 109–45. On pecado nefando accusations and defamation, see James A. Brundage, "The Politics of Sodomy: Rex V. Pons Hugh De Ampurias (1311)," in *Sex in the Middle Ages: A Book of Essays*, ed. Joyce E. Salisbury

(New York: Garland, 1991), 239–46. For a detailed analysis of hundreds of sodomy trials in Spain, see Rafael Carrasco, *Inquisición y represión sexual en Valencia: Historia de los sodomitas (1565–1785)* (Barcelona: Laertes, 1985). On colonial Mexico, see Serge Gruzinski's path-breaking study of multiple individuals accused of the pecado nefando in a single trial ("Las cenizas del deseo: Homosexuales novohispanos a mediados del siglo xvii," in *De la santidad a la perversión: O de porqué no se cumplía la ley de Dios en la sociedad novohispana* [Mexico City: Editorial Grijalbo, 1986], 255–81).

4. I have modernized the spelling of all personal names, adding accents where required.

5. Modern-day Sucre, Bolivia.

6. For Trent's impact on colonial Latin America, see many of the articles in *Sexuality and Marriage in Colonial Latin America,* ed. Asunción Lavrin (Lincoln: University of Nebraska Press, 1989).

7. For insightful analyses of sexuality based on individual-centered histories, see Guido Ruggiero, *Binding Passions: Tales of Magic, Marriage, and Power at the End of the Renaissance* (Oxford: Oxford University Press, 1993).

8. On the early history of the virgin of Copacabana, see Sabine MacCormack, "From the Sun of the Incas to the Virgin of Copacabana," *Representations* 8 (1984): 30–60.

9. For a detailed analysis of the colonial church hierarchy, see John F. Schwaller, *The Church and Clergy in Sixteenth-Century Mexico* (Albuquerque: University of New Mexico Press, 1987). I use here his English translations of the titles of the various church offices.

10. Archivo General de Indias, Seville (AGI), Charcas 144.

11. The main source for both cases involving Dr. González is AGI Charcas 140; hereafter, all direct quotations are from this manuscript, unless otherwise indicated (translations mine). The document (97 folios in length) is a copy drawn up for the final appeal process; as such it is incomplete, including only the "essential witnesses" (f. 1), essential, that is, to the prosecution. The document does not contain either Dr. González's confession or his various appeals, though it is possible to reconstruct his final appeal from the prosecutor's very detailed response (ff. 85–94).

12. Both Carrasco (*Inquisición,* 115, 189) and Gruzinski (*Las cenizas del deseo,* 276) note that in the cases they studied there was little information on affection or love.

13. That the divine omens should have come in the form of fire is no surprise, given the destruction by fire of Sodom and Gomorrah and the cremation of executed sodomites. Interestingly all the witnesses interpret the fiery omens as signs from God that Dr. González and don Diego Mexía must be punished; they do not seem to fear an impending cataclysmic (and collective) divine punishment, as was the case in medieval and early Renaissance Europe (see Ruggiero, *The Boundaries of Eros,* 109, 111, 112; and Brundage, *The Politics of Sodomy,* 239; but see Brundage's comment on p. 240).

14. In 1568, just five years after the closing of the Council of Trent, Pious V issued a papal bull stipulating that priests convicted of the pecado nefando in ecclesiastical court could be defrocked and handed over to secular authorities for trial and punishment (Carrasco, *Inquisición,* 40); in his argument before the court, the prosecutor in the case referred directly to this papal bull (AGI Charcas 140, f. 92v).

15. AGI Charcas 135 and AGI Charcas 415, L. 2, f. 257v.

16. On actives, passives, and dishonor, see Stewart, *Honor,* 55; Ruggiero, *The Boundaries of Eros,* 121–24; Mary Elizabeth Perry, *Gender and Disorder in Early Modern Seville* (Princeton, NJ: Princeton University Press, 1990), 125; Carrasco, *Inquisición*; and Ramón A. Gutiérrez, *When Jesus Came, the Corn Mothers Went Away* (Stanford, CA: Stanford University Press, 1991), 76, 210. For an extended (though problematic) discussion, including a consideration of feminization, see Richard C. Trexler, *Sex and Conquest: Gendered Violence, Political Order, and the European Conquest of the Americas* (Ithaca, NY: Cornell University Press, 1995), especially chapters 1, 2, and 7.

17. Trexler attempts to explain this paradox (see *Sex and Conquest,* 35–37).

18. Though interestingly, Dr. González did so by noting how attractive Mexía was to women.

19. An interesting (and very modern-sounding) usage, equating sexual and monetary domination. The verb used here is *cabalgar,* literally meaning "to ride" or "to mount" and used colloquially to refer to the "active" in sexual intercourse; "screw" seems the most appropriate translation in this context.

20. Whereas Mexía's affairs with women do not seem to have affected the public perception of him as passive in his relationship with Dr. González.

21. In usage linked directly to the pecado nefando, *puto* derived from *puta,* or female whore (more pejorative in intent and meaning than prostitute); *bujarrón* meant literally one who had been perforated, penetrated. For early seventeenth-century definitions of these terms, see Sebastián de Covarrubias, *Tesoro de la lengua castellana o española* (Barcelona: S. A. Horta, [1611] 1943), 244, 698, 889). Trexler (*Sex and Conquest,* 169) argues that *puto* most often was used to refer to passives.

22. In his study of contemporary Nicaragua, Lancaster notes that the stigma associated with the passive can extend to the active if the latter becomes emotionally attached and if the nature of their relationship becomes publicly known; *Life is Hard: Machismo, Danger, and the Intimacy of Power in Nicaragua* (Berkeley: University of California Press, 1992), 244. Dr. González's sexuality may have been cast into doubt, given his occupation as priest (see Trexler, *Sex and Conquest,* 48, 50, 51); however, as I argue above, the nature of his relationship with Mexía was far more important.

23. Pitt-Rivers, "Honour and Social Status," 24, 25.

24. There was one possible exception: Padre Sánchez, the priest of Guaqui, testified in 1608 that three years previously there were rumors of an intimate relationship between Dr. González and Licenciado Carbajal, who had served as priest of Paucarcolla and who had also been suspected of committing the pecado nefando.

25. For example, see Ann Twinam, "Honor, Sexuality, and Illegitimacy in Colonial Spanish America," in *Sexuality and Marriage in Colonial Latin America,* ed. Asunción Lavrin (Lincoln: University of Nebraska Press, 1989), 118–55.

26. For a discussion of similar strategies calculated to retain masculine honor while minimizing potentially violent repercussions, see Steve J. Stern, *The Secret History of Gender: Women, Men, and Power in Late Colonial Mexico* (Chapel Hill: University of North Carolina Press, 1995), 184–87.

27. In fact, the fate of Dr. González's successor exemplifies the political uses of sodomy.

Pedro de Arandia replaced González as cathedral canon of La Plata, only to be accused himself of having committed the pecado nefando. After a protracted litigation, Arandia was acquitted of the charge, which was apparently cooked up by his enemy, the vicar general of La Plata, Bartolomé de Zervantes. Absolved of guilt but scandalized and in shame, Arandia was offered the same option as Dr. González—separation from his church district. In their 1634 letter to the king requesting that Arandia be reposted, the cathedral chapter attached a copy of the 1614 royal order from the king concerning Dr. González. For the Arandia case, see AGI Charcas 20 R. 12 N. 121 and AGI Charcas 20 R. 16 N. 190; the 1634 letter is in AGI Charcas 140.

28. While the intensity of Dr. González's passion for don Diego Mexía comes through very clearly in the court transcript, it is difficult to judge to what extent Mexía reciprocated his feelings. The tenderness of their affective behavior, the contents of their love letters, and the considerable risks posed by the openness of their relationship (for which Mexía paid dearly at the hands of judicial authorities) would all argue for the depth of Mexía's emotional bond. But don Diego's amorous attentions were somewhat divided, judging from his affairs with women, and the great inequalities of wealth and power that characterized his relationship with González did place him in a dependent position.

CHAPTER THREE

THE NEGOTIATION OF HONOR
Elites, Sexuality, and Illegitimacy in Eighteenth-Century Spanish America

ANN TWINAM

AN INTRODUCTORY TALE

On the first of January in 1786, the Havana city council met to elect officers for the coming year. The members deadlocked twice in their choice before sparring factions divided their votes evenly between don Mariano de las Casas and don Antonio Basilio Menocal. Following legal custom, the two men then cast dice to see who would hold the office of *procurador general,* and don Mariano, a Havana lawyer, emerged the victor. Normally that would have settled the issue, but factionalism on the council surfaced as the losing side tried to overturn don Mariano's win by attacking his family's reputation. Although the rival faction never questioned that don Mariano was legitimate, they challenged his honor and therefore the validity of his election because he descended from a "bastard through his maternal line."[1] They argued that the lottery results were not valid, because such a casting of lots should only occur "when the subjects are equal." This was not the case, they argued, because the illegitimacy of don Mariano's mother deprived her of honor, and so she could not have passed on this fundamental requirement to her son.

What started as a triumphant election for don Mariano now turned into a public challenge to his honor. Bitterly complaining of his enemy's "daring spirit of malevolence, hatred, and rancor," don Mariano tried to repair the damage.[2] Three times he appealed the city council's decision to award the post to another; and he obtained a statement from the governor that he was qualified to hold any position "to which he might be elected." Yet his efforts proved futile, for it was his competitor rather than don Mariano who gained the coveted post.

Don Mariano then decided to prevent any further challenges to his honor. After collecting supporting testimony, he appealed in 1792 to the Cámara, the small group of the Council of the Indies members who dealt with such petitions. He asked them to legitimate his seventy-one-year-old mother, doña Antonia del Rey Blanco. However, he had difficulty in finding anyone still alive who could testify to those long-ago events surrounding her birth. He eventually dredged up three witnesses in their seventies and eighties who recalled what must have been a well-known scandal in the Havana of their infancy and childhood. They verified that don Mariano's mother was the illegitimate daughter of doña Beatris Blanco de la Posa. This doña Beatris had left the convent of Santa Catarina due to health reasons, was courted and promised matrimony, began a sexual relationship, and became pregnant. However, her marriage plans had to be canceled when her family discovered that her 'fiancé,' don Lázaro del Rey Bravo, already had a wife in Spain.

Little is known of the later history of the unfortunate doña Beatris, but twenty-one years later her illegitimate daughter, doña Antonia, was married to don Juan Andrés de las Casas (1721). Don Juan was an accepted member of the Havana elite who had confirmed his high status with election to the Havana city council in 1739. Yet several decades later (1786), city council officers denied the same position to don Juan's legitimate son, don Mariano, due to his mother's illegitimate birth. The reverberations of a sexual relationship that had occurred more than seventy years before compelled don Mariano to petition Spanish officials to legitimate his mother and thereby restore the family honor as well as his own eligibility for civil posts.

Don Mariano's tale of discrimination found a receptive audience when it reached the Cámara of the Indies. Royal officials noted that his mother was now "seventy-one years old, that she had been married to a distinguished person and had legitimate succession." Therefore they legitimated her so there would be no "pretext to embarrass" her family concerning "those effects of pure distinction and honor to which they might aspire . . . as has occurred in the case of don Joseph Mariano her son."[3] Yet even royal intervention was not sufficient in this instance, for although the newly legitimated doña Antonia could now retroactively pass honor on to her son, don Mariano never secured a seat on the Havana city council.

What is going on here? The tale of don Mariano's search for acceptance introduces three themes essential for understanding how members of colonial elites defined and defended their honor. First, although the judgments of the Havana council may seem cruel or even petty, they were faithful to tradition when they refused to accept a person who lacked honor onto their selective body. Second, the cabildo's rejection of don Mariano demonstrates that mem-

Figure 9. Love letters such as this one allowed contact between elite men and women. Sometimes these contacts escalated into sexual relationships that could threaten honorable status and family reputation if revealed. (Carta de amor de Diego Rodríguez del Pozo, ramo Inquisición, vol. 1100, exp. 2, fol. 53, no. 4853, Archivo General de la Nación, Mexico City.)

bers of the elite conceptualized honor as a condition inherited from both parents. It was not sufficient that don Mariano's father was a former council member and man of honor, if his mother lacked that essential quality. Third, even though the illegitimacy of don Mariano's mother meant that she could not pass on honor to her son at his birth, this was not necessarily a permanent problem. Don Mariano was able to purchase a royal decree that not only legitimated his mother and restored her honor, but also his own, even though he never became a cabildo member. Tracing the evolution of historic definitions of honor, how its presence or absence affected intimate relationships between men and women, and how honor might be negotiated and lost or gained, introduces themes critical to any understanding of hierarchy, sexuality, and social mobility in colonial Latin America. Before proceeding it is essential not only to consider what has gone before, but to understand how those requests for legitimation known as the *gracias al sacar* inform the following analysis.

METHODOLOGY, SOURCES, AND APPROACHES

The tale of don Mariano and his mother challenges us to discover what elite eighteenth-century Latin Americans meant by the concept of honor. Although don Mariano lacked honor because his mother was illegitimate, circumstances of birth were not the sole determinant of who did and who did not possess honor. Since honor has been a topic on which much has been written, and even more confused, a consideration of what has gone before can set the agenda for what follows.

An extensive and valuable historiography on the issue of honor must be approached with a degree of caution. Unfortunately, assumptions derived from research concerning honor in one time and place have too often become assimilated into generalizations concerning honor in other centuries and other cultures. For example analyses of Spanish medieval law and literature have promoted influential stereotypes as to how honor shaped the lives of Hispanic women. Statements such as "no wife could be permitted to commit adultery" or "no daughter could be permitted to have sexual relations out of wedlock" have been followed by extreme conclusions, including that sexual misconduct led to "total collapse of social esteem and personal pride," or to severe reactions by males who "avenged the deed, usually by violent means." Sixteenth-century literature has been another frequent source, promoting images of swashbuckling Don Juans or other protagonists similarly obsessed by issues of honor. More recent anthropological studies of the Mediterranean have added to the mix with discussions of how honor has influenced gender relationships in twentieth-century Greece, Italy, and Spain.[4]

There is no question that an understanding of the honor codes of medieval Spanish matrons, sixteenth-century Don Juans, or modern Greek peasants might provide insight into the uses of honor in colonial Latin America. However, such comparisons should be generated without any assumption of transferability. Yet Latin American historians have been overly influenced by extreme interpretations. One colonial scholar concluded in a pioneering article in 1917 that "among the families of the distinguished classes, offenses [against] honor are only erased with the death of the guilty, and the religious profession of the injured."[5] Patricia Seed's more recent (1988) analysis of honor in colonial Mexico relied on generalizations derived from sixteenth-century Spanish playwrights such as Lope de Vega and Calderón de la Barca to forward a concept of honor as "virtue," which was presumably characteristic of seventeenth-century Mexico.[6] This model was then contrasted with twentieth-century anthropological definitions of honor as "status," which supposedly influenced the honor paradigm in eighteenth-century Mexico. The question is whether either sixteenth-century playwrights or twentieth-century anthropologists should set any fundamental agenda for analyzing how the seventeenth or eighteenth-century Mexican elite conceptualized honor. The more rigorous process would be first to determine what Mexicans in one period or another said and did concerning honor and then to compare their formulations of honor with those of other times or other places.

Recent research on honor, such as Elizabeth S. Cohen's investigations of early modern Rome, provide an alternative model. She insists that honor be viewed as a "complex of values and behavior" that varies widely in its meaning and practice. Even cultures that share similar theoretical conceptions of honor may act out these values in different ways. Cohen's work provides both a warning and a challenge:

> To understand honor, it is important to distinguish region from region, urban from rural, elite from popular, male from female and one era from the next. Furthermore, despite its rhetoric, honor is seldom absolute, but rather subject to negotiation. However clear honor culture may appear in the scholar's theoretical construction, its application in social practice is riddled with ambiguity.[6]

Different historical sources, at different times and places, will give different definitions and descriptions of honor; these differences need to be acknowledged and clarified.

Given that colonial Latin Americans from all castes and classes might hold varying conceptions of honor, it is important to discover the similarities as well as the differences in how a Spanish viceroy, a mestiza housewife, or a mulatto muledriver might define their distinct versions. This essay limits exploration to one facet of the honor complex in eighteenth-century Latin America. It relies on the collective biographies of 244 elite families whose life histories occur in petitions for legitimation known as gracias al sacar.[8] Some were local notables who possessed honor but who had engaged in sexual relationships that had threatened their own or someone else's honor. Others were the illegitimate offspring of elite members who lacked honor because of their birth, but who wanted to gain it. Others were family members or friends, who were concerned by the absence of honor in someone close to them. Applications for legitimation include tens and sometimes hundreds of pages of testimony in depositions that beg royal officials to grant civil legitimations and to restore honor.

Such petitions originated in every corner of Spanish America, as an increasing number of illegitimate individuals from New Orleans to Concepción, from

Buenos Aires to Havana, applied throughout the eighteenth-century. In these testimonies witnesses recounted family histories over generations. They not only detailed how the norms of honor affected the courtship and sexual relationships of elite men and women who produced illegitimate babies, but also chronicled what occurred as these children became adults and confronted lives devoid of honor. These testimonies reveal that illegitimate petitioners skated at the edge of acceptance by elite society. Since many had grown up in the homes of their mothers and fathers alongside their legitimate half-brothers and sisters who possessed honor, their views reflect customary elite perceptions of honor. Their testimonies reveal that even though Latin Americans of other castes and classes believed that they possessed honor, only the elite considered it to be solely attached to themselves. This conviction was so intense that members of the elite would deny the presence of honor in their own blood relatives—much less in anyone else—who did not meet their honor criteria. To understand the elite definition of honor is not only to explore how those at the social apex defined their exclusivity but also how they rationalized such superiority.

Yet sometimes answers to the simplest of questions can be the most difficult: What was honor, what did it mean to have it or not to have it? How could it be lost? Could it be regained? When don Mariano asked the Cámara of the Indies for restoration of his honor, he spoke in a code understood by his contemporaries but that is much less intelligible today. To understand what gracias al sacar petitioners meant by honor, we need to discard preconceived notions and to listen to their voices as they explain how its presence or absence affected their lives. The testimony of the colonial elite reveals that even though honor was not a physical attribute, they conceived of it as tangible—perhaps more like intelligence than eye color, but nonetheless heritable and under specific circumstances unmistakably passed from parents to children. Nor did the elite qualify the issue of honor. Unlike academic investigators, who have industriously chopped up the honor complex into pieces—honor as virtue, honor as status, honor and shame—members of the colonial elite simply used the single word "honor" to encompass a variety of shifting meanings and situations.

How then, did the colonial elite decide who possessed honor and who did not? Testimony suggests that elite recognition of honor depended on both historic guidelines and popular practices, a conclusion that runs through the essays in this volume. Historic meanings of honor included those culturally specific ways that Spaniards had always rationalized discrimination due to defects in birth (illegitimate, nonnoble), religion (non-Catholic), and race (nonwhite). Such patterns had evolved over the centuries to shape the nature of prejudice and to distinguish the privileges of those with honor from those without. Yet these overarching guidelines were not the sole honor criteria, for honor was also subject to negotiation. Popular practices, including the phenomenon of passing, provided social spaces where the elite might exercise choice as to whether discriminatory norms would be carried out. Situational variables including wealth or prominence, geography or epoch, or even the extent to which damaging information was known in public, might also affect whether a person possessed or lacked honor. Let us first explore those historic agendas that set the discriminatory standard, before examining the degree to which these guidelines might be negotiated in the daily worlds of colonial Latin Americans.

HONOR AS A HISTORIC ATTRIBUTE

Spanish legislation provides a historic chain of evidence for the succession whereby illegitimacy eventually became synonymous with absence of honor. Long before the Council of Trent (1545–63) unmistakably defined Catholic marriage, Spanish legal codes such as the Siete Partidas (1256–65) already discriminated against a person "not born of legal matrimony according to the command of the Church."[9] The Partidas characterized such an illegitimate individual as "*infamado*," for the lack of "*fama*," or reputation, which the Partidas defined as "the good state of [a] man who lives rightly, and according to law and proper customs." The penalties for those without fama were exclusion from "any dignity or honor (honra) among those who might be chosen as men of good reputation." Although the Partidas specifically forbade those without fama to become counselors to the king, the law conceded that these might still serve as judges of courts (audiencias) and in "all the other offices." The very wording of the code suggests the linkage between natal defect and civil effect: since illegitimate men lacked fama, they could not achieve honra, and thus should not be permitted to serve in designated prestigious public capacities.

Another significant stage in discriminatory legislation against the illegitimate occurred in 1414, when Pope Benedict XIII approved the foundation and the constitution of the Spanish college (*colegio*) of San Bartolomé. The college's constitution linked illegitimacy and another prejudicial marker, the concept of purity of blood, or limpieza de sangre. The application of this criterion ostracized anyone who had Jewish, Moorish, or heretical heritage. Entering college members had not only to supply proof that they possessed fama, that is, that they were legitimate; but they also had to prove their "pure blood." By 1430 the connection between limpieza and legitimacy was even more explicit in the constitution of the college of Naples, which demanded that medical doctors have "no excommunicated or infamous ancestors. . . . If dead they must be publicly declared good and serious men without . . . illegitimate birth."[10]

As the fifteenth century progressed, discrimination against those without legitimacy or limpieza not only became more common, but the two conditions were increasingly tied together in a single prejudicial marker. In the beginning illegitimate individuals who were officially recognized by their parents and their grandparents might be able to prove limpieza—that they lacked Jewish or Moorish ancestry for at least three generations. However, many could not, given that it was customary for parents to refuse to identify themselves on their illegitimate baby's baptismal certificate. One of the first candidates to face discrimination under a crucial Toledo city council statue of 1449 may or may not have actually had Jewish ancestry. However, since he was "a secret bastard of unknown father and mother," he could not prove that he had "purity of blood" in any case, and was therefore barred from the office of notary public. He was, as one historian noted, "without father, without mother, and without genealogy."[11]

The tightening association between legitimacy and limpieza is also revealed in the evolution of regulations for the office of notary public. By the seventeenth century, city ordinances that forbade those without limpieza to serve as notaries had been extended to imperial legislation and had been expanded to discriminate against illegitimate individuals as well. Even as late as 1609, the royal provision for notaries only required that they be a certain age and demonstrate expertise before obtaining their office. However, by 1679 candidates not only had to provide proof concerning their "life and customs," but they had to certify both their limpieza and legitimacy. Thus local ordinances against those without "purity of blood," which included those illegitimate individuals who could not prove their ancestry, eventually expanded to become imperial regulations that explicitly prejudiced all those of illegitimate birth. By the eighteenth century, the legislation that regulated legitimation (gracias al sacar) reflected this earlier linkage, as it included a special provision to legitimate those whose birth precluded their service as notaries.[12]

The Royal Pragmatic of 1501 marked another phase in discriminatory legislation, for it contained a list of more than forty offices barred to those who could not prove limpieza de sangre. Unlike the earlier Siete Partidas, which had essentially excluded illegitimate men from service on royal councils, but which permitted them to serve elsewhere, the new prohibitions extended to every civil post. Royal councillors, judges of courts and chancelleries, secretaries, and other imperial officers: all had to demonstrate limpieza. Even local officers such as *corregidores, regidores,* and *alcaldes* had to meet such requirements, which extended to every "public office" throughout the realm. The effect was to inflict on those who could not document their purity of blood what one seventeenth-century writer aptly characterized as a "civil death," since they were barred from most sources of political power.[13]

In contrast to the case of the notaries, the Pragmática was not followed by explicit legislation extending discrimination by denial of public office to everyone who was illegitimate. Instead the laws that governed officeholding remained ambiguous. Although the Laws of the Indies required that local alcaldes be "honored persons," they did not explicitly discriminate against men of illegitimate birth. Even a royal degree of 1549, which commented that there were "laws and pragmatics" that kept the racially mixed and illegitimate from holding public office, failed to cite any legislation.[114]

Yet even if there was no overt prohibition against illegitimate individuals holding public office, the implicit assumption that officials must be legitimate and persons of honor appears in some of the earliest legitimation degrees issued in the Americas. When the son of the earlier Inca ruler Huascar Inca applied to legitimate numerous illegitimate sons in 1544, the decree noted that his offspring would now be "honored" and therefore able to serve in "royal offices" and "councils." A 1591 decree gave limited permission to the viceroy of Peru to legitimate selected mestizos who were not previously able to hold office, given both their "mixture" and their "illegitimacy." In the seventeenth century, a decree assured a newly legitimated resident of Quito that he: "would have . . . and be admitted to all the royal offices, councils and public [offices] . . . as fully as [if you were] of legitimate marriage." By the eighteenth century the linkage was clear: when individuals of illegitimate birth applied for gracias al sacar, they noted that their birth deprived them of "honor," while men additionally explained that this defect barred them from "honorific posts."[14]

As the centuries passed, limpieza and legitimacy became preconditions not only for holding offices but also for practicing certain professions. The 1501 Pragmática had also detailed entire occupations barred to those who could not prove their limpieza. Not only public notaries but lawyers, surgeons, pharmacists, and smelters had to provide proof of purity of blood, and as time passed, of legitimacy as well. The existing ordinances of military orders, religious congregations, colleges, and universities also prohibited those who could not prove limpieza and legitimacy from joining their ranks. When colonial American institutions such as colleges and universities wrote their own ordinances, they based them on Spanish models and included such discrimination as well.[16]

At some unknown time the American colonies added an explicit racism to the prejudices of birth and religion encompassed in the classic Spanish concept of limpieza de sangre. When colonists defined those who possessed purity of blood, they added the stipulation that candidates be "white" and "without any mixture of . . . mulatto" in addition to the traditional discriminations against "commoner, Jew, Moor, . . . or converso." Since Jews and Moors had been prohibited from settlement in the Americas, the colonial limpieza ordinances became targeted almost exclusively against the illegitimate and the racially mixed.[17]

By the eighteenth century several discriminatory traditions in Spanish history had merged. Added to the original Partidas definition of illegitimate individuals as without fama and thus prohibited from certain offices of honra were the more detailed limpieza ordinances, which expanded political and economic discrimination and which often explicitly prejudiced those of illegitimate birth. Later on American colonists added racial discrimination as yet another prerequisite for purity of blood. Both legitimacy and limpieza became linked in the Hispanic mentality to form essential conditions subsumed under the broader category of "honor." Embedded within eighteenth-century colonist references to honor was the implicit understanding that such a deficit produced a civil death that barred those so marked from most prestigious, authoritative, and lucrative positions in society.[18]

In certain cases—and don Mariano's is one of them—there was a cause and effect linkage between historic patterns of prejudice and specific discrimination. The Havana cabildo excluded him because his lack of honor technically disqualified him from public service. However, even in this case issues of honor were seldom straightforward or direct. Rather, written laws and historic traditions set potential guidelines; they rationalized potential discrimination by members of the local elite against those without honor, which might or might not be put into effect, depending upon local circumstances.

However, before we consider how members of the local elite might affect decisions concerning honor, we must first confront another deceptively simple question: How, after all, could a monarch really change something so seemingly irreversible as the religious heritage of someone's ancestors, or illegitimacy of birth, or race? To answer this query is to explore the fundamental ways that Hispanic culture distinguished between private and public spheres and how that duality affected the concept of honor.

Underlying the monarch's ability to transform status was a mentality that differentiated between the private and the public and that accepted the possibility of a distinction between private reality and public reputation. Even before the era of Ferdinand and Isabella, Spanish monarchs had consistently intervened to alter an individual's public status, no matter the actual circumstances. The possession of Jewish, Moorish, heretical, illegitimate, or racially mixed ancestry was not necessarily a permanent condition. What one Spanish historian described so succinctly for purity of blood holds true for the rest: "The king counts more than blood."[19]

Yet how could a king really remove "Jewishness" or "Moorishness"? How could he make an illegitimate, legitimate or a mulatto, white? He could do these things because Hispanic society made conscious distinctions between individuals' status in their private and public worlds. Spaniards and Spanish Americans consciously and constantly distinguished between a private world populated by an inner circle of family, relatives, and intimate friends and a public world inhabited by everyone else. Witnesses continually spoke of the "secret," the "intimate," and the "private"; and contrasted it with what was "public and notorious."[20] An individual's standing in the private world—whether known to be Jewish, illegitimate, or mulatto—need not always be congruent with status in the public world of laws, reputation, and honor.

Thus the monarch could alter public status so that individuals were treated as if they were born with the desired condition. Creative examples of this dichotomy abound in Spanish history. One notable transformation occurred in 1604, when Phillip III effectively laundered the blood of the descendants of the most famous of Jewish rabbis, Pablo de Santa María. The decree conceded that the case was "unique," but then went on to grant limpieza de sangre to don Pedro de Ossorio de Velasco, as well as all the other descendants of this Jewish convert. Included in the royal grant was the provision that such heirs would be eligible for "all the honors, offices, benefices and patronage" that would go to "gentlemen, nobles, [and] Old Christians free of taint." While not as liberal, other monarchs granted concessions to Jews who converted to Catholicism.[21] Even the most prejudicial condition in early modern Spain—descent from Jewish ancestry—might officially be altered at the will of the king. Although the descendants of Pablo de Santa María were "really" of Jewish ancestry, this status was not held against them in the public world, where they enjoyed the honors of "Old Christians."

The historic prerogative of the monarch to create public status distinct from private reality also affected illegitimate individuals. Starting in 1475 an unbroken chain of documents attests to thousands of legitimations through the nineteenth century. Although the process, the goals of applicants, and the results of legitimation differed throughout the centuries, the underlying assumption that the monarch could effectively intervene and elevate the public status of deserving subjects provides an underlying continuity.[22] Included in these thousands of cases is that of doña Antonia, don Mariano's mother. Even though she had been born illegitimate, the state changed her public status with a royal legitimation degree so that she might enjoy the privileges of a woman of honor, who could pass that public condition on to her son.

To what extent did doña Antonia's legitimation degree actually alter her past? In one case royal officials explicitly noted that a person who had been born illegitimate could not change what had occurred, and they insisted that the baptismal documents proving there had been an irregular birth remain as the official record. What altered was that the state entitled an illegitimate to enjoy the prerogatives of a person of honor in public, no matter what their private reality.[23]

Such a transformation was facilitated by the conception of honor as a characteristic marking status in the public world. Honor used in this historical and cultural context did not describe ethical conduct; it had nothing to do with being "honorable," although proper action might be required to maintain a reputation as a person of honor. This does not mean that the colonial elite did not internalize ethics or have a moral compass, but it suggests that they were much more likely to use other words—for example *conscience* rather than *honor* to describe such ethical considerations. Elizabeth Cohen's description of the meanings of honor in early modern Rome captures some of the ethically neutral and public components that composed the colonial elite version of honor: "In honor culture a person's sense of worth lies not in internal virtue—as manifested in good intentions or a guiltless soul—but in the external of bearing and deed, and in society's appreciation of them. . . . Virtue and vice thus exist only when visible to onlookers."[24] Seen from this perspective, honor did not describe a code of personal integrity, honesty, or virtue. Nor did honor demand congruity between a person's private reality or secret actions and public persona. Private sins or defects need not affect public honor, as long as such transgressions remained secret. One Chilean lover explicitly expressed this understanding when he admitted that he had had sexual relations with "a subject of quality." Yet he went on to conclude that he had not damaged her "honor, since that intercourse was without anyone knowing of it."[25]

Honor identified those who could maintain public reputations of belonging to the political, economic, and social elite because they were descended from generations of ancestors characterized by legitimacy, limpieza, and whiteness. Yet—as the confession of the Chilean seducer also shows—honor was not defined solely by these historic attributes; it was also negotiated on a day-to-day basis, for those with honor had to act (at least in public) according to established norms in order to maintain it. Their peers made ongoing judgments concerning who merited public reputations as persons of honor, just as they weighed who had lost honor and who had regained it. Since don Mariano's

Figure 10. A wealthy Brazilian sugar planter and his wife travel together on horseback, followed by their slave, who carries an umbrella to protect them from the sun. (Jean Baptiste Debret, Albúm de aquarelas da região meridional do Brasil datadas de 1827, Inéditas, Coleção Conde de Bonneval, São Paulo.)

plight uncovers some of the spoken and unspoken rules that governed such ongoing negotiations of honor, let us return to him.

GENDER, SEXUALITY, AND HONOR

Although don Mariano had suffered a stinging rebuff from the Havana cabildo, it should not be forgotten that the status of the women in his family were at the heart of his difficulties. His grandmother, doña Beatris, had lost her virginity, become pregnant, and produced his mother, doña Antonia, whose illegitimacy foreclosed the transmission of honor to her legitimate son. Don Mariano's plight precisely illustrates why the definition of honor gave not only elite men but also elite women public personalities and defined roles in the public sphere. Even though colonial patriarchy denied elite women the political offices or economic activities reserved to men with honor, women still had to possess and to maintain their honor or they would prejudice not only their

own status but that of succeeding generations of officeholding and economically active males.

Issues of honor affected generations in distinctive fashions. Lovers such as
doña Beatris and don Lázaro had to bear the personal consequences of their
sexual relations and their violation of the honor code. Doña Antonia and don
Mariano were innocent victims who might lead lives deprived of honor because their ancestors had defied prescribed norms. It is therefore important to
consider not only how honor shaped the conduct of the generations who had
it, but also how its absence affected their heirs. Although the questions are
simple, the answers are complex. What were the rules for the transmission of
honor? What happened to those who violated them? What were the remedies
for those whose parents' actions had deprived them of honor?

Although both elite men and women shared aspects of honor, they manifested it in different ways. Both strove to preserve their public reputations as
persons of honor, worthy of the perquisites of hierarchy. Both recognized the
historic imperative that honor was inherited from ancestors and that it could
only be passed to the next generation through legitimate marriages and births.
However, biological and culturally defined differences meant that men and
women expressed and maintained their honor distinctly. Since the passing of
honor was dependent upon circumstances surrounding the birth of the next
generation, honor involved sexual issues and therefore the most intimate relationships between men and women.

Obvious biological differences established parameters for sexuality and procreation and influenced cultural norms that defined the presence or absence of
honor. Unlike females, males could never physically demonstrate proof of their
virginity at the time of first intercourse, so male sexual abstinence was never an
issue of honor. Since males never become pregnant, they never had any potential to manifest overt signs of their sexual activity in public, and so the ensuing
consequences of intercourse never directly threatened their personal honor. A
critical corollary was that men could never, ever, be absolutely certain that they
had fathered a particular child.

In contrast, female honor could rest on tangible proofs of virginity, and
women physically showed that they had been sexually active when they became
pregnant or gave birth. Women who consented to intercourse risked their personal honor in ways that men could not. Given the realities of biology as well as
the double standard inherent in patriarchy, female honor necessarily revolved
around the control of reproduction and the authentication of paternity.

Legitimation depositions nevertheless suggest that members of the colonial
elite did not consider female honor to be absolute. Rather they viewed honor as
an elastic commodity, somewhat analogous to a bank account. Elite women

Figure 11. Two wealthy women, attended by a servant, travel across the Mexican countryside in a sedan chair mounted between two mules. The honor of elite women was protected by isolating them from any opportunity for insult. (Claudio Linati, Costumes civils, militaires et religieux de Mexique . . . *[Brussels: Ch. Sattanino, 1828].)*

effectively received an honor deposit from both parents at birth. Through their own proper actions, such as control of their sexuality, marriage, and the production of legitimate children, they made deposits on their own and passed their share of the honor account to the next legitimate generation. However, they might suffer potential losses of their honor balance with unfavorable investments such as the loss of virginity or out-of-wedlock pregnancy. Personal honor might be maintained or restored in spite of such circumstances with further investments, either by eventual marriage or by the concealment of sexual activity and pregnancy so that such activities never became public knowledge and therefore never threatened honor.

Popular traditions surrounding sexuality, courtship, and marriage reflected the divergence between the ideal of a virgin bride and the reality, in which women might be sexually active. Customs that surrounded the promise of matrimony (*palabra de casamiento*), the potential for restoration of honor through a later, or post hoc, matrimony, as well as the arrangements characterized as private pregnancy: all provide evidence of customary occasions on which elite women might engage in sexual relationships, bear illegitimate children, and not necessarily bankrupt their own honor account.

Many elite women were not virgins on their wedding day yet maintained their honor. Although an elite male might presume the virginity of an intended wife, he expected her to prove this aspect of her honor at the time of first intercourse, which often occurred after the couple had exchanged the promise of matrimony. The engaged pair might then engage in sexual relations for months or even for years and even have illegitimate offspring (*hijos naturales*) before an eventual wedding ceremony.[26]

Evidence for the acceptability of such a custom comes from witness testimony that as long as sexual activity occurred within the context of a betrothal, it did not threaten a woman's honor. Elite women also received the benefit of the doubt even in questionable situations where marriage may not have been promised, for witnesses assumed that a woman of honor would never engage in intercourse without such assurances. Don Mariano's case provides such an example, for one commentator noted the "impossibility" that his grandmother would have begun a sexual relationship without a promise of matrimony, given her "retirement, honest way of living . . . and because she is a woman of honor." A witness from Cuba remembered the "honesty and honor" with which doña Rosalia Ramos had lived "in the states of virgin, wife, and widow," so that she "never would have engaged in intercourse with the indicated gentlemen . . . unless she had received a contract of marriage." Another vouched that a Vera Cruz unwed mother, doña Juana Díez de Estrada, "would never have accepted" her lover's "communication unless he promised to be her husband." Although one Colombian witness admitted that he did not know for "absolute certain" how doña Catarina Casafús became pregnant, he "had heard truthful persons say" that if she had a sexual relationship, it "would not be less than under the palabra de casamiento."

The most acceptable denouement to premarital intercourse or out-of-wedlock pregnancy was marriage, which fulfilled the promise of matrimony, erased any question of female honor, and fully transferred honor and inheritance potential to any offspring. Such post hoc matrimonial customs found their basis in Roman and canon law and were codified in the Spanish medieval code, the Fuero Real. Evidence of this practice appears in baptismal registers throughout the empire, which not only recorded an illegitimate infant's reception of the sacrament but might later register his or her parents' eventual marriage. Don Juan Cavallero, a Spaniard resident in Mexico City, initiated such a sequence in 1722. He explained that he and his lover, doña Teresa Maldonado y Zapata, had been "single and able to marry" when they produced a son, don Andrés, who had been baptized as an *hijo natural.* Since then the couple had married "as the certificate proves," and so they requested yet another document to authenticate that their child was "a legitimate son of a legitimate marriage."[27]

The presumption that such post hoc legitimations could occur significantly affected the status of elite women. As long as they and their lovers remained able to marry, the issue of honor remained in limbo, for they might at any time be converted into respected and honorable matrons and their children into fully legitimate offspring. Such flexibility meant that any judgment by peers as to whether a woman had engaged in dishonorable sexual activity might be hedged or delayed for years or even for decades.

But what if marriage were never a possibility? If a woman engaged in intercourse with a married man or a priest, or was married and became pregnant by another man, or the single lovers decided not to marry, couples might choose the option of private pregnancy. Elsewhere I have described such a practice, which exhibited several classic signs.[28] The woman, her lover, family, kin, and intimate friends collaborated so that even while those within the private circle might be aware of her pregnancy and motherhood, such conditions were never acknowledged to outsiders. In such cases the Catholic Church cooperated to protect female identity and honor, for the mother's name would not be listed on her infant's baptismal certificate. Illegitimate don Joseph Antonio Betancourt clarified this process when he explained that his mother's name was not made public on his baptismal certificate because she was "a white woman of distinction, for whose honor her name has always been suppressed." The disparities between private reality and public reputation could be acute: in Mexico, doña Magdalena de la Vega died in childbirth yet maintained her public reputation as a virgin. Such spaces between the private and the public could only be sustained, however, if a woman surrendered all connections with her illegitimate baby. The traditional arrangement in private pregnancies was for the babies' fathers or the relatives of the mother to take the infant. Of the 187 mothers of illegitimate children who appear in legitimation cases, more than a third had identifiable private pregnancies, where the mother's identity was not revealed on the baptismal certificate and she did not take the child.[29]

In sum, Hispanic women could pay a high price if intercourse with a lover became public knowledge due to a resulting pregnancy. However, popular customs provided escape mechanisms to maintain or restore honor even in these circumstances. Female honor might be preserved if sexuality had occurred as part of a process (palabra de casamiento, post hoc matrimony) that eventually led to the altar or if the awareness of a woman's sexual relationship and illegitimate baby were confined within the private sphere (private pregnancy).

In sharp contrast, masculine honor was threatened neither by sexual activity nor by the birth of illegitimate offspring. The lack of commentary in legitimation documents as to how pre- or extramarital sexuality or single fatherhood affected the honor of men is suggestive. It signals a documentary vacuum where the absence of evidence may be as telling as any testimony. The record is mute even in cases where a man might pledge to marry, take the virginity of his fiancée, and then renege on the promise of matrimony. It might be assumed that such duplicity would threaten or compromise masculine honor. However, witness commentary does not support this conclusion, for neither friends, relatives, nor outsiders, nor even the men who had failed to keep their promises ever conceded that such refusal to wed diminished a man's honor. Rather when witnesses testified concerning such broken masculine pledges, they invariably described them as failures to heed the obligations of "conscience" rather than as deficits of honor.

Unlike honor, which was a public phenomenon, matters of conscience belonged to the private sphere and to matters of ethics and of religion. Considered from this perspective, the promise of matrimony reflected a pre–Council of Trent practice, where couples might promise and then marry themselves without a formal church ceremony. Even after the Council weakened the significance of such promises with the decree that marriages could only be sanctified by priests, the deep religiosity of colonial Latin Americans meant that they considered God to be a third party whenever they exchanged such pledges, which then became matters of conscience. Historian María Emma Mannarelli provides an illustrative example of such a linkage from seventeenth-century Lima, where an abandoned fiancée formally cursed her lover after he rejected her. When her fleeing suitor was subsequently shot dead in Spain, she considered his precipitous end to be a judgment from heaven in her favor.[30]

Colonists often made distinctions between issues of morality and the public face of honor. Guatemalan don Rafael García Goyena specifically differentiated between the demands of honor, or the "respect of the world," which had initially led his parents to arrange a private pregnancy for his mother and to raise him "secretly," and the "interior sentiments of conscience," which had eventually motivated his father to send for him and to care for him after he was seven. While masculine honor might not have been threatened by sexual affairs outside of matrimony, by the procreation of illegitimate children, nor by broken promises of matrimony, the pressure of conscience might ultimately have served as a powerful lever to compel action.

A failure to heed the demands of conscience rather than a failure of honor appears in other depositions as a traditional rationale for why men should fulfill their promises. When one Peruvian mother testified about her engaged daughter's love affair, which had resulted in two illegitimate sons, even she candidly admitted that her own daughter had been "dishonored" in public, given that her lover, don Antonio León Cataluyd, had abandoned her and fled to Spain. Yet doña Juana never suggested that her daughter's lover was similarly tainted. Instead she charged that he had an "obligation in conscience" to marry her daughter.

Considerations of conscience also seemed to motivate Cuban don Pedro Díez de Florencia, who had abandoned his lover even after he signed a promissory note guaranteeing that he would marry her. Decades later, when he finally decided he should marry his abandoned fiancée, he never mentioned that he might do so for reasons of honor. Rather he explained that it was to "fulfill his obligation" and to "discharge his conscience." Similarly in Colombia, one rejected fiancée charged that her lover, don Joseph Sánchez, had disregarded the "obligation of conscience" when he had abandoned her to marry another. One of her relatives seconded the charge and indicted the erring male as one who had "forgotten the obligations of conscience and justice." Yet another Bogotano, don Lorenso de Parga, spoke of his "mournfulness" in not marrying his deceased fiancée "according to the charge of his conscience." Failure to act ethically did not diminish a man's honor, although it was a charge against his conscience.

The ultimate irony was that even though male honor was not personally diminished by sexual activity nor out of wedlock fatherhood, men could ultimately be bound by the honor code.[31] It does not appear that men were pressured to "do the right thing" out of fear, since the exaggerated vendetta stereotype, whereby the rejected woman's relatives sought revenge against a man who had dishonored her reputation, never appears in any of the legitimation case histories. Yet even if men who seduced and then abandoned fiancées did not suffer physical harm, they still paid immediate and long-term personal prices. Their failure to wed risked the reputation of the closest members of their private circle, for it diminished the honor of their sexual partner, who might in the course of time become their wife; and it deprived their closest blood kin, their often cherished children, of a life of honor. Thus males might eventually act not to defend their own honor but because their failure to wed had damaged the reputations of others.

Even when males refused to heed their conscience, and even when their own honor was not compromised, they still might act to defend the honor of their lover. Unlike stereotypical renditions of *machismo* described for later centuries, where masculine boasting of sexual prowess was customary, the colonial code often demanded silence or at least discretion from elite males. A traditional masculine priority was the protection of their partner's honor, rather than any advertisement of their own sexual exploits.

Private pregnancies required the greatest secrecy. Even though Venezuelan don Joseph Francisco Betancourt often visited the family to whom he had entrusted the care of his baby son, he never mentioned the identity of his partner, for he noted that "she was a white woman of honor which necessitated silence." Guatemalan don Joseph García Goyena would only reveal that his baby was "the son of that same woman whom he has privately and secretly disclosed to the vicar." Such discretion transcended the generations, as fathers impressed their sons with the necessity for continued reticence. Don Rafael, the illegitimate son in that case, also explained that he also could not name his mother, for he had only received "secret information concerning her condition, quality, and single state."

Even decades after the fact, men maintained silence concerning the identity of women protected by a private pregnancy. Such discretion could endure even when fathers recounted the history of their love affairs in their petitions to the Cámara of the Indies. Of sixty-seven private pregnancy cases, the identity of the mother appeared in less than a quarter at the time of the petition, even though such specificity might have promoted a favorable decision. Since legitimation petitions usually occurred years and often decades after an illegitimate birth, this silence as to maternal identity is striking. Even more stunning is that more than half of male lovers continued to protect the names of their female partners so that they remain unknown even today. Elite men guarded the honor of lovers with such steadfastness that when the identity of a woman protected by private pregnancy became public, it was most often through the initiative of the mother rather than the father.[32]

As the years passed, men became prime candidates for yet another challenge to their conscience and their honor. As their illegitimate infants grew into young adults, fathers now faced the ultimate repercussions of their failure to wed and pass on honor to their blood kin. They had to face the reality that their illegitimate offspring had become the innocent victims of their sexual promiscuity or their failure to fulfill their promises. A father might cherish a daughter, yet find that he had prejudiced her status; he had to realize that a favorite son might never be esteemed as a man of honor in the community.

Many unwed fathers expressed their guilt when they saw how their failure to marry had prejudiced the futures of their children. Even when his illegitimate daughter was still young, naval lieutenant don Agustín Herrera spoke of his "remorse" and saw her as an "indispensable obligation and charge to [his] conscience." Oidor don Gaspar de Urquizu spoke of the "weight" of illegitimacy against the "admirable person" of his adult son Santiago and his own "continued sentiment" of the prejudice that his offspring suffered, given that he "loved him." Even though a man's personal honor might not have suffered when he engaged in intercourse with a social peer, broke a pledge of matrimony, or produced an illegitimate child, he still might become caught in the trap of honor, for his actions would have prejudiced the honor of his lover as well as the future honor of succeeding generations. It is to the fate of these latter, including such innocent victims as doña Antonia and don Mariano that we now turn.

GENDER, ILLEGITIMACY, AND HONOR

In what ways might the absence of honor have affected the lives of doña Antonia and don Mariano? How typical was their experience? Petitions initiated by adults are particularly revealing in this regard, as those of illegitimate birth commonly chronicled the long-term frustrations that led to their applications. In some cases illegitimate individuals suffered from the historic prejudices developed over centuries of Spanish history that were levied against those without honor. For example don Mariano was among fifteen men who petitioned to hold public offices and presumably to end the "civil death" attached to an absence of honor. Eleven requested the special legitimations granted to notaries, who had to prove their legitimacy before they might receive a license to practice. Five mentioned that they applied in order to matriculate or graduate from American universities. Four asked for dispensations to practice medicine, two to become lawyers, two to serve in the army, one to practice as a smelter, and twelve to enter or advance in the priesthood.[33]

However, even a cursory examination of legitimation cases shows that any linkage between historic norms and the daily prejudices faced by illegitimate individuals was seldom consistent nor even usually so direct. Rather written laws and traditions established customary agendas for discrimination that might or might not be carried out. In some situations illegitimate men seemed able to bypass traditional modes of discrimination and to gain office or to practice occupations supposedly barred to them due to their birth, ethnicity, race, or religion. The resulting dialectic between ascriptive norms prejudicing people of illegitimate birth and any potential for individual achievement can best be explored through the analysis of a complex of actions that I have characterized as "passing."

Passing occurred when illegitimate individuals were able to establish public reputations as persons of honor, the private defects of their birth notwithstanding. Passing proved to be the informal, local equivalent of the gracias al sacar. Just as the monarch might officially issue a royal decree that authorized treatment as a person of honor in the public sphere, so the local elite might informally choose to overlook someone's private defects and publicly treat him or her as a peer. Often legitimation petitions originated when such efforts at passing were challenged. It should not be forgotten that don Mariano had passed to the extent that half of the Havana city council had initially been willing to overlook his absence of honor and to elect him to office. It was only after that vote tied and he faced a challenge that don Mariano began official proceedings to restore his honor. Investigating such day-to-day workings of honor is to enter an ambiguous arena where the presence or absence of honor could be constantly "subject to negotiation."[34]

The case of don Mariano illustrates that passing was never an all-or-nothing affair. An illegitimate man or woman accepted for one purpose as a person of honor might find his or her status challenged or blocked on another occasion. Sometimes such a person might pass in small but socially meaningful ways, only to be thwarted when seeking more substantive mobility. It mattered socially, for example, whether members of the local elite publicly addressed illegitimate individuals as don or doña, for these were appellations generally reserved for social equals who possessed honor. People of illegitimate birth might also pass when they were addressed with familiarity by members of the local elite, invited to their homes, or considered worthy of shared confidences.[35] Members of the elite may have been more willing to enhance the status of illegitimate individuals with such social concessions than with access to political or economic privileges.

Each attempt to pass balanced the interests of the private and public spheres. The private circle, which included the illegitimate person and his or her relatives and friends, provided group solidarity and functioned to forward the interests of its members, including illegitimate kin who sought to pass. Contraposed to the private sphere was the public world, where the imperial as well as the local elite enforced written and unwritten discriminatory practices, defended the privileges reserved to those who possessed honor, and thereby maintained the exclusivity of their existing hierarchy. Each attempt to pass was a balance between historic norms of discrimination and the unofficial decisions by the elite as to whether those norms would be put into practice.

Such private and public interests naturally conflicted, although evidence of such personal decisions rarely appears in the historic record. An elite male might be expected, for example, to use his influence so that a member of his private circle, perhaps an illegitimate nephew, might avoid "civil death" and hold a political position normally closed to him by the "defect" of his birth. Yet that same elite male, in his public persona as defender of the hierarchy, would not be hypocritical if he opposed the appointment of someone else's illegitimate nephew to the same post. Both of these positions would be consistent with his private and public interests. An elite male had yet another option, however, for he might simply accept such passing. If he did so, he would make a personal choice to treat someone else's illegitimate nephew as a person of honor. His concession would only be effective to the extent that it was supported by other members of the elite.

A complex of variables influenced the extent to which this process might occur. The gender of the illegitimate person, the extent of his or her ambition and achievement, the degree of family influence, the intensity of local prejudice, and the timing of an attempt carried weight in every such attempt. The interplay of variables was so complex that one illegitimate might be rebuffed at the very point where another with roughly similar credentials might pass. Local popular culture variably determined whether an illegitimate might or might not be treated as a person of honor. Yet within this diversity underlying processual patterns emerged. Understanding how gender, locality, and chronology affected individual attempts to pass provides fundamental insight into the tensions between the honor hierarchy and social mobility in colonial Latin America.

Since gender profoundly molded the roles of men and women, it correspondingly shaped the impact of discrimination. Given that women were foreclosed from political or economic positions where lack of honor could lead to discrimination, the most adverse response they faced was social ostracism. Members of the colonial elite practiced what one historian characterized as a "fierce endogamy," in that they strongly preferred to marry peers who possessed honor.[36] When an illegitimate woman passed, it was to overcome that discrimination, to marry a man of honor, and to be treated as a woman of honor in the local community. The life story of don Mariano's mother, doña Antonia, illustrates such a process, for she had married don Juan Andrés de las Casas, a man of honor who served on the Havana cabildo.

Doña Antonia's history equally demonstrates why illegitimacy and the resulting lack of honor might dramatically prejudice a woman's marital choices. A long-term cloud might hover over an elite family who accepted an illegitimate bride into their midst. Decades could pass with local society accepting and even treating the illegitimate as a woman of honor; however, if the family became involved in any kind of competition or quarrel, skeletons in the family closet could be exposed, to the advantage of opponents. Even if an illegitimate woman brought a competitive dowry to an elite marriage and could be generally accepted, she still carried the potential for future family humiliation.

Since the Latin American elite not only concerned themselves with the past and present but also with future implications of honor, it was usual for families to discriminate against women who sought marriage into their private circle if they might become weak links in the chain of honor. Anticipation of such prejudice was one of the primary motivations for the legitimation of women. In Bolivia the guardian of doña Gregoria de Rivera y López of La Plata admitted as much when he applied for her legitimation, for he hoped that she might "contract a marriage worthy and equal to the circumstances and honor of the family." Civil legitimation made twenty-two-year-old doña Gregoria a more acceptable bride, for it foreclosed any future challenges to her or her children's honor.

The discrimination on the part of a family against females who threatened its honor might be intense. It led one Venezuelan widow, doña Juana Figueroa, to apply to erase her illegitimacy, the apparent reason why her potential husband's family urged him not to marry her. She forwarded the love letters from her fiancé, don Juan Antonio de Echevarría, to the Cámara of the Indies, to illustrate the exact nature of her problem. Ostensibly, any delay in matrimony did not originate from any lack of passion on the part of don Juan Antonio, for he addressed her as the "greatest love of my heart" and pledged his total devotion: "I am dying for you, . . . I never eat nor sleep but I only think of you." The hindrance to any happy ending was his family's pressure against accepting an illegitimate woman into their private circle, for don Juan Antonio also confessed: "but if I marry as you wish, my brother will not be friendly with me, nor others that I know." Even though her fiancé repeatedly offered to die for her, he seemed unwilling to marry her, if it meant alienating his brother and assorted relatives.

Doña Juana was understandably upset with such tactics, for his family's objections to their marriage had challenged her passing and her informal status as a woman of honor. In her petition she defended this public reputation, noting that she "had always behaved with honor and esteem and had been treated as a notable woman of that city." Nor had "that defect served as any obstacle in the first marriage she had contracted with don Bartholomé Ramirez." She must have made her position very clear to her fiancé, for don Juan Antonio lamented that he "felt very upset that you do not treat me with affection." Thus while it may have been relatively easy for an illegitimate woman unofficially to pass as a woman of honor, the long term "stain" of her illegitimacy might surface at anytime to prejudice her, her children, or her family.

Such was the situation faced by don Mariano, who rightly perceived his rejection by the Havana cabildo as a direct result of his mother's illegitimacy and as an insult to his status in the community. Cabildo service carried with it

Figure 12. Elite and middle-class women communicated their honor and wealth to society through their opulent dress. The more impractical the clothing, the higher the woman's status. (Baltasar Jaime Martínez, Compañon Trujillo del Peru a fines del siglo XVIII *[Madrid, 1936].)*

much more than just a fleeting year of local power. Men elected to the city council were distinguished in their neighborhoods as persons of responsibility and substance, and such a distinction lasted throughout their lifetimes. This was why even though colonists continually complained that city council service was onerous, they still accepted election and considered it a high point in their public career. Service on the cabildo marked a man as a member of the local inner circle, for a fraternity of peers had elected him as a man of honor to be included among their elite ranks.

Whenever city councils elected new members, they chose much more than just a procurador or a sheriff; they permanently enhanced the public reputations of a favored few. One of the decisions they could make was whether to include eligible illegitimate men in this select group. If their decision was negative, it could provoke situations such as don Mariano's, in which illegitimate individuals who had passed in other arenas petitioned to overcome local prejudice against them. The extent to which they could pass in different cabildo jurisdictions provides a telling indication of local variations in discrimination throughout the Spanish empire.

The comparative situations of don Mariano from Havana and don Manuel Antonio Vásquez y Rivera from Tegucigalpa provide a sharp contrast illustrating the substantially different levels of discrimination that prevailed in the Caribbean and Central America. The contrast becomes even more compelling given that both men served, or tried to serve, as procurador general on their respective cabildos within seven years of each other (1786–93). Their local elites showed wildly different levels of tolerance toward these ambitions.

Don Manuel Antonio seems to have experienced comparatively little discrimination in Tegucigalpa. He was the natural son of a royal official and a woman of "first distinction." By the time of his petition in 1793, he had already successfully passed, for the local elite had elected him procurador general of the cabildo in spite of his illegitimacy. Don Manuel Antonio had risen even further, for he had recently purchased the more prestigious city council office of regidor. It was not local but imperial prejudice that prompted his legitimation petition, for he feared that he would not obtain the necessary royal confirmation of his rank if he were illegitimate. Thus he wrote the Cámara of the Indies and asked for "your royal dispensation of that defect" before he took up his post.

Several striking themes emerge in any comparison of the careers of don Manuel Antonio and don Mariano. First is the manifest difference in the attitudes of the local elite toward their passing. In Tegucigalpa they elected don Manuel Antonio as their procurador general, even though he was illegitimate. In Havana the elite denied the same post to don Mariano, who was legitimate, because of the "stain" attached to his mother. Such differences show why passing and turning point moments were so distinctive, for they mirrored the varying levels of discrimination practiced by local elites throughout the empire. Although the topic of regional variation is beyond detailed consideration here, patterns in passing suggest that discrimination was greatest in the Caribbean and northern South America and was particularly fierce in late colonial Havana, which may explain why don Mariano experienced such difficulties. Prejudice against those of illegitimate birth seems to have been somewhat less severe in Mexico, followed respectively by the southern cone, Central America, and Andean Ecuador and Peru. Members of the Central American elite were among the least discriminatory, which accords with the easier mobility experienced by don Manuel Antonio in Honduras.[37]

As the eighteenth century drew to a close, prejudice against those who could not prove their honor was on the rise throughout the empire. Social and racial tension increased, as members of the elite who rationalized their place in the hierarchy by their honor, and their honor by their whiteness and legitimacy, now felt increasingly challenged from below. A new society had formed after three centuries of conquest and slavery, one in which the simple natal, social, and racial dividers were no longer as stark nor as effective as prejudicial markers. Centuries of racial mixture had produced a blended population; stability among the racially mixed populace led to increased legitimacy, while economic development added pressures for social and racial mobility that challenged the mechanism of passing and the customary equilibrium between exclusion and inclusion.[38] The traditional mechanisms through which those at the top discriminated against the majority and privileged the few were starting to come apart. The response by local elites was to tighten ranks and to restrict passing.

One indicator of such heightened prejudice was the appearance of a cluster of cases between 1789 and 1799 in which relatives petitioned to legitimate elderly or even dead family members whose birth status clouded family genealogies. Attempts to confront rising discrimination and to avert social embarrassment motivated one Puerto Principe family to admit that one of their ancestors, don Joseph de Zayas, was the son of a priest. Even though he was of sacrilegious birth, don Joseph had been able to pass in his own time as a person of honor. He not only married a woman of "distinguished reputation," but served in the high status office of captain of the local militia. Nor had don Joseph's legitimate son, don Santiago, seemed to suffer much from his father's illegitimacy, for "he had obtained positions of honor in politics and the military."

It was family concern for the next generation, for don Santiago's legitimate son, don Mariano, that led to their petition in 1799. As was common in Cuba militia units, don Mariano had followed his legitimate father and sacrilegious grandfather and had begun to serve as a cadet. However, the family now feared that his promotion might be threatened by the stain of his grandfather's birth. Thus don Mariano and his father applied so that don Joseph's sacrilegious birth "would not serve as an impediment [for the family] to continue to enjoy the honors, privileges, and grants" usual to families of honor. Unstated was the obvious question as to why don Mariano was now encountering this problem, when his father and illegitimate grandfather had not.

The royal official who reviewed the petition expressed a certain bewilderment concerning the request. He noted that don Joseph had held office in the militia even though he was illegitimate, as had his son, and so the bureaucrat wondered "why would [his grandson] need such a dispensation?" Underlying the official's response was the assumption that if the grandfather and father could pass as persons of honor, then the grandson should be able to do so as well. The family's answer to this query was inherent in the very fact of the petition itself: the climate in Puerto Principe, which had tolerated passing for the son of a priest and for his legitimate son in turn, was no longer as permissive for his legitimate grandson. If don Mariano could not document his descent from legitimate ancestors, his career was in jeopardy.

This case is also notable in that don Joseph did not follow customary procedure and personally request his own legitimation, but rather his son and grandson appeared as petitioners. Since the family could not provide his baptismal certificate, given that the Puerto Principe archive had burned, it is impossible to know how old he was when his descendants made their request, nor did they informally provide this information. Such absence of data suggests that don Joseph could have even been dead when his son and grandson requested his legitimation.

If so, this case would join three other petitions submitted in 1789, in which families from Mexico, Peru, and Cuba requested that the Cámara of the Indies legitimate their dead relatives. Such requests made a certain sense, given that elite individuals viewed honor as an entity that passed from honorable member to honorable member and from one legitimate generation to the next. Legitimation of the dead would presumably restore the weak links in the family chain of honorable ancestors.

Such was the hope of Mexican don Venturo Escrivanis, who asked the Cámara to legitimate his "dead wife," doña Francisca. Doña Francisca had been left an orphan when her unwed father dropped dead of a fever and her unwed mother went into premature labor and died upon hearing of the death of her fiancé. Adopted and lovingly raised by a prominent Jalapa family, doña Francisca had effectively passed as a woman of honor when, at age twenty-three, she married don Venturo, who could trace his ancestry back to the seventeenth century and who had served as captain and lieutenant colonel in the militia. Apparently the couple had felt no pressure to legitimate her during her lifetime, but don Venturo now expressed concern that his deceased wife's illegitimacy might prejudice the military career of their sons. Although royal officials provided extensive commentary on this application before they approved it, it is notable that they never considered the issue that doña Francisca was dead. Instead they reviewed the considerable documentation, noted the "preeminence" of don Venturo, and applauded the intentions of his sons to follow a military career. In the eighteenth century, members of the elite viewed honor as an entity that might be attached to an individual after death. A gracias al sacar might reach beyond the grave to convert an illegitimate relative who could not pass on honor into a legitimate family member who could.

CONCLUSION

When don Mariano petitioned the Council of the Indies to restore the honor of his seventy-one-year-old mother, he did so within a centuries-old tradition in order to resolve an immediate crisis. Constructions of honor could be both historic and negotiated. Honor could stretch back as far as the Siete Partidas; it could be purchased through a royal decree; it could be withheld or granted to individuals on a daily basis. In his case, don Mariano proved to be in the wrong place at the wrong time. As the eighteenth century drew to a close, the Cuban elite proved among the most discriminatory, so don Mariano was not only unable to pass informally as a person of honor, but he found that even the official legitimation of his mother failed to secure a coveted political post. Yet the very extremity of his case illuminates the process by which others at the margins of elite society might informally pass or officially achieve significant mobility through the gracias al sacar.

Honor proved to be a prism through which the private and personal histories of colonial elites became public and political. Yet the conceptual division between the private and the public could also create significant social space for deviance and flexibility. Elite women who violated sexual norms might negotiate public reputations that maintained or eventually restored their honor; illegitimates could informally pass and be treated as persons of honor, or they could petition for legitimation and the official restoration of honor. The gracias al sacar depositions pinpoint how constructions of honor differed for elite men and women, varied by localities, and changed over the eighteenth century. Yet it is essential to remember that this social process proved to be but one part of an even more complex system by which Spaniards and Spanish

Americans of differing genders, classes, and castes variously defined, pursued, and defended that elusive phenomenon called honor.

NOTES

1. Archivo del Consejo Municipal [ACM]—Museo de la Habana [Havana, Cuba], 1 de enero de 1786, contains the tally and the *cabildo* discussion. ACM-Habana, 27 de enero de 1786, 20 de marzo de 1786, 28 abril de 1786; ACM-Habana, 24 de noviembre de 1786 also provide information on his quest for office. A search of city council officers through the rest of the eighteenth century suggests that don Mariano never served on that body.

2. To reduce the length and frequency of footnotes, citations or quotations from specifically cited gracias al sacar legitimation cases can be identified by family name in the text and then correlated with the following archival locations in the Archivo General de Indias: Betancourt (Caracas 299, no. 22, 1787); Borboya y Vega, Vega (Mexico 1771, no. 6, 1785); Casas (Santo Domingo 1483, no. 38, 1792); Casafús (see Muños); Cataluyd (Lima 910 no. 53, 1785); Escrivanis (Mexico 1776, no. 6 1789); Estrada (Santo Domingo 421, no. 1, 1723); Figueroa (Caracas 299, no. 1788); Florencia (Santo Domingo 425, no. 2, 1741); García Goyena (Guatemala 609, no. 2, 1798.); Herrera (Santo Domingo 1471, no. 6, 1787); Muños (Santa Fe 717, no. 8 1793); Parga (Santa Fe 720, no. 26, 1796); Ramos (Santo Domingo 1488, no. 15, 1796); Rivera y López (Charcas 560, no. 15, 1795); Sánchez (Santa Fe 677, no. 19, 1766); Urquizu (Lima 893, no. 42, 1778); Vásquez y Rivera (Guatemala 605, no. 4, 1793); Vega (see Borboya); Zayas (Santo Domingo 1498, no. 49, 1799). For a discussion of the sources that compose the legitimation petition databases, see note 8.

3. AGI, Santo Domingo 1483, no. 38, 1792.

4. Lucy A. Sponsler, "Women in Spain: Medieval Law versus Epic Literature," *Revista de Estudios Hispánicos* 7 (October 1973): 433.

5. José María Ots Capdequi, "Bosquejo histórico de los derechos de la mujer casada en la legislación de Indias," *Revista General de Legislación y Jurisprudencia* 137 (1917–20): 149.

6. Patricia Seed, *To Love, Honor and Obey in Colonial Mexico: Conflicts over Marriage Choice, 1574–1821* (Stanford University Press, 1988): 9, 62, 240. I question Seed's temporal frame, given that variables she considers of primary significance in seventeenth-century manifestations of honor-virtue, such as the protection of feminine reputation, are equally viable indicators in the eighteenth century. Similarly, issues she sees as key for eighteenth-century honor-status, such as economic standing and race, were important earlier (see p. 225).

7. Elizabeth S. Cohen, "Honor and Gender in the Streets of Early Modern Rome," *Journal of Interdisciplinary History* 22 (Spring 1992): 599–600.

8. The 244 cases used in the most complete database include: 101 cases with full petition from the Americans and subsequent legitimation decree; 41 with full petition (incomplete cases or those denied); 69 cases of legitimation decree (but no petitions); 5 cases from

Cámara internal records. The 28 remaining cases are "lost," as they derive from index references to cases from the period 1799 to 1820 that appear in nineteenth-century handwritten indexes to each audiencia and that, with the exception of Santo Domingo, cannot be located in the archive. The database includes nine legitimations granted prior to 1721, although there certainly were others that cannot be located. After that date the reorganization of the Cámara led to a systematic collection such that internal evidence (eighteenth-century inventories, citation of earlier cases as precedents) suggests that coverage is close to complete.

A SAS package provided simple percentages and cross tabulations of relevant variables into four databases: n = 244 (henceforth DB 1–244) for total distribution over time and geography; n = 216 (DB 2–216) for the number of illegitimate individuals (minus 28 missing cases); n = 187 (DB 3–187) for the number of mothers or fathers (some had more than one illegitimate child); and n = 67 (DB 4–67) for private pregnancies.

While it is doubtful that there would be much proportional congruity between gracias al sacar data and the "real world" of illegitimacy, the comments of colonists as to "customary" practice and the documentation of macrotrends and common practices do reveal social patterns of historic import. Geographically 36.5 percent (n = 89) of the petitions originated in Santo Domingo (mostly Cuba), 39 percent (n = 95) came from South America, and 24.5 percent (n = 60) came from Panama northward. Although individuals of illegitimate birth applied throughout the eighteenth century, the years from 1780 through 1799 accounted for slightly more than half of the total number of petitions (53.3 percent). There were 9 petitions before 1700, 7 in the 1720s, 2 in the 1730s, 10 in the 1740s, 5 in the 1750s, 14 in the 1760s, 11 in the 1770s, 59 in the 1780s, 71 in the 1790s, 27 in the 1800s, 28 in the 1810s and 1 in the 1820s; DB 1–244.

9. Relevant sections quoted from the Siete Partidas (henceforth SP) are: SP, part. 7, tít. 6, ley 2; SP, part. 7, tít. 6, ley 1; SP, part. 7, tít. 6, ley 7.

10. The 1414 constitution can be found in Albert A. Sicroff, *Los estátuos de limpieza de sangre: Controversios entre los siglos xv y xvii* (Madrid: Taurus Ediciones, 1979): 117–18. The 1430 constitution is found in Miguel Eugenio Muñoz, *Recopilación de las leyes, pragmáticas, reales decretos y acuerdos de real protomedicato* (Valencia: Imprenta Viuda de Antonio Bordazar, 1751): 72.

11. Sicroff, *Los estátuos,* 189.

12. Imperial legislation is collected in *Novísima recopilación de las leyes de España* (Madrid: Imprenta Real, 1805), lib. 7, tít. 15, ley 6; the gracias al sacar legislation is found in Archivo Nacional Histórico-Madrid, Consejos Libros 1498, no. 38, 1795.

13. Muñoz lists the offices that were excluded, *Recopilación,* 72.; Sicroff quotes from Fray Gerónimo de la Cruz, who wrote a 1637 treatise concerning nobility and limpieza de sangre, *Los estátuos,* 293.

14. Juan de Solorzano y Pereyra, *Política Indiana* (Madrid: Ibero-Americana, 1930 [1647]), libro 3, cap. 6, commented in the mid-seventeenth century that many illegitimate individuals had been successful in obtaining political office. He noted that "there is no law that gives them the note of infamy nor excludes them from dignities nor magistrates but only that in equality of merits they ought to be placed behind [those who are] legitimate." The

Laws of the Indies are found in *Novísima recopilación,* lib. 5, tít. 3, ley 4; Richard Konetzke, *Colección de documentos para la história de la formación social de hispanoamerica, 1493–1810* (Madrid: Consejo Superior de Investigaciones Científicas, 1958–1962), 5 vols. (henceforth cited by volume, number of document, and year; note that volumes 2 and 3 have two parts). Konetzke, *Colección* I, no. 98, 1536 reprints a royal decree of 1536 that notes that alcaldes in Santiago de Cuba should not only know how to read and write but be *honrados;* Konetzke, I, no. 167, 1549.

15. These decrees can be found respectively in Konetzke, I, no. 151, 1544; Konetzke I, no. 473, 1591; and Konetzke, 2:1, no. 349, 1663.

16. Sicroff notes that conversos might enter but could not graduate from the universities of Salamanca, Valladolid, and Toledo, *Los estátuos,* 119–20. On distinctions between law and practice, see John Tate Lanning, *The University in the Kingdom of Guatemala* (Ithaca, NY: Cornell University Press, 1955), 193–95.

17. Comments on particular American variants appear in *The Royal Protomedicato: The Regulation of the Medical Professions in the Spanish Empire,* ed. John Tate Lanning and John Jay TePaske (Durham, NC: Duke University Press, 1985), 179–80.

18. José Antonio Maravall, *Poder, honor, y élites en el siglo xvii* (Madrid: Siglo XXI, 1989), 128, links limpieza with the "condition for receiving honor."

19. Sicroff traces the concept that the king was the ultimate or the "only source of political and civil nobility" to the Siete Partidas, for the king "can bestow the honor of nobility to those that are not so by lineage," *Los estátuos,* 343; Maravall, *Poder,* 84, quotes Velez de Guevara: "Mas pesa el rey que la sangre."

20. In one case witnesses noted that they accepted an illegitimate individual "publicly and secretly" (AGI, Guadaljara 368, no. 6, 1761); another distinguished between "private" and "notorious" communication (AGI, Santo Domingo 421, no. 1, 1723); yet another noted that an illegitimate baby was recognized in "private" and in "public" and that her illegitimacy was a "notorious public fact" (AGI, Santo Domingo 1470, no. 14, 1786). In Peru one illegitimate individual was only recognized "in secret" (AGI, Lima 826, no. 57, 1788). Other historians have also pointed out such conscious distinctions. For example María Emma Mannarelli, *Pecados públicos: La ilegitimidad en Lima, siglo xvii* (Lima: Ediciones Flora Tristan, 1994), 99, 125, 141, speaks of "properly public culture," an "interior world," and of the "frontiers between the public and the private"; she also quotes documents that use the customary divisions of *público* and *secreto.* Richard Cicerchia, "Vida familiar y prácticas conyugales, clases populares en una ciudad colonial: Buenos Aires 1800–1810," *Boletín del Instituto de Historia Argentina y Americana Dr. E. Ravigani,* tercera serie no. 2 (1990), 95, also describes the family as a "mixture of public and private relations."

21. Sicroff, *Los estátuos,* 218, quotes the royal grant that was awarded because the converted rabbi then became the bishop of Burgos and supposedly converted forty thousand Jews with his preaching; grants of similar dispensations by Ferdinand appear in Antonio Dominguez Ortiz, *Los judeoconversos en españa y america* (Madrid: Ediciones Istmo, 1971), 242.

22. The Archivo General de Simancas (Registro General del Sello) contains a comprehensive index of more than two thousand Spanish legitimation cédulas dating from 1475 through 1543. Remaining years of the sixteenth and seventeenth centuries are uncatalogued.

Some 290 eighteenth-century-Spanish legitimation petitions and cédulas (1716–1800) are catalogued in Archivo Histórico Nacional (Madrid) under Consejos. I am at present collecting these documents for a comparative study of sexuality and illegitimacy in Spain and the Americas.

23. AGI, Santo Domingo 1468, no. 6, 1786. The extent to which the decree "worked" varied widely. If civil officials had leverage, they were usually effective, given that they might pressure authorities to permit the newly legitimated to graduate from the university or to practice a profession. Where the potential for state control was nebulous or dispersed and local elites had a say in issues such as elections to the city council or marriage partners, the outcome varied by region, epoch, and the particularities of each case.

24. Cohen, "Honor and Gender," 617.25. Eduardo Cavieres F. and Rene Salinas M., *Amor, sexo y matrimonio en Chile tradicional,* Serie Monografías Históricas no. 5 (Valparaíso: Universidad Católica de Valparaíso, 1991), 53.

26. DB 3–187 shows that forty-three, or 23.0 percent, had exchanged the promise of matrimony; forty-six, or 24.6 percent, had not; and the situation of the remaining ninety-eight, or 52.4 percent, is unknown. See Ann Twinam, "Honor, Sexuality and Illegitimacy in Colonial Spanish America," in *Sexuality and Marriage in Colonial Latin America,* ed. Asunción Lavrin (Lincoln: University of Nebraska Press, 1989), 118–55, on such extended engagements. Other authors confirm similar customs. Cavieres F. and Salinas M., *Amor,* 91, describe the custom of sexual relationships after engagements as "very common"; Lee Michael Penyak, "Criminal Sexuality in Central Mexico 1750–1850" (Ph.D. diss., University of Connecticut, 1993), 50, also confirms that many couples initiated sexual intercourse during engagements; Asunción Lavrin, "Sexuality in Colonial Mexico," in *Sexuality and Marriage in Colonial Latin America,* ed. Asunción Lavrin (Lincoln: University of Nebraska Press, 1989), 61, finds that the exchange of a gift, or *prenda,* was customary for Mexicans, although my own research suggests this was not as common in other parts of the colonies.

27. The original Spanish law is cited in the Fuero Real: Opúsculos legales del Rey don Alfonso el Sabio, 2 vols. (Madrid: Imprenta Real, 1836), Libro III, Título 6, Ley II; the post hoc example from Mexico comes from Archivo General de la Nación-México, Bienes Nacionales 1016, exp. 12, 1722. Other examples of post hoc legitimations include: Twinam, "Honor, Sexuality," 153; Cavieres F. and Salinas M., *Amor,* 105; Juan Ignacio Arnaud Rabinal, Alberto Bernárdez Alvarez, Pedro Miguel Martín Escudero, and Felipe del Pozo Redondo, "Estructura de la población de una sociedad de frontera: La Florida española, 1600–1763," *Revista Computense de Historia de América* 17 (1991): 102; Donald Ramos, "A mulher e a família em Vila Rica do Ouro Preto: 1754–1838," in *História e populacão: Estudos sobre a América Latina,* ed. Sérgio Odiolon Madalin, Maria Luiza Marcílio, and Altiva Pillati Balhana (São Paulo: Fundacão SEADE, 1989), 156.

28. Twinam, "Honor, Sexuality" 125–34.

29. DB 4–67: sixty-seven, or 35.8 percent.

30. Mannarelli, *Pecados públicos,* 229.

31. On male obligations see Ann Twinam, "Honor, paternidad e ilegitimidad: Los padres solteros en América Latina durante la colonia," *Estudios Sociales* 3 (September 1988): 9–32.

Men had to pay for the upbringing of hijos naturales, or illegitimate children where both parents were single. They were not obliged to maintain bastard (adulterous, sacrilegious) offspring. This obligation was not a matter of honor but was included under the obligation of *crianza* as outlined in SP, part. 4, tít. 19, ley 1.

32. DB4–67: The mother's identity appeared in sixteen, or 23.9 percent. Of the rest, the identity of one mother (1.5 percent) became public at her death, five (7.4 percent) were made known at the time of the petition, the disposition is unknown in six cases (9.0 percent), and the identities of thirty-nine (58.2 percent) of the mothers remain unknown (total, 100 percent). The data base (DB4–67) also reveals specific occasionos why private pregnancy mothers' identities might be revealed: five women (7.5 percent) came forward publicly at the time of the petition to acknowledge their illegitimate child, in six other instances (9.0 percent) they solely acknowledged their offspring, and in three others (4.5 percent), they and the fathers jointly acknowledged their children. Private pregnancies also became public when the mother openly lived with (two cases, 3.0 percent) or married (one case, 1.4 percent) her lover. Only in the three cases of lawsuits (4.5 percent), the one public scandal (1.4 percent), or where the outcome was unknown (seven cases, 10.5 percent) might fathers independently have broken their promise of silence and threatened the honor of their lovers. Thirty-nine private pregnancy mothers (58.2 percent) remained protected (total, 100 percent).

33. DB 2–216.

34. Cohen, "Honor and Gender," 599–600; "Central to all was the valuing of a persona according to a publicly established reputation which was always at risk in the arena of daily affairs" (p. 598).

35. Twinam, "Honor, Sexuality" 151.

36. Juan Javier Pescador C., "La nupcialidad urbana preindustrial y los límites del mestizaje: Características y evolución de los patrones de nupcialidad en la Ciudad de México, 1700–1850," *Estudios Demográficos y Urbanos* 7(1) (1992): 141. Verena Martínez Alier, "El honor de la mujer en Cuba en el siglo xix," *Revista de la Biblioteca Nacional José Martí* 13(2) (1971): 51 also noted that "one can say that honor defines the frontiers of class endogamy."

37. This subject is explored in my *Public Lives, Private Secrets: Gender, Honor, Sexuality and Illegitimacy in Colonial Spanish America* (Stanford, CA: Stanford University Press, forthcoming). Another indication of differentiation can be found in the ratio of male to female applications for legitimation. Overall men were twice as likely to apply for legitimations as women (DB 2–216, 143 men, or 66.2 percent, as opposed to 73 women, or 33.8 percent). Yet breaking down this gender ratio by colonial geographical divisions shows that women were much more likely to apply where discrimination was fiercest, since—as in the case of don Mariano—the lack of limpieza extended to the next generation. Women applied on a one-to-one basis with men only in the Caribbean and in northern South America (Colombia and Venezuela). Fewer Mexican women applied per male (one to three), while even fewer women petitioned from the Andes and the southern cone (one to four). No women applied from Quito or Panama. These data suggest that the balance between passing and discrimination may have varied such that Caribbean and northern South American

elites may have discriminated the most against illegitimate individuals, followed by their Mexican, Andean, South American, and Central American peers, a conclusion also substantiated by anecdotal case histories.

38. Konetzke, *Colección* 3:2, no. 300, 1788, reprints a typical white expression of the problem of pardo mobility, which surfaced as part of the Royal Pragmatic of 1776–78. The classic exposition is Magnus Morner, *Race Mixture in the History of Latin America* (Boston: Little Brown, 1967). For more recent treatments see: Cicerchia, "Vida familiar," 43; Daisy Rípodas Ardanaz, *El matrimonio en Indias: Realidad social y regulación jurídica* (Buenos Aires: Fundación para la Educación, la Ciencia y la Cultura, 1977), 34, 45; Eduardo R. Saguier, "El combate contra la 'limpieza de sangre' en los orígenes de la emancipación argentina: El uso del estigma de la bastardía y del origen racial como mecanismos de defensa de las élites coloniales," *Revista de Historia de América* 10 (July/December 1990): 185–86; Steve J. Stern, *The Secret History of Gender* (Chapel Hill: University of North Carolina Press, 1995), 23, 28, 35, 185, 289; Guiomar Dueñas-Vargas, "Gender, Race and Class: Illegitimacy and Family Life in Santa Fe, Nuevo Reino de Granada, 1770–1810" (Ph.D. diss., University of Texas-Austin, 1995), 29–31, 133–35.

CHAPTER FOUR

AN URGENT NEED TO CONCEAL
The System of Honor and Shame in Colonial Brazil

MURIEL NAZZARI

In 1815 donna Anna Margarida de Mello Dormo, who was single and over forty years old, petitioned the Desembargo do Paço (the Portuguese Royal High Court) to legitimize her daughter, Maria Perpetua.[1] She stated that as the result of human weakness, she had had this illegitimate child many years before.[2] She added that now, under the guidance of her spiritual advisers, she wanted to legally recognize her daughter so that Maria could inherit her estate. She explained that she had been "living under her father's authority at the time her daughter was born and it had therefore been necessary to conceal the birth so as not to damage her reputation and that for this and other reasons that modesty would not allow her to reveal, she had had the child baptized as a foundling." Maria Perpetua's baptismal certificate therefore read that she was the daughter of "unknown parents." donna Anna Margarida added, however, that she had always treated Maria Perpetua as a mother treats a daughter (modern *dona,* abbreviated as "D." before names).[3]

How can we reconcile this last statement with D. Anna Margarida's previous words about concealing the birth and protecting her reputation? Continuing her life at home under her father's authority, she certainly could not have raised the baby herself. But if she later considered that she had always acted like a mother, neither could she have in fact left the child on the doorstep of the church or a family home to be found and reared as a true foundling. Instead she herself or some accomplice must have arranged to have the baby raised by a foster family, maybe even paying them for their services. All these maneuvers entailed subterfuge and secrecy, which were the main strategies used by people to retain their reputation after human frailty led them to break the code of

Figure 13. The elites of Latin America were able to isolate themselves from the lower classes in many ways. One method was to travel through the rowdy streets in sedan chairs with accompanying servants, who protected the honor of their employers. (Jean Baptiste Debret, Albúm de aquarelas da região meridional do Brasil data-das de 1827, Inéditas, Coleção Conde de Bonneval, São Paulo.)

honor. That this was a well-known fact can be seen in the words of the eighteenth-century governor of the captaincy of São Paulo, Antonio Manoel de Mello Castro e Mendonça, when he wrote about the "innocents whose birth must be hidden because of their mothers' circumstances."[4]

The system of honor and shame in Brazil, as elsewhere in Latin America, predicated that single women should be virgins until they married, wives should be faithful, and widows chaste.[5] The system of family honor thereby sought to prevent and constrain the sexual activity of single daughters and married women. Yet colonial society had contradictory expectations. The honor system led men to protect the women in their own family from sexual assault and thereby preserve the family honor, whereas contemporary views on masculinity led them to attempt to seduce women in other families, thereby dishonoring them. Men's status and reputation within male culture rose as a function of how many women they were able to conquer.

Figure 14. Elite and middle-class women were expected to be exemplary Christians. Here a well-dressed Brazilian woman goes door to door asking for alms for the sick and poor. (Jean Baptiste Debret, Albúm de aquarelas da região meridional do Brasil datadas de 1827, Inéditas, Coleção Conde de Bonneval, São Paulo.)

This explosive mix of contradictory expectations had several consequences in colonial society. Because it was not usually men's sexual conduct that could dishonor a family, the system of honor and shame served to reinforce the double standard of morality. The system of honor and shame also served to differentiate society into classes, since it was much easier for the families of the upper classes to seclude and protect their daughters and wives from unwanted sexual advances than it was for the lower classes. In addition to relatives, wealthy families also had servants and slaves to serve and protect their female members. Women in lower-class families not only had fewer persons to protect them, but they also were not as sequestered, having many activities outside the home, which made them vulnerable to seduction or sexual attacks.

Thus the system of honor and shame upheld not only morality but also reinforced class stratification.[6] The Spanish colonial elite distinguished between people who had honor, *gente decente,* and people who did not, *gente baja.*[7] This was true in colonial Brazil, too, where one of the words most used in colonial times to describe an honorable family was *grave,* which not only meant "serious" but also "important, noble, illustrious." I have found countless uses of this word, especially in betrothal suits, in which a pregnant girl whose fiancé refused to marry her tried to convince the ecclesiastical court that her family was of such a station and honor that her not marrying would result in disastrous dishonor.[8]

Under this system, women's sexual behavior was therefore not only a question of personal morality but impinged on the status of the family itself. This paper will argue that one of the consequences of the system of honor and shame was the creation of a hypocritical society in which much was concealed and things were not always as they appeared.

FAMILY HONOR AND WOMEN'S SAFETY

The honor of a family was so vital to its status that many women in colonial Brazil who had dishonored their families by conceiving a child out of wedlock feared for their lives (and that of their seducers). For instance, in 1771, Francisca Xavier, a widow belonging to "one of the principal families" of São Paulo, started an ecclesiastical betrothal process after she became pregnant, in order to oblige Antonio Gomes Machado to keep his promise to marry her. Two different witnesses testified to the danger both she and Antonio faced from the wrath of her relatives.[9] In fact the words "she is in danger" were used frequently by witnesses in betrothal cases.[10] This was a realistic fear.

Policies of the Portuguese and Brazilian church confirm the danger of physical violence to women whose conduct affected their family's honor. The eighteenth-century Brazilian ecclesiastical law code spells out its instructions to the clergy very explicitly. Regarding adultery it states that if a married woman is found to be having an affair, and if "her husband is the kind of person who leads to the fear that there is a danger to her life or of her suffering considerable injury," the priest should proceed with caution. If there is no way to have her appear in court without danger, the parish priest should only admonish her in secret. And if the married woman's partner in sin is to be prosecuted in the ecclesiastical court, her name should never be mentioned.[11] A case in which this occurred was that of Simão Pinto Guede, who was admonished in 1750 in the São Paulo ecclesiastical court for the sin of concubinage with "a certain married woman."[12]

The ecclesiastical code included similar policies regarding the sin of fornication or concubinage involving single women. Another paragraph of the code stated that "if a single woman has still not lost her reputation, especially if she belongs to an illustrious [grave] family," and there is danger that her father or brothers could mistreat her, "the priest should proceed with the same caution."[13] This concern of the church for the safety and reputation of women who committed sexual sins was quite realistic, for civil law came down very hard on them and very leniently on their husbands, should their husbands find them in the act and kill wife and lover. On most such occasions, the husband would be acquitted of murder and only penalized if the status of the lover were much greater than that of the husband.[14]

The church's concern for the safety of women was long-standing. A seventeenth-century confessor's manual (a book to guide priests on how to conduct confession) states that penitents "should never name the persons with whom they sinned." In fact, the manual continues, if the sin committed is especially heinous, such as incest with one's mother or daughter, it is best to keep silent when confessing to one's regular confessor, who knows the mother or daughter. In such cases the penitent should look for a confessor who does not know him or his family.[15] The manual also advised penitents to refrain from confessing a sin if it was impossible to confess without implicating someone else.[16]

Because of its concern for an individual's or a family's reputation, the church therefore not only concealed a sinning woman's name from the rest of society, but tried to prevent even the clergy from knowing the names of women who had sinned grievously. In this respect the situation in colonial Brazil was very different from that of the Protestant English colonies, where women who sinned sexually were shamed publicly in their church and ostracized.

CONTRADICTIONS OF THE HONOR SYSTEM

In practice the system of honor and shame had two contradictory results. On the one hand it did in fact constrain the sexual conduct of single and married women. But on the other, precisely because of the great importance of a family's honor, it led to a system of concealment of transgressions of the code that in fact made them difficult but possible. As long as the reputations of a woman and her family were maintained, she could get away with quite an irregular lifestyle.

An example of this is the life of Isabel Fernandes Buena of the city of Curitiba, who wrote her will in 1799. She was a woman of elite status, the daughter of a militia captain and a property owner in her own right. She declared in her will that even though she was single, she had had four children, whose births she had concealed and whom she had subsequently abandoned as foundlings. She stated further that her children were: João Francisco, who had been left in the home of Maria das Neves e Sá, who had raised him and with whom he still lived; Felisberto, left to Escolastica Maria e Sá, with whom he resided; Manoel, left with José da Rocha Dantas, whose family had raised him and still sheltered him; and Antonia, abandoned at the home of Bento de Freitas, but whom Isabel had later covertly brought to her own house and who was therefore living with her. She declared that she wanted to institute her children as her heirs for reasons of conscience and to save her soul.[17]

Isabel Fernandes Buena had her reputation and status to protect. Yet the fact that she had four children points to a long-lasting relationship, undoubtedly with someone who could not marry her, perhaps a priest or a married man.[18] She had never recognized her children, having them baptized as foundlings. She had, however, selected their foster homes carefully, choosing what might be two sisters to raise the first two and then respectable married men for the last two. She also appears to have been following her children's progress in their foster families and may have waited until her parents died to bring her daughter to her own home, where she probably maintained the fiction that she had taken in a foster child. All these elaborate precautions could not have been entirely foolproof, so that it is quite possible that quite a few persons knew the truth. Her situation may be seen as analogous to that of homosexuals in the United States Army in the twentieth century. Concealment was necessary to her life and reputation but was probably not complete.

Since single daughters were expected to continue living with their parents until their parents died, actual or probable negative reactions on their part to their daughter's illegitimate child were strong motives for giving the child to foster parents. This was especially true in a period in which so much of a family's honor depended on the sexual conduct of its female members. The constraint that some women felt is clearly expressed by D. Francisca de Silveira e Souza, when she declared in her petition to legitimize her two sons that they had been abandoned to another family because of the scandal of her situation, that she had nevertheless always watched over them, and that their father, a priest, had supported them. She added that during her sons' early childhood, she had been constrained in the home of her parents, but that when she came to live on her own, she had publicly acknowledged her children.[19] These strategies were not uncommon; in studying the processes of legitimation in the Desembargo do Paço, I found that in at least 8 percent of the cases, it openly states that the child was baptized as a foundling and raised as such, at least during its early years.

Moreover illegitimate children were experienced differently by mothers and fathers. The baptismal records of most illegitimate infants did not include the name of the father but did include that of the mother, who thereby lost her honor. Thus the only way to protect the mother's reputation was to abandon the child and have it raised as a foundling. The difference between foundlings and other illegitimate children, then, was that foundlings had not been recognized by their mothers.

Protection of the mother's honor and reputation is also evident in several cases where the father recognized his child at baptism or later had the baptismal certificate redone but retained the phrase "born of an unknown mother." Such was the case of the 1819 baptismal certificate that read "natural son of Doctor Amaro Baptista Pereira and an unknown mother."[20] When Judge José Mascarenhas Salter de Mello e Mendonça wrote a declaration in his own handwriting in 1783 recognizing his two sons and had it duly witnessed, he stated that he had had the boys with "a concealed lady."[21] This kind of protection of a woman's honor could last many years, for I found that the mother's name was never mentioned in 15 percent of the legitimation processes in the Desembargo do Paço.

The situation may not be as clear cut as it appears, however. There are a few cases where the mother's name was not mentioned because of her lowly status. This seems to be the case in the preliminary inquiries made by the priest before the wedding of Ensign José da Silva de Oliveira with Mariana de Araújo Lima in 1802 in São Paulo.[22] When they married, she was listed as the daughter of Adjunct Domingos de Araújo Lima da Silva (who was a witness at the wedding) and an unknown mother. In the preliminary inquiries, the baptismal certificate she presented stated that she was the daughter of Domingas, a slave belonging to Anna da Rocha, and an unknown father. Omitting her mother's name was clearly not meant to protect her mother's honor and reputation but rather her own, now that her father seemed to have taken her under his wing.

What the former case confirms is that circumstances frequently changed during the lifetime of the child, and the unknown father or unknown parents might become known and acknowledge their child. Another such case is that of Anna Thereza da Conceição, who married in São Paulo in 1795, stating she was the natural daughter of Ensign Ignacio Alvares de Toledo and Maria Ferreyra. However, her baptismal certificate only gave her mother's name, giving her father as unknown. Something changed in the intervening years, for her relationship to her father had become close enough for him to be a witness to her wedding.[23]

These changes might occur in a relatively short time. For instance when Dr. Amaro Baptista Pereira's son was baptized in 1819, the baptismal certificate stated that the mother was unknown. Nine years later he legitimated his son, naming the child's mother, D. Luiza Escolastica Botelho Correira de Mesquita.[24] Though the documentation gives us no more information about her, her name itself, the use of the term *donna*, and the long string of surnames tell us that she belonged to a distinguished family. We can only speculate on what had happened in the intervening years to make it possible for her to officially reveal her identity as the boy's mother.

The case of D. Anna Clara Freire, the widow of Captain José Barboza de Mendonça, provides us with one example of what could change over the intervening years. It was her husband's death that made the difference, allowing her to legitimize in 1818 the nine children she had had with Bacharel José Soares Pereira da Silva, who had legitimized them four years before without naming their mother. In this case it was only in the official documentation that the situation had not been recognized, for D. Anna Clara had lived openly with Bacharel José Soares Pereira during those years in which the children were born and raised. She had been informally separated from her husband, with whom she had no children, and her irregular situation would certainly not have existed had there been divorce and remarriage laws at the time. Legitimizing her children after she became a widow was important, because it made it possible for them to inherit from her thereafter.[25]

REPUTATION AND POVERTY

Thus though not all silences in relation to the mother can be attributed to a desire to protect her reputation, one could still argue that the great number of foundlings in colonial Brazilian society was one of the consequences of the system of honor and shame. Though poverty and economic hardship were undoubtedly also causes of child abandonment, we should pay attention to the issue of contemporary mores and their effect on mothers of illegitimate children, who might abandon them only to protect their reputation and not because of the financial impossibility of raising the child.[26]

The two hypotheses involve mothers of different classes. If we use the former hypothesis, that poverty drives mothers to abandon their children, foundlings would originally come from the poorest strata; under the second hypothesis, that it is concern for their reputation, it would be women of a higher socioeconomic position who would be damaged the most by acknowledging their illegitimate children, and who would therefore more frequently abandon them. It is probable that both hypotheses are true, and that foundlings were of

de Español y Negra

Figure 15. There was a strong color prejudice in colonial Latin America. In this eighteenth-century painting the European husband is assaulted by his black wife. The painter's message is that honor and status were likely to be overturned by a marriage that ignored social conventions. (Museo de América, Madrid.)

two kinds, those abandoned for economic reasons and those abandoned for reasons of honor.

If we use race as an approximation to class, the white as the higher class and the colored as the lower, the statistics concerning illegitimate children and foundlings can point to what was actually happening. The baptismal records of the rural parish of Santo Amaro in São Paulo started to classify free infants by race in 1799, either as white or *pardos* (colored). The statistics are very illuminating. In the five years between 1799 and 1803, only 15 percent of white illegitimate children were acknowledged by their mothers at the baptismal fount, whereas 85 percent were abandoned. On the other hand, 64 percent of pardo illegitimate children were acknowledged by their mothers, and only 36 percent were abandoned.[27] That is, white mothers were nearly two and a half times more likely to abandon their illegitimate children than were pardo women.

Using the example of Santo Amaro, we can conclude that leaving their infants on a doorstep was the more usual behavior of white women caught in

Figure 16. The absence of privacy separated the lives of the poor from those of the rich. The poor lived much of their lives in public spaces like this plaza, where barbers shaved and cut the hair of their clients. In an environment such as this, honor was tested by insults and physical challenges. (Jean Baptiste Debret, Albúm de aquarelas da região meridional do Brasil datadas de 1827, Inéditas, Coleção Conde de Bonneval, São Paulo.)

illicit relationships than of freed colored women—women of the higher (white) status, concerned with their honor, abandoned their illegitimate children more frequently. White mothers clearly had greater difficulty acknowledging their transgressions of social mores than pardo mothers.[28]

Each group of mothers of illegitimate children may have been making realistic choices. Scholars have found that marriage was not very frequent in colonial Brazil, something that contemporaries were aware of and blamed on the great expense of legal marriage. Of those who married, most belonged to the upper (white) classes.[29] It was therefore women of the class most able to marry who stood to lose the most if their illicit relationships became widely known. Since lower-class women had fewer opportunities for marriage, they might realistically wish to keep their children with them and even enter into long-term relations of concubinage, in which they might find happiness despite the dishonor attached to them.[30]

INCEST

Because of the church's concern to prevent incest the ecclesiastical processes of marriage inquiries are an excellent documentary source to recover the identities of illegitimate children's parents who were not named at baptism. The church was especially concerned about the marriage of foundlings, for fear that they would unknowingly marry close relatives.[31] Thus, despite the admonitions to the clergy about not divulging people's sins, the clergy was also urged to learn as much as possible about an illegitimate child's parents. And future spouses themselves were desirous of fulfilling all necessary requirements, in order to make their marriage a valid one.

Such a case is that of Joaquim Xavier de Oliveira who married Gertrudes Joaquina de Almeida in São Paulo in 1799 with a dispensation for consanguinity in the fourth degree. According to her 1781 baptismal certificate, Gertrudes was the illegitimate child of Izidora Maria de Araújo and an unknown father. Her godparents were Sergeant Thomé de Almeida Lara and his mother. At the marriage inquiries eighteen years later, Gertrudes declared that she was the daughter of Izidora and the now Captain Thomé de Almeida. The consanguinity between the spouses was traced through her father, the captain, who had a common great-grandparent with the groom, so the spouses could not have avoided incest if she had not known who her father was.[32]

Another such case is that of Gertrudes Maria do Espirito Santo, who married Salvador Pires de Lima in São Paulo in 1798 with a dispensation for consanguinity. She was related to her husband through her mother, Rita Maria de Jesus, who had had her baptized as a foundling. During the ecclesiastical inquiries, Gertrudes explained her mother's actions saying, "Since my mother was single, she had me baptized as a foundling in the home of José . . ., and now it has been clearly discovered that, though registered as a child of unknown parents, I am the child of that same Rita Maria, who raised me on her own milk."[33]

However, the processes of marriage inquiries also show that many foundlings never learned who their parents were. These true foundlings appear as prospective marriage partners throughout the marriage processes. We must thus be careful not to assume that all foundlings later learned who their parents were. If we assume that there were two kinds of foundlings, those whose mothers felt the need to conceal the birth to protect their reputation and those whose mothers simply did not have the resources to raise a child, it seems probable that those who had no resources would more likely abandon their children forever. This is speculation, however, and it could just as easily be that some of those who abandoned their children to protect their own honor never recognized them either.

FALSE FOUNDLINGS

There was another possibility in this widespread web of concealment, when a single mother raised her illegitimate child herself but presented the child to the church in baptism and to society in general as a foundling. This was the case of Bernardina Joaquina do Nascimento, who in 1828 sought to legitimize her fifteen-year-old daughter. She declared that her daughter had been baptized as a foundling and that she had raised and educated her as such from the time she was an infant.[34]

Thus baptismal records are not always to be trusted. Though foundlings were supposed to be children with unknown parents who were being baptized and raised by foster parents, this was not always the case. Sometimes the supposed foster parent was in fact the birth mother or father. A few baptismal records show some ambiguity; although the wording used was generally "unknown parents," one baptism tellingly records that "the parents are hiding."[35] Another says that a little girl was "from unknown parents born in Tereza's home." Interestingly enough, the child was also named Tereza.[36] How could a child be born in a certain house without its members knowing who the mother was? What these cases suggest is that the circle of persons who knew the foundling's parentage might have included the foster parents, who colluded with the parents in keeping the information from the church and other official sectors of the community.

A complex web of concealment was created in the process. Consider the case of Captain João Gonçalves da Cruz of the town of Guaratinguetá, who had five illegitimate daughters, born between 1787 and 1803 to Theodora Gonçalves de Oliveira, while he was married to another woman.[37] He also had had five children with his wife. When she died, he married Theodora and had two legitimate children with her. Because the captain's illegitimate daughters were born during his first marriage, they were adulterine children.[38] He tried to have his illegitimate daughters legitimized in 1827 before the Desembargo do Paço; their respective baptismal certificates revealed that all were baptized as foundlings. All five children were abandoned to families living in the same neighborhood as the captain, the first two to people bearing the surname Gonçalves, who were therefore probably his relatives or relatives of the children's mother. The last two daughters were baptized as foundlings abandoned to the captain himself. The choice of godparents is also interesting, for the second child had her mother as godmother and the fourth had her father as godfather.

Thus we have a situation in which, to preserve their honor, parents deliberately managed the supposed abandonment of their illegitimate offspring, and quite a few people besides the children's parents apparently colluded in the secrecy that was adopted. Both foster parents and godparents were obviously chosen by the captain and Theodora, who also decided to themselves be the godparents of two of their daughters, a course forbidden by the church.

Yet these were not the only parents to become their own children's godparents. The ploy of having the father become his illegitimate child's godfather seems to have served in the case of Carlos Manoel Gago da Camara as a way to legitimize his continued interest in the child. He was single when he had a son with D. Anna Maria de Araújo, a doctor's widow. When his son, Joaquim Manoel Gago da Camara, petitioned to be legitimized after his father's death, he presented as evidence several letters written by his father to his mother, in which he called Joaquim his godchild, showed much interest in his education, and sent sums of money to help pay for his support. After Carlos Manoel married a wealthy widow in Bahia, he had the boy brought to Bahia to live in his own home.[39] The court legitimized Joaquim Manoel, clearly viewing Carlos Manoel's behavior as going far beyond that expected of a godfather.

HONOR AND THE CENSUS

The system of honor and shame also had effects on what persons reported to the census taker. Studying the late eighteenth- and early nineteenth-century São Paulo censuses, we find that some children were listed as children of single mothers and were therefore born out of wedlock, whereas others are listed as foundlings and therefore are presumed to have no blood relationship to members of the household. But when one studies the census for several years, tracing families through several censuses, one finds great variations that suggest efforts to conceal relationships.[40]

The case of Clemente Rodrigues and his wife Maria de Siqueira of the rural neighborhood of Santana in São Paulo appears to be a case of a true foundling. They had no children but Anna, called a foundling in the census of 1787 and 1795. In the census of 1796, she is called an *agregada* (a nonrelative who lives in the household), whereas in 1798 she is simply called "daughter." This is clearly a couple with no children of their own who were raising a child, whom they or the census taker designated in different ways for different censuses.

Another example illustrates that there were more devious ways to call a child a foundling in the census. Anna Ferreira was called the daughter of João Ferreira dos Santos and Tereza Roiz in the Santana censuses of 1778, 1796, and 1798. She was called "foundling" in the censuses of 1783, 1787, and 1795, whereas in the census of 1780 she was called an agregada (a nonrelative living in the household). Since the couple appear to have had no other children, she would seem to be, in fact, a foundling they raised. However, she was an adult woman throughout those censuses, and in 1780 a two-year-old child, Maria, also called a foundling, was added to the household. This child was the right age to be Anna's daughter, despite being called a foundling, and the suspected relationship appears to be confirmed in a later census, when Maria had grown and married, and her husband was referred to as Anna's son-in-law.[41]

From these and similar cases, we can deduce that many times the word *exposto* ("foundling") was used appropriately in the census, that is, to denote a child of unknown parents being raised by foster parents, but examples like that of Maria suggest that the word might also be used to conceal a relationship and preserve public honor. Another case of the latter is that of the widow Izabel de Siqueira, who in the 1783 census had in her household, among others, a twenty-eight-year-old single daughter called Josefa and two little girls called foundlings. These children were also called foundlings in the 1787 census, but by 1795 and 1796 they were openly designated as Josefa's children and Izabel de Siqueira's granddaughters. Two opposite interpretations are possible. Josefa's children could have been called foundlings in the first censuses as a means of concealment, or Josefa's true foster children could have come to be called her children as time went on. Without outside corroboration we can therefore not be certain that suspicious uses of the term actually represented a cover-up.

Outside documentation does confirm the use of the term exposto in the census list as a cover-up in the case of the household of Captain José Antonio da Silva, commander of the militia of the rural neighborhood of Santana in São Paulo from before 1778 until he was assassinated in 1797. He and his wife were childless, but at the settlement of his estate, his widow declared that she and the captain had given a small farm within their property to Gertrudes Pires, who was the mother of his seven illegitimate children.[42] Baptismal records reveal that the children had been baptized as natural children of Gertrudes and an unknown father.[43] In the 1783 census Gertrudes and her first child, Damazio, appeared as white agregados of José Antonio da Silva's household, although the fact that Damazio was her child was not mentioned. Moreover in 1787 Damazio and his younger sister and brother, who were born in the interim, were characterized as foundlings. Eight years later, in the census of 1795, Gertrudes and her children were again all categorized as agregados, and no relationship was shown between mother and children. In the following year's census, that of 1796, Gertrudes was called an agregada, but her children were all identified as foundlings, as they were in the 1797 census as well, in which their mother's name was not even recorded. The relationship of José Antonio da Silva to his children and to his mistress was thereby obscured, as it had been in every previous census, thereby protecting the family honor.

Yet to preserve their honor with so much secrecy required the help of many persons who were in the know. This fact is quite evident in the case of Colonel Francisco de Amorim Lima, who in 1815 instituted his son as heir in his will. For the legitimation process, his son, Francisco de Assis de Amorim Lima, presented a notation made out by his father, stating that "On Sunday, November 4, 1781, a son was born to me around two o'clock in the morning named Francisco, who was baptized in the Parish of Sé. My brother, Domingos de Amorim was his godfather." The baptismal certificate reads: "Francisco, son of unknown parents exposed to Boaventura de Faria, whose godfather was Domingos de Amorim" (there was no godmother). The colonel's sister declared at the legitimation process that she well knew that Francisco de Assis was her nephew, for her brother treated him as his son from the moment of his birth, arranging to have him raised and later bringing him to live in his own home. She added that her brother had told her before Francisco was born that the child was his and asked her to take care of matters regarding the birth so that the reputation of its mother would not suffer, since she was held by everyone to be a maiden. Furthermore eight letters were produced for the legitimation process, written by the godfather, Domingos de Amorim Lima, and addressed to his "godson and nephew," showing that Francisco came to be openly addressed as a relative.[44]

Thus quite a few people were needed to help conceal a birth and protect a family's honor. The reputation of Francisco de Assis de Amorim Lima's mother and her family was shielded during the first few years by his father and several of his relatives and friends, including his paternal aunt and uncle and the foster family who raised Francisco during his early years. By the time Francisco was legitimated, at the age of thirty-four, his mother's name was openly used in the legitimation process.

Because he could do so without losing his honor, it was Francisco's father who saw that he was raised as an infant and who later took him into his own home to see to his education. His mother had nothing to do with her son, like a birth mother in the twentieth century who gives up her child for adoption.

FATHERS AS SOLE RECOGNIZED PARENTS

This pattern was quite frequent in colonial Brazil. In many cases where it was important to preserve the mother's honor, it was the father who raised the child. This was made explicit in over 10 percent of the cases in the Desembargo do Paço. In many of these cases, moreover, it was the father's wife who did the actual raising. Such is the case of Manoel Carlos de Abreu Lima, who petitioned in 1812 to have his nineteen-year-old daughter legitimized. He declared that she had been born to a married woman during his own marriage and that from the time of her birth, he had openly recognized her and raised her in his home. His wife agreed to the legitimation, probably because they had no children of their own.[45]

A case in which the father's wife helped raise his illegitimate daughter despite their having children of their own is that of Manoel Estanislao de Castro e Cruz, an officer in the Brazilian navy. Witnesses declared that Manoel had brought his small daughter back from Montevideo or Buenos Aires when he was still single, but that after his marriage she continued to be raised by her father and stepmother, together with their other children.[46]

That so many people knew the secret means that in the long run others would learn it. This did happen in the case of Francisco de Assis de Amorim Lima, discussed above, for his mother, D. Roza Maria de Jesus, was named in the legitimation process; she also appears to have been illegitimate. Francisco's process of legitimation did not proceed smoothly, because his grandmother, wishing to inherit her son's estate herself, threw out doubts about whether Francisco could in fact be considered a 'natural' son who could inherit from his father. According to Portuguese law, a natural child was the child born out of wedlock to single or widowed parents, who had no canonical impediment to marriage; that is, to parents who could have married if they had so wished.[47] Excluded from the possibility of inheriting were 'spurious' offspring. Spurious children were either adulterine, that is, born during the wedlock of at least one of the parents to a third party, sacrilegious, the offspring of a monk or priest, or incestuous, the children of an incestuous relationship.[48]

It was this latter possibility that Francisco's grandmother used to bolster her objections to his recognition as her son's child. His grandmother declared that before she married Francisco's grandfather, he had had a mistress whose daughter became Francisco's mother, Rosa Maria de Jesus. His grandmother added that therefore Francisco's mother, Rosa Maria, was thought to be his father's half-sister, which would mean that he had been born from an incestuous union and could never inherit from his father. Some of Francisco's uncles sided with their mother, but his aunt and his uncle (and godfather) Domingos sided with his father and his explicit wishes in the will. It was the latter position that won out in the Desembargo do Paço, for Francisco was duly legitimized after the will of Francisco's grandfather was presented to the court, in which he explicitly denied having any other but his legitimate children.

HONOR AND APPEARANCES

I have presented this part of the case in order to highlight the kind of society that evolved when many individuals resorted to such subterfuges to conceal their sexual transgressions in order to protect their honor. It was a society in which appearances were important, but people knew appearances did not always conform to reality. Because of this knowledge, individuals naturally tended to try to make deductions based on whatever limited information they had. People knew that the maternal grandmother of Francisco de Assis had been the mistress of his paternal grandfather for a time, for instance, and therefore assumed that any children she had were his. Since the children's birth was most likely concealed, and they were probably raised as foundlings the first few years, few persons besides the parents would know when a child was born. Speculation could therefore proceed. We cannot learn whether his mother and father were in reality half-brother and half-sister. People might have assumed the worst, when in fact that situation might not have existed.

Subterfuge became even more important in the case of married women who had children with men other than their husbands. In the cases treated at the Desembargo do Paço, there were relatively few illegitimate children born to married women—only around 3 percent of the cases. Most of these were the offspring of women abandoned by their husbands or separated from them. For instance Maria da Costa de Faria had had a child with Dr. Placido da Silva de Oliveira Rolim while they were both single, but her parents then forced her to marry another man; because she so despised him, their marriage was not consummated and was later annulled. After that she had five more children with Dr. Placido.[49]

There was only a handful of cases of married women who were cohabiting with their husbands when their adulterine children were born. Of all the situations of danger to the life of a woman who was transgressing the norms of the honor and shame system, this was the worst. And the church, with its constant concern for the safety of women who sinned sexually, had very explicit instructions for what should be done under such circumstances. The confessor's manual told priests that they could absolve a penitent married woman who bore an adulterine child while cohabiting with her husband. Furthermore they could absolve her without informing her husband about her sin, especially if she were afraid he would kill her, or even if it were only to preserve her reputation. It added that the priest must not tell her husband, even if it meant that he would suffer by raising as his a child who was not his. The manual recommended further that when the son became an adult, if he was virtuous, he be told by his mother about his birth, so that he could leave his share of the inheritance to his siblings. Or else, it suggests, he could become a priest and, without need for explanations, his siblings would automatically inherit.[50] The church therefore became a reluctant accomplice in the web of concealment created by the system of honor and shame. Confirmation of this conclusion is found in the case of D. Josefa Maria Francisca de Paula, who in 1816 petitioned the Desembargo do Paço to legitimize her son Nicolau, who was born while she was still married to her first husband. She declared that after her first husband died, she had married the father of her son and now wanted to change his baptismal certificate, because when Nicolau was baptized, "by the ecclesiastical authority he was declared to be my son and the son of my first husband."[51]

Another such case is that of Antonio João da Costa Carneiro, who argued for his own legitimation before the Desembargo do Paço, presenting a legal document of recognition made out in his lifetime by his deceased father (and godfather), Judge João da Costa Carneiro de Oliveira. He had been raised by his mother and her husband for the first three years of his life, then had gone to live with his father. His baptismal certificate was made out in the name of his mother and her husband, and Antonio João explained that this was done "so as not to divulge his mother's failing, and in consideration of the decency of her marriage."[52] Making Antonio João's real father his godfather also allowed the judge to maintain appearances when he received his son into his household, probably calling him his godchild.

Despite the double morality and the fact that it was women who suffered the greatest loss of honor through their transgressions, men could also suffer in their family honor if they were brazen about their own infractions. We can see this in the two following examples involving men of great social standing. The first was Colonel Lourenço Maria de Almeida Portugal, illegitimate son of the Marquis of Lavradio, Dom Luiz de Almeida Portugal, who was the viceroy of Brazil from 1769 to 1779. The colonel's 1776 baptismal certificate stated that he was a foundling taken up by Catherina Joanna de Sena, though he was later raised by Field Marshal Pedro Nolasco Pereira da Cunha, whose daughter he married. When he petitioned to be legitimized in 1823, after his father had died, we learn that he was the son of a very respectable widow, D. Marianna da Fonseca Costa Araújo. The field marshal testified that after the marquis returned to Portugal in 1779, he wrote him several letters asking him to continue educating his son "until circumstances would permit him [the marquis] to have his son join him in Portugal." In his own testimony the colonel declared that his father had not kept his word to send for him, probably because of his premature death, and also "to preserve the laws of decency."[53] Thus it was not only women who could not openly acknowledge their illegitimate children, but also men.

Another example of this kind of care for appearances in men's lives is that of Major Luis Deodato Pinto de Souza, who requested legitimation as the natural son of Councilman José Manoel Pinto de Souza, who died in Rome in 1818, as envoy extraordinaire of the Portuguese crown to the Italian government. Several distinguished witnesses testified to his being the councilman's son, including his aunt, who declared that she knew he was her brother's son, "not only because he had told her so, but also because of Luis Deodato's physical structure and mannerisms that left no doubt in her mind that he was her brother's son." After his father died, the major received several letters from the executor of his father's will. The first one informed him of his father's decease and of the sizable amount he had bequeathed to the major. The second is in answer to the major's letter in which he had described his wish to go to Lisbon to visit his father's grave. The executor quite clearly discouraged him from doing this, suggesting that the major "examine such plans more maturely. I believe that you will show sufficient piety and thankfulness to your father's memory if you continue in your present career, or another that is equally honorable, with the same decorum and probity that you have heretofore shown."[54] The executor was apparently concerned either with the major's or his father's reputation, should he go to Lisbon and openly refer to his filiation.

In another case Domingos Ferreira Lopes in 1823–24 petitioned the Desembargo do Paço to be legitimized as the son of Admiral D. Francisco de Souza Coutinho, already deceased. His cousin wrote a strong letter against his legitimation, arguing that his uncle had given Domingos an excellent education and property, and that to insist on legitimation would be to discredit his uncle's reputation. The admiral had professed in the Order of Malta; for Domingos to try to obtain legitimation now would denigrate the admiral's memory and exhibit to the world the weakness he showed with Domingos's mother, contrary to the solemn vows he had made.[55] Despite the fact that Domingos's cousin's letter was undoubtedly tainted by his desire to inherit from his uncle, the fact that he used this argument so extensively means he felt it would be effective, that people believed a man's reputation could also suffer from having an illegitimate child.

CONCLUSION

To learn about the consequences of the system of honor and shame in colonial Brazil, we have examined the actions of a minority of the parents of illegitimate

children, mostly the people with sufficient money to be able to seek to legitimize themselves or their illegitimate children in the Desembargo do Paço or to
write wills. Only a relatively small percentage of the population of colonial
Brazil married, and there were therefore many illegitimate children and foundlings, which means that the system of honor and shame was not sufficient to
suppress people's natural instincts. Instead the system of honor and shame
combined with the expense of marriage to reinforce class stratification. It was
mainly white upper-class women and their families who retained their honor,
though lower-class people aspired to do so and were often successful. Moreover
giving an illegitimate child up as a foundling provided complete anonymity to
the parents, preserving their reputation. Thus the system of honor and shame
undoubtedly contributed to the large number of foundlings in colonial Brazil.

The system of honor and shame limited the sexual choices and freedom of
women; it constrained their sexuality, whether they were single, married, or
widowed. This research has shown, however, that not all women and men
conformed to these constraints, and mechanisms evolved in the society to
conceal their infractions to the code. Men, women, and families did not lose
their honor, as long as they kept up appearances of an honorable life. But to be
able to keep up appearances required the collusion of quite a number of people,
including ecclesiastics, so that many persons in fact knew the truth. Thus the
honor of most families was based on the actual chastity of daughters and the
faithfulness of wives, but that of some families was based on subterfuge.

NOTES

The research for this paper was supported by a Fulbright Area Research Grant and an
award from the Joint Committee on Latin American Studies of the Social Science Research
Council and the American Council of Learned Societies.

1. The Desembargo do Paço was a Portuguese high court that was transferred to Brazil
when the king and his court moved to Rio de Janeiro in 1808; it was used in Brazil until 1828
to legitimize illegitimate offspring. Most of the persons requesting the legitimizing were
fathers, but some, as in the case above, were mothers. In some instances it was the children
themselves. The process in the Desembargo do Paço was long and probably expensive, so it
is possible that only wealthy individuals carried it out. For other cases of legitimation and
other uses of that high court, see Maria Beatriz Nizza da Silva, "A documentação do
Desembargo do Paço e a história da família," in *Ler História* 20 (1990): 61–77. Illegitimate
children were also legitimated in European nations. Edward Shorter, "Illegitimacy, Sexual
Revolution, and Social Change in Modern Europe," in *The Family in History: Interdisciplinary Essays,* ed. Edward Shorter, Theodore Rabb, and Robert Rotberg (New York: Harper,
1972), found that the proportion of legitimated children (compared to all illegitimate

children) rose in Paris from 7.2 percent in 1822 to 35.3 percent in 1910–14 and in Belgium from 34.7 percent in 1851–60 to 61.1 percent in 1911–13.

2. I use *illegitimate* in this paper as a blanket term to cover all types of children born out of wedlock. For issues of succession, Portuguese legislation differentiated between "natural" children (those born of single or widowed parents who could have married), who had many rights in relation to their parents and their parents' estates, and "spurious" children (born of adulterous, incestuous, or sacrilegous unions—the latter involving a priest). See Linda Lewin, "Natural and Spurious Children in Brazilian Inheritance Law from Colony to Empire: A Methodological Essay," *The Americas* 48 (3) (January 1992): 351–96.

3. See Arquivo Nacional, Desembargo do Paço, Legitimações (hereafter called Legitimações), caixa 123, pac. 1, doc. 12, 1815.

4. Antonio Manoel de Mello Castro e Mendonça, *Memória econômico-política da Capitania de São Paulo,* as quoted in Alzira Lobo de Arruda Campos, "O Casamento e a família em São Paulo colonial: Caminhos e descaminhos" (Ph.D. diss., University of São Paulo, 1986), 325.

5. Though Brazil shared these customs, there have been few studies made. For references to family and women's honor in Brazil, see Mary del Priore, *Ao sul do corpo: Condição feminina, maternidades e mentalidades no Brasil colônia* (Rio de Janeiro: José Olympio, 1993), 62, 71, 74. For issues of honor in Spanish America, see essays in this volume and Ann Twinam, "Honor, Sexuality, and Illegitimacy in Colonial Spanish America," in *Sexuality and Marriage in Colonial Latin America,* ed. Asunción Lavrin (Lincoln: University of Nebraska Press, 1989), 123; and Ramón A. Gutiérrez, "From Honor to Love: Transformation in the Meaning of Sexuality in Colonial New Mexico," in *Kinship Ideology and Practice in Latin America,* ed. Raymund T. Smith (Chapel Hill: University of North Carolina Press, 1984), and "Honor Ideology, Marriage Negotiation, and Class-Gender Domination in New Mexico, 1690–1846," in *Latin American Perspectives* 12 (1) (Winter 1985): 86 in particular. Also see Verena Martinez-Alier, *Marriage, Class and Colour in Nineteenth-Century Cuba: A Study of Racial Attitudes and Sexual Values in a Slave Society* (London: Cambridge University Press, 1974), especially chap. 1; and Patricia Seed, *To Love, Honor, and Obey in Colonial Mexico: Conflicts over Marriage Choice, 1574–1821* (Stanford, CA: Stanford University Press, 1988), 61.

6. See also Muriel Nazzari, "Sex/Gender Arrangements and the Reproduction of Class in the Latin American Past," in *Gender and Power in Latin America: Methods, Theory, and Practice,* ed. Elizabeth Dore (New York: Monthly Review Press, 1997).

7. Twinam, "Honor, Sexuality," 123.

8. See for instance, Arquivo da Cúria Metropolitana de São Paulo (hereafter ACMSP), Processos de esponsais (uncatalogued), 1762 and 1771, Mariana Rodrigues, autora, Francisco Duarte do Rego, réu. Also see Muriel Nazzari, "Concubinage in Colonial Brazil: The Inequalities of Race, Class, and Gender," *Journal of Family History* 21 (2) (April 1996), and del Priore, *Ao sul do corpo,* 62, 71, 74.

9. ACMSP, Processos de esponsais (uncatalogued), São Paulo, 1771, Maria Francisca Xavier, justificante, Antonio Gomes Machado, justificado.

10. See, for instance, ACMSP, Processos de esponsais, São Paulo, 1761, Ana Maria de Medeiros, justificante, João Dias Linhares, justificado.

11. Constituições primeiras do Arcebispado da Bahia, feitas e ordenadas pelo Ilustríssimo e Reverendíssimo Senhor dom Sebastião Monteiro da Vide, arcebispo do dito arcebispado e do Conselho de Sua Majestade; propostas e aceitas em o sínodo diocesano que o dito senhor celebrou em 12 de junho do ano de 1707 (Coimbra: Real Colégio das Artes da Companhia de Jesus, 1720) (hereafter Constituições), liv. 5, tit. 23, par. 990.

12. See Nazzari, "Concubinage," 115.

13. *Constituições*, liv. 5, tit. 23, par. 991.

14. See Eni de Mesquita Samara, "Mistérios da 'Fragilidade Humana': O adultério feminino no Brasil, séculos XVIII e XIX" (paper presented at the conference Familia y Vida Privada: América, Siglos XVI a XIX, Universidad Autónoma de México, May 1993). On p. 6 she quotes title 38 of the Portuguese code (*Código Philippino: Ou Ordenações e Leis do Reino de Portugal*), which is entitled "Of him who kills his wife when finding her in adultery."

15. Dr. Martin de Azpilcueta Navarro, Manual de Confessores y Penitentes, que contiene quasi todas las dudas que en las Confessiones suelen ocurrir de los pecados, absoluciones, restituciones, censuras e irregularidades (Valladolid: Francisco Fernandez de Cordova, 1670), 39, 55.

16. Ibid., chap. 28, p. 10.

17. See ACMSP, uncatalogued wills, Isabel Fernandes Buena, Curitiba, 1799.

18. She asked José da Rocha Dantas to be her executor and the tutor of her children, but he refused both tasks, claiming illness. One wonders whether he was not the married father of these children.

19. Legitimações, caixa 125, pac. 3, doc. 44.

20. Legitimações, caixa 123, pac. 1, doc. 6. Other cases where the father recognizes his child but the mother remains unknown are found in caixa 121, pac. 2, doc. 27; caixa 123, pac. 1, doc. 6; and in caixa 124, pac. 1, doc. 21, and pac. 2, doc. 29.

21. Legitimações, caixa 127, pac. 1, doc. 10.

22. These were required before every wedding and were called *processos de casamento*. The bride and bridegroom had to provide proof of baptism and proof that they were single or widowed. The latter entailed a certificate from the parish priest of every place the bride or bridegroom had lived for longer than six months. Usually it was the groom who had traveled extensively and moved around in the world, making this a very expensive process. They were also asked questions meant to reveal their status, such as how much they expected to inherit (see Nazzari, "Concubinage"). This case is found in ACMSP, Processos de casamento, 1802, no. 7–25–2756, Alferes José da Silva de Oliveira, Mariana de Araújo Lima.

23. ACMSP, Registros de casamento da Sé, liv. 3, 1795, fol. 15 v., and Processos de casamento, Domingos Veigas Lisboa and Anna Thereza da Conceição.

24. Legitimações, caixa 123, pac. 1, doc. 6.

25. Legitimações, caixa 123, pac. 1, doc. 11.

26. This is also the opinion of Maria Beatriz Nizza da Silva, "O problema dos expostos na Capitania de São Paulo," *Revista de História Económica e Social,* 5 (January–June 1980) and *Anais do Museu Paulista* 30 (São Paulo, 1980–81).

27. Source: ACMSP, Livro de batiasados brancos e pardos livres, paróquia de Santo Amaro, SP, 1799–1803. A. J. R. Russell-Wood, *Fidalgos and Philanthropists: The Santa Casa*

da Misericórdia of Bahia, 1550–1755 (Berkeley: University of California Press, 1968), 313, also shows that more white than pardo children were abandoned to the Santa Casa in Salvador in 1757 and 1758. See also Felipe Arturo Avila Espinosa, "Los niños abandonados de la casa de niños expósitos de la ciudad de México, 1767–1821," in *La familia en el mundo iberoamericano* (Mexico City: Instituto de Investigaciones Sociales/Universidad Nacional Autónoma de México, 1994). Avila shows that white children were abandoned in Mexico City for reasons of honor more frequently than Indian or mestizo children; see especially his figures on pp. 307–8.

28. Russell-Wood, *Fidalgos and Philanthropists*, 311, reaches the same conclusion: "The honour of the white girl had to be preserved at all costs."

29. See Donald Ramos, "Marriage and the Family in Colonial Vila Rica," *Hispanic American Historical Review* 55 (2) (May 1978); Maria Beatriz Nizza da Silva, *Sistema de casamento no Brasil colonial* (São Paulo: Queiroz, 1984), 50–56; and Nazzari, "Concubinage."

30. Nazzari, "Concubinage." For an analysis of such strategies elsewhere, see Robert McCaa, "Marriageways in Mexico and Spain, 1500–1900," *Continuity and Change* 9 (1) (1994): 11–43.

31. For this concern in an earlier period in Europe, see John Boswell, *The Kindness of Strangers: The Abandonment of Children in Western Europe from Late Antiquity to the Renaissance* (New York: Pantheon Books, 1988).

32. Marriage registered in ACMSP, Registro de casamentos da Sé, liv. 3 (1794-1812), fol. 84. The marriage inquiries are found in ACMSP, Processos de casamento, 1799, Joaquim Xavier de Oliveira, Gertrudes Joaquina de Almeida. Gertrudes's mother was an agregada (nonrelative resident) of Captain Thomé de Almeida's household. See AESP, Listas nominativas de São Paulo, Segunda companhia de ordenanças da capital, 1795 and 1797.

33. ACMSP, Precessos de casamento, no. 6–63–22–89, Dispensa de consanguineidad, 1798, Salvador Pires de Lima/Gertrudes Maria do Espirito Santo.

34. Legitimações, caixa 124, pac. 1, doc. 6.

35. ACMSP, liv. 04–01–27, 1765, fol. 224 v., Vicente. The words *filho legítimo* or *filha legítima* were not always used in eighteenth-century parish registers; I have counted as legitimate any child listed as the child of a named man and a named woman, unless the child was called *natural.*

36. ACMSP, Livro de batisados, no. 04–01–27, 1735, fol. 41 v., Tereza.

37. Legitimações, caixa 125, pac. 3, doc. 39.

38. His second marriage was delayed after his first wife's death, because he had also had sexual relations with two of Theodora's cousins; this was considered incest by the church, and they therefore needed a dispensation to marry.

39. Legitimações, caixa 126, pac. 1, doc. 15. Other cases where the father was his illegitimate child's godfather were those of Joaquim Francisco Leal (Legitimações, caixa 126, pac. 2, doc. 31) and Desembargador João da Costa Carneiro de Oliveira (Legitimações, caixa 125, pac. 3, doc. 50).

40. The following analysis is of successive censuses of the rural neighborhood of Santana in the parish of Sé, within the municipal limits of the city of São Paulo. The data come from Arquivo do Estado de São Paulo (hereafter AESP), Maços de população, Cidade de São

Paulo, Listas nominativas do bairro de Santana. The censuses studied are for 1778, 1779, 1780, 1783, 1787, 1795, 1796, 1798, 1802, 1807, 1816, 1825.

41. Of course the circumstances could have been just the opposite—that the child whom Anna was raising came over time to be called her child.

42. AESP, Inventários não publicados, José Antonio da Silva, 1797, no. de ordem 569, c. 92.

43. See ACMSP, Registro de casamentos, 7–31–2815, for the marriage of Damazio Antonio da Silva in 1803, which includes a copy of his baptismal certificate of 1780.

44. Legitimações, caixa 124, pac. 3, doc. 50.

45. Legitimações, caixa 128, pac. 1, doc. 7.

46. Legitimações, caixa 128, pac. 1, doc. 10. Other cases where the father subsequently married and his wife continued raising the child even though they had children of their own are found in Legitimações, caixa 124, pac. 2, doc. 31, and caixa 128, pac. 1, doc. 8. In another case it was the paternal grandmother who raised the child, Legitimações, caixa 123, pac. 1, doc. 16.

47. According to Portuguese law, two-thirds of the estate of the deceased had to go to his or her necessary heirs. Necessary heirs were the children of the deceased, whether legitimate or natural, or if the deceased died childless, his or her parents; see *Ordenações*, liv. 4, tit. 96 and tit. 82, n. 5; and Linda Lewin, "Natural and Spurious Children." Since the colonel had a surviving mother who was his necessary heir, in order for his son to inherit, he had to be recognized in the will and thereby made his father's necessary heir.

48. See Lewin, "Natural and Spurious Children."

49. Legitimações, caixa 128, pac. 1, doc. 43.

50. Aspílcueta, *Manual,* 178–79.

51. *Legitimações,* caixa 127, pac. 2, doc. 21.

52. *Legitimações,* caixa 125, pac. 3, doc. 50.

53. *Legitimações,* caixa 127, pac. 3, doc. 29.

54. *Legitimações,* caixa 127, pac. 3, doc. 35.

55. *Legitimações,* caixa 125, pac. 1, doc. 15.

CHAPTER FIVE

DANGEROUS WORDS, PROVOCATIVE GESTURES, AND VIOLENT ACTS
The Disputed Hierarchies of Plebeian Life in
Colonial Buenos Aires

LYMAN L. JOHNSON

INSULTS AND VIOLENCE

At midday on February 17, 1782, the journeyman carpenter Francisco Escola entered a *pulpería* (neighborhood shop selling dry goods, food, and drink) in the Barrio Concepción in Buenos Aires. As was his custom, he brought his lunch (bread, a peach, and some cheese) with him to the shop and ordered a quarter real's (about eight cents) worth of cheap brandy. The journeyman shoemaker Pasqual Duarte, a neighbor, was standing at the pulpería's rough plank bar drinking brandy when Escola arrived. Because the men lived near each other, they occasionally met at this or other drinking spots and had occasionally talked or played cards together. Standing next to each other, the two men talked easily, manifesting the loud good spirits of casual masculine conversation.

In the course of this easygoing exchange, Pasqual Duarte reached across and casually pulled a wood chip from Escola's beard. Almost without warning, this scene of masculine fellowship exploded in violence. According to witnesses Escola flew into a rage, drew a short knife from his leather apron, and struck Duarte in his arm and side. The second blow pierced the victim's lung and nearly proved fatal. Following the attack the assailant fled from the city to escape immediate arrest. Nevertheless he stayed in the area and was soon located working on a nearby farm. He was apprehended there by agents of the courts. Surviving records of his interrogation by the *alcalde de barrio* (local peace officer) suggest that Francisco Escola was unrepentant, justifying his assault on Duarte by asserting that he had responded naturally to an insult.[1] Implicit in his justification was the assumption that no man could receive an

Figure 17. A colonial pulpería *in Buenos Aires where plebeian men socialized. In this scene men wager on a cockfight. Notice that the shopkeeper is protected from his customers by iron grillwork over his window. (Archivo General de la Nación, Buenos Aires.)*

insult without responding violently. As one recent commentator has put it, "[a]t root honor means don't tread on me."[2]

Neither Francisco Escola nor his victim used the word *honor* in their efforts to explain this event to the authorities. Indeed few members of late colonial society believed that artisans and other men who worked with their hands possessed this quality. Honor, as Mark Burkholder pointed out in chapter one, was assumed to have a clear class character. In Buenos Aires, as elsewhere in the Spanish Empire, the successful assertion of personal honor depended on an individual's inherited characteristics, such as European birth or descent, legitimacy, family social status, and personal attainments such as social influence, wealth, education, reputation for honesty, courage, and restraint. Only members of the wealthy and powerful propertied groups who controlled government, the church, and the economy, commonly referred to as the gente decente (decent people, or people of substance), could publicly claim to possess personal honor without fear of ridicule or dispute.

Few social historians of colonial Spanish America would deny that a desire to protect individual honor defined in essential ways relations among members of the elite. Civil lawsuits, bureaucratic conflicts over status, and, with decreasing frequency, interpersonal violence all helped to define colonial meanings of personal and familial honor and establish social contexts within which the claims of honor were asserted and defended. The connection between honor and violence was clearest in the early colonial years, when conflicts among conquistadors often led to bloodshed. The violent conflict between Cortés's followers and his enemies, noted in the introduction, and between the Pizarro and Almagro factions in early Peru provide good illustrations of this pattern.

By the end of the eighteenth century, however, the inclination of elite males to defend their honor in face-to-face confrontations had largely been tamed by the augmented authority of state and church. Burkholder is correct when he suggests that by the last decades of the colonial era, the culture of dueling existed only at the margins of Spanish colonial culture. Hierarchical relations among elite males were neither challenged nor defended in duels or spontaneous acts of violence. Competition among them was instead focused on efforts to acquire wealth and influence, the material and political manifestations of honor. As a result litigation and bureaucratic infighting came to replace interpersonal violence as the means for resolving questions of honor among male members of the colonial elite and professional groups.

It was extremely rare for plebeian men and women to contest the elite's claimed monopoly of honor. Among successful colonial artisans in the most prestigious fields, such as the wealthiest goldsmiths of Lima or Mexico City, the word *honor* was sometimes asserted in ways that imitated elite usage. As pointed out by Sonya Lipsett-Rivera in chapter seven, in some small towns and villages far from the centers of power, men and women of modest means and resources sometimes used the word *honor* in referring to themselves and their families. However, in colonial capitals such as Buenos Aires, Lima, or Mexico City, where wealthy families and powerful representatives of church and state resided, surviving documents suggest that plebeians avoided using the word even while imitating the values and behaviors associated with this cultural system. In these places it was assumed that men who worked with their hands, no matter how skilled, were tainted by the physical nature of their work. A plebeian male's effort to assert or defend personal honor was undermined by his poverty, lack of privacy, and subservience to the commands of his employer. The colonial elite believed that what it regarded as the base character of plebeian life segregated the working poor from the world of honor. Nevertheless it is clear that Francisco Escola's explanation of his violent assault on Pasqual Duarte followed closely the language and symbolism of masculine honor.

Although artisans, laborers, and other plebeians of late colonial cities were inhibited in their use of the word *honor*, it is clear that by the late eighteenth century, the culture of honor had penetrated every level of masculine society and informed nearly every male interaction. Even though the word was commonly reserved for conflicts among the rich and powerful, plebeians were every bit as sensitive to the experience of shame and humiliation as elite members of Spanish American society. Indeed plebeians were more likely to resort to violence to prevent or avenge an insult than were their social betters. Unlike elite males, who had a strong preference for the courtroom rather than the dueling ground as an arena for the defense of honor, plebeians more closely replicated the values and behaviors of the sixteenth-century conquistadors, responding violently to perceived insults and slights.

Among the artisans and laborers of eighteenth-century Buenos Aires, a man who failed to defend himself against the challenges of his peers found life intolerable. He was, in essence, feminized and became the target of endless jokes, pranks, and insults. Unless he was willing to "act like a man" and defend himself, he was essentially exiled from full participation in the society of men. The often brutal enforcement of this behavioral template resulted in an ongoing cycle of challenge and reply. In this masculine world of confrontations and conflict, insults and the revenge they provoked defined interpersonal relations in work, residence, and social life.

As suggested by Ann Twinam in chapter three, Mediterranean codes of honor provided the foundation for the system of honor that developed in colonial Spanish America, although important differences appeared in response to local conditions and experiences.[3] Both codes of honor closely connected a man's honor with the sexual behavior and moral reputation of his female relatives. As a result words or actions that challenged the reputation of wife, daughter, or mother often provoked a violent response in both cultures. In this volume, Ann Twinam and Muriel Nazarri discuss often intense efforts to conceal or disguise out-of-wedlock pregnancies and the births of illegitimate children, in order to protect family honor and avoid violence directed against women who were presumed to have injured the reputations of husbands, fathers, or brothers.

Among plebeians in particular, the weakness or even temporary absence of a father or husband could put a woman at risk. Demeaning comments, rumors of promiscuity, and assaults were the common experience of unprotected plebeian women, who conducted much of their daily lives in streets and markets. Men who failed to respond adequately to insults or physical challenges seemed to invite assaults on the reputations of female family members. Masculine culture judged that a man's failure to act with proper courage and physical skill was, in effect, an admission that his wife or other female family members could not be defended. His cowardice and incompetence, manifested as a failure to avenge shame or humiliation, was therefore understood to mean that liberties could be taken with his female relatives.

These potent connections between masculine honor and the reputation of female relatives were altered in important ways by the nature of the colonial economy and the opportunities and constraints this economy imposed on plebeian life. Artisans, day laborers, and other plebeians were more likely to remain single, defer marriage into their twenties or even thirties, or live apart from families in the Spanish colonies than were their counterparts in Spain. Colonial plebeians were also less likely to be members of guilds, lay brotherhoods, or other formal structures where reputation, once acquired, would be hard to alter. Colonial plebeians experienced greater geographic mobility as well; many Buenos Aires artisans, for example, remained in the city for less than two years before trying their luck in another colonial city. Finally slavery and the colonial racial hierarchy inhibited slave and free black plebeians from responding to challenges and threats in the same ways as white plebeians. Given the mechanisms of racial oppression they faced, slaves and black freemen simply could not protect female relatives from insult without great danger to themselves.

Colonial Buenos Aires's largely illiterate plebeian class left few records for modern historians to examine: no private letters, diaries, or autobiographies. Historians, therefore, are forced to discover the values and opinions of these mostly inarticulate men in records produced for other purposes. Among the most useful sources for illuminating plebeian understandings of honor are surviving records of violent crimes, especially homicides and aggravated assaults.[4] Although tainted by the efforts of both perpetrators and victims to influence judicial outcomes, testimonies collected during criminal investigations reveal popular understandings of masculine honor and the circumstances in which it was challenged and defended.

HONOR IN THE ARENA OF EVERYDAY LIFE

The records of the police and courts suggest that the city's small number of premeditated homicides were seldom occasioned by a perceived need to avenge injured honor.[5] More commonly insults or physical challenges, like Duarte's gentle tug on Escola's beard, provoked among plebeian males responses that entered the criminal record as aggravated assaults or unpremeditated homicides. Most of these violent acts occurred in public places, and nearly all were preceded by drinking. Because colonial legal authorities pursued their inquiries with a patient thoroughness and an eye for detail, criminal records include often dense testimonies offered by witnesses, victims, and perpetrators. Victims and perpetrators were nearly always identified by marital status, race, birthplace, occupation, length of residence in the city, and location of their workplaces and residences. Care was also taken to record the spoken words and physical acts that preceded these violent attacks. It is this rich contextual detail that allows us to explore and illuminate the connections between violence and honor among the plebeian males of colonial Buenos Aires.

Daily life among these men was commonly lubricated by substantial quantities of alcohol. Brandy was often taken at noon with food. After the workday ended, brandy and (much less commonly) wine accompanied the games, sports, and conversation of leisure time. One gunsmith arrested in 1783 for wounding a customer during an argument acknowledged that prior to the attack he had had his first glass of brandy at eleven in the morning and then drank more brandy at noon, at sunset, and at six in the evening.[6] Without a doubt alcohol also acted as a catalyst in transforming a concern for personal honor into a predilection for violence. The blacksmith Joseph González, for example, nearly killed his friend, the barber Matheo Arias, with a knife after a long drinking bout led to the expression of "hot words."[7] The alcohol-induced expression of fighting words or direct physical challenges preceded many of the violent confrontations among working-class men. Most insults involved sexual allusions.

Allegations of sexual incompetence or the unfaithfulness of a wife or kinswoman were provocative insults, and no man of this class could let them pass without grievous consequence to his reputation. Not every man, however, responded violently when confronted in this way. When in 1793 Bernardino Luque called the wife of the shoemaker Andrés Morales "a fox and a whore," Morales went to court and forced a retraction and apology.[8] Because criminal action could be brought for the offense of *malas palabras,* or "bad words," men could satisfy their injured honor without accepting the dangers of physical confrontation with their tormentors. Nevertheless no man uttered these incendiary words confident he would avoid physical confrontation.

Pushing, grabbing, and other forms of rough-and-tumble were everyday occurrences among plebeian males and could be interpreted as either a sign of affection or as a challenge. Knocking a man off his feet or forcing him to submit was, like the most provocative insults, likely to produce violence, because it so directly challenged his manhood. Touching the face or pulling the beard of an adult male was not always seen as a provocation. The elderly, especially women, could commonly presume this right, especially if the male was a familiar in the woman's home. Young children, wives, or lovers might affectionately touch or pull a man's beard. Among male peers in public places, as was the case with Duarte and Escola, this gesture was very dangerous indeed, since the beard was viewed as the outward manifestation of virility.

Honor was gained and lost by male plebeians in face-to-face and often rit-ualized exchanges of insults and physical provocations. The logic and dangers of this endless cycle of challenge and riposte was sometimes clearly revealed in criminal documents. The journeyman carpenter Antonio Pilmo customarily took his noon meal in a pulpería located two doors away from his employer's shop, in the barrio Merced. On December 8, 1794, he walked into the street after his second noontime brandy and saw a neighbor, the recently arrived matador José María Troncoso, crossing the small plaza that fronted the pul-pería. Both men wore capes and, according to one witness, Pilmo carried a sheathed sword. For unknown reasons Pilmo accosted the matador, yelling out that he would "unmask" him. This was a dangerous and insulting challenge, since no man of honor could allow someone to suggest that he was not what he appeared to be, but was instead a fraud and a counterfeit. It may be that Pilmo was dismissing Troncoso's performance in the city's bullring, but witnesses offered the investigator few details. A loud confrontation followed, and one witness stated that Pilmo struck the matador. Bystanders intervened and sepa-rated the men. However, within hours Troncoso had armed himself, found his tormentor, and run him through the heart.[9] Although the perpetrator sought refuge in a nearby church, he was soon dragged out and arrested.

Why did the victim initiate this dangerous game, and why did Troncoso respond so violently? Testimony suggests that Pilmo and Troncoso knew each other casually from the neighborhood. On a few occasions the men had shared drink and talk in the local pulpería. It is possible that Pilmo thought that his earlier relationship created a context where his taunt would be interpreted as playful banter. More likely Pilmo believed that his loud public challenge would humiliate Troncoso and thereby elevate his own status. Given the accumulated effect of Pilmo's words, bearing, and tone, and given the public nature of the insult, Troncoso could hardly allow the incident to pass without being shamed. Could he have appeared again in the bullring, if his cowardice were common knowledge? Did Pilmo actually think the matador was a coward? We might suggest that the victim miscalculated Troncoso's reaction and his skill with a sword, but he certainly understood the dangerous game he was playing. In this culture, the physical courage and athletic skill required in the bullring were symbolic of masculine identity. Pilmo's public challenge, even if uttered in jest, represented an effort to appropriate Troncoso's reputation. Just as Troncoso dominated a bull, Pilmo would dominate Troncoso. As one modern commen-tator put it, "[t]he shortest road to honor was to take someone else's."[10]

The need for men to defend themselves against insults was inculcated in them from their early years. As a result these patterns of provocation and violent response dominated the relationships of even the youngest members of the working class. In colonial Buenos Aires it was common for young men in their early teens to leave home and enter the city's large workforce of day laborers or take up apprenticeships in the artisan trades. Both at work and during leisure time, they experienced an environment of rigid hierarchy differentiated by rank, seniority, and strength. They were subject to severe discipline and humiliating corporal punishments by both employers and older workmates.

At the same time they were ceaselessly admonished to "act like men," to respond violently to insult and challenge. For these young men, masculine relationships were constructed in the dangerous arena of teasing and challenging taunts that sorted out leaders and followers (bullies and their victims) in both work and play. However, not every jest or prank required a violent response. If the challenger used the right tone and carefully avoided unambiguously provocative topics, playful challenges could help build intimacy and lead to friendship. Every young man needed to learn to distinguish between what could be tolerated and what could not. A male who failed to protect his honor jealously was diminished in stature—in effect feminized—by those who were stronger or more quick-witted. Failure to recognize the line between affectionate teasing and insult was dangerous, because it led inevitably and relentlessly to loss of reputation or to angry confrontation and violence.

On the evening of July 1, 1783, taunts and insults exchanged by two groups of young men led to bloodshed. A fourteen-year-old apprentice shoemaker, the pardo José de la Cruz (*pardo* was another word for mulatto) and two workmates, an older pardo apprentice and a young Spanish boy (*mozo*) were on their way to a dance, a *fandango,* in the Retiro neighborhood. The group had already visited a pulpería, where they each had at least two brandies. Walking through the narrow streets of the city, they were filled with boisterous good spirits. Trouble began when they crossed paths with an eighteen-year-old wagoner's helper named Ygnacio. Ygnacio claimed to have heard an insult. In the argument that followed, Ygnacio pushed the youngest and smallest of José's group to the ground. He then walked off, returning within minutes with two allies. Ygnacio used a sling to throw a brick fragment at José, who then rushed to the attack with a small knife he said he used to cut plug tobacco. Ygnacio was quickly dispatched by a stab wound that narrowly missed his heart. His honor protected, José de la Cruz and his two friends left Ygnacio bleeding in the street and went on to the fandango. After being arrested by the alcalde de barrio, José showed no remorse, stating simply that he had responded naturally to Ygna-cio's insults and assault.[11] He was exonerated by the courts.

The three cases discussed so far illustrate the explosive potential for violence embedded in the masculine culture's central concern with preserving and pro-tecting individual honor. Violence was the predictable result of direct physical challenge or intolerable insults. It could also be unintentionally triggered by teasing, taunts, or in the case of the carpenter Escola, by an acquaintance's uninvited presumption of intimacy. Two other contributory factors can be isolated. First, a taunt or insult issued in front of witnesses was clearly more dangerous than one spoken in private, because it could not be ignored by the victim without loss of honor. And second, consumption of brandy or other strong drink dramatically increased the likelihood that any misunderstanding or argument might lead to violence. Few working men passed a day without consuming alcohol in some form. It was an essential prop of masculine social activity—associated with gambling, games of chance and skill—indeed, almost all off-hours activities. Every male, therefore, would be aware of alcohol's predictable effect, the precipitation of dangerous risk-taking among casual acquaintances and strangers.

FAMILY AND FRIENDSHIP IN THE CULTURE OF HONOR

It might be presumed that kinship or long friendship and association would have greatly reduced the potential for masculine conflict, but the historical records suggest a somewhat different story. Even among friends and kinsmen, jests, pranks, and roughhousing could provoke violence. The master shoe-maker José Escobar, a pardo immigrant from the Canaries, often entertained his journeyman, Justo Gorordo, in his rented room. On October 17, 1793, Gorordo and two other journeymen shoemakers, together with a soldier who had spent the evening drinking at a pulpería, went to Escobar's room. Friendly banter and teasing led to rough horseplay. When the three younger men began fighting in earnest, Escobar tried to separate them. After being pulled from his rivals by Escobar, Gorordo lost his temper and slashed his employer's arm with a knife.[12] This case is distinguished from the three earlier examples by the greater intimacy and longer association of the victim and assailant. Why attack your employer and occasional drinking associate rather than one of the three men with whom you had been fighting? Gorordo's testimony provides some help. Although he denied cutting Escobar, he seemed to see his employer's intervention in the fight as an act of disloyalty. In the culture of honor, failure

Figure 18. Central plaza and market in colonial Buenos Aires. Artisan shops were located under the arched walk at the back of the plaza. (Archivo General de la Nación, Buenos Aires.)

to support a friend in whatever circumstance was commonly viewed as a betrayal. Escobar was attacked because he had failed in his role as a friend; his lack of loyalty was seen by Gorordo as an act of bad faith.

Family members were also potentially at risk if they violated the fundamental understandings of masculine culture. Intervention in a kinsman's fight or the public correction of a kinsman's actions could be seen as an intolerable provocation. In 1788 Marcos de Mesa was stabbed when he attempted to pull his brother-in-law from the scene of a violent, late-night quarrel. Mesa's brother-in-law had been drawn into a fight when a stranger pulled his hat from his head "as if he were a child." While he struggled in the street with his tormentor, his wife ran to get her brother. After reaching the fight, Mesa grabbed his brother-in-law, who then wounded him in the leg with a knife. The wife sought to explain her husband's drunken assault on Mesa as "un efecto del aguardiente" (an effect of the brandy), despite the fact that no weapon had been drawn in the precipitating quarrel.[13] It was only when Marcos de Mesa attempted to pull his brother-in-law away that blood was

Figure 19. Interior of a shoemaker's shop. In this scene the master shoemaker disciplines one of his journeymen by striking his upturned hand. The master's wife looks on from the doorway. (Jean Baptiste Debret, Albúm de aquarelas da região meridional do Brasil datadas de 1827, Inéditas, Coleção Conde de Bonneval, São Paulo.)

shed. Mesa had failed to recognize that his kinsman would take this public "correction" by a younger man, even if that younger man was his brother-in-law, as a humiliation. Kinship, even more than friendship, demanded loyalty.

Loyalty to one's family was a central feature of colonial culture, and there were very few criminal cases where men violently attacked their parents or siblings. The family was a fundamental source of individual identity and provided a social environment where traditional masculine defensiveness could be relaxed. Nevertheless even the relationships among family members, work-mates, and neighbors of long standing held the potential for violence. As Marcos de Mesa discovered, the desire to protect a relative from harm could be interpreted as an effort to establish primacy. Once a man undertook a public quarrel, even if drunk and wrong-headed, he persisted until he believed himself satisfied. Intervention was dangerous. These conflicts were only indirectly about right and wrong; they were more directly about the fundamental concerns of male identity: power, autonomy (defined in relationship to class and racial hierarchies), and honor.

PARADOXES OF PLEBEIAN HONOR

Plebeian men found it as difficult to accept a public slight or physical challenge as a direct insult. Even when a man's own behavior was clearly and obviously provocative, he often appeared genuinely surprised and enraged by a response in kind. Juan Montanche, journeyman bricklayer, entered a pulpería located near the Convent of the Catalinas at around eight in the evening on August 14, 1786. He asked for a quarter real of cheese and a quarter real of bread. After being served by the young shop assistant, Vicente Buzeta, Montanche claimed that he had been shortchanged. The shopkeeper said he had paid with a half-real coin, while he claimed he had given a full real and was owed a half real. A heated argument ensued. The issue was not merely who was telling the truth or who was honorable, but also who had the right to compel agreement. As the discussion grew in intensity, Montanche drew his knife and attacked the unarmed counterman, cutting his face and stomach. As pointed out by many commentators on the gaucho culture of the Río de la Plata region, contestants in knife duels commonly sought to cut the face of their rivals, in order to leave a visible sign of their domination. The surviving testimony suggests that Montanche also aimed for his victim's face, transforming an argument over making change into a tableau of machismo. In the end, however, the victim wrestled his attacker to the ground and called for help.

Testimony presented by the victim and other shopkeepers from the neighborhood suggested that Montanche was a troublesome customer, who often alleged that he had been shortchanged and commonly abused the credit custom of shopowners. Would not a man who so blatantly and routinely tried to cheat in petty business dealings expect disagreement and confrontation? What made this particular exchange so dangerous? Montanche emphasized in his statement to the judge that Buzeta had called him a liar, thereby claiming to unmask him as Pilmo had threatened to unmask the matador Troncoso.[14] To question a man's honesty, or his courage or sexual potency, was to question his place in male society. A direct allegation of dishonesty, even when the allegation was abundantly justified by evidence, was likely to provoke violence. Just as no man in that culture could permit another man to call him a coward or a woman, no man could passively accept being branded a thief or a liar without losing face. Even though plebeians were not overly concerned with honest dealings nor particularly scrupulous with the property of others, direct allegations of dishonesty were clearly provocative.

A deadly assault at a local brick factory in 1780 provides an additional illustration of this point. With the owner away from the city, the factory's ten *casta* (mixed-race) employees and an acquaintance from a nearby farm spent the morning gambling at cards. During the card game the young peon visiting with the brickyard workers began to argue with an older man, Ramón, over a bet. As the two men argued, one of the other brickyard laborers, Joseph, intervened, calling Ramón "a shit from Santiago del Estero" and "a son of a whore who had been thrown out of the tent." Ramón replied in kind, calling Joseph "a son of a whore." Soon the two men were throwing bricks at one another. Finally, with the others looking on, Ramón pulled a knife and fatally stabbed Joseph through the heart. He was then subdued by the witnesses and handed over to the authorities.

This case illuminates some of the most important characteristics of plebeian life in late colonial Buenos Aires. A very large percentage of plebeian men lived outside ongoing family relationships. Many remained unmarried well into their middle years and, among the married men, many lived away from their families for long stretches of time. Very few plebeians maintained long-term relationships with employers or workmates. Many worked only a day at a time, seeking employment anew each morning. Even in their housing arrangements, male plebeians were unlikely to establish intimate or lasting associations. Few lived independently in their own apartment or house. More commonly they slept on makeshift beds at the back of a shop or factory, changing residence as often as they changed employer. Relationships tended to be casual, guarded, and wary.

When the brickyard workers were questioned by the authorities, no one knew or could confidently provide either the last name or racial identity of either the assailant or his victim, even though they took their meals together and shared living quarters in a small shed on the factory grounds. These circumstances tended to produce a dangerous superficial intimacy among workmates. In this case the barracks-like residential arrangement and the desultory pattern of work at the brick factory worked to encourage both the clumsy effort at cheating and the verbal challenge that served as preface to the homicide.[15]

Criminal records demonstrate that disagreements about the terms of a lease, the repayment of a loan, and unpaid wages also could challenge the honor of artisans and laborers.[16] Given the colonial culture's inclination toward sharp business practices, artisans and laborers often found themselves in conflict with clients and employers of superior status. Because artisans and laborers seldom worked under the protection of a formal contract, clients and employers routinely attempted to force down costs or completely escape their obligations by withholding payment. Regardless of the provocation, however, colonial authorities would not permit a physical attack on a member of the gente decente by a plebeian. Punishment in such assaults was predictably harsh.

Colonial society was hierarchical, and plebeian males acknowledged the superiority of the educated and propertied classes by forswearing both physical and verbal violence when challenged by members of the gente decente. Instead artisans and laborers attempted to satisfy their threatened honor by forcing a legal proceeding. The opportunity to give testimony and require written responses from upper-class defendants offered a symbolic equivalence to the physical confrontation that more commonly settled similar differences between social equals.

When disputes over wages, contracts, and property arrangements involved only laborers and artisans, there was always a potential for violence similar to that found in the other common venues of masculine conflicts—the pulperías, plazas, and streets. Once a confrontation among plebeian males was framed in narrow terms that allowed only for winning or losing, triumph or humiliation, gaining or losing honor, violence was predictable. During the summer of 1797, Pedro José Gonzales Peña, a stonemason, took his son to harvest prickly pears at his deceased mother's farm. While the estate remained in probate, Gonzales Peña's older brother, as executor, had rented the farm. Gonzales Peña had no dealings with the renter and did not even know him by name. He had made no effort to ask the renter's permission before visiting the farm. As he and his son collected prickly pears, Gonzales Peña was confronted by the renter, who ordered him off the property. Although it was not yet true that the estate had legally passed to his brother and himself, he replied that he owned the farm and would do as he chose. The two men pushed each other and exchanged insults, while a crowd gathered. Gonzales Peña, armed with a club, forced his way into the farmhouse, where a violent struggle began. It ended when Gonzales Peña was struck in the arm by the renter's knife.[17]

The flash point for this bloody struggle was Gonzales Peña's presumption of hierarchy and his high-handed effort to ignore the renter's contractual status as the householder, treating him in effect as a dependent and peon. Restraint was valued among male members of the elite. A conflict of this nature between elite males would most likely have been resolved through face-to-face negotiations, through the mediation of a third party, or by the courts. Among plebeian males such conflicts were potentially explosive, especially if one or both of the parties acted in Gonzales Peña's insulting manner, because they put individual honor at risk. Angry direct confrontations left participants with only two possible outcomes: domination of or humiliation by one's rival.

HONOR AND RACE

The working class of late-colonial Buenos Aires was a racial and ethnic montage created in large part by international and internal migratory flows. Among male plebeians, employment-based hierarchies were complicated by the society's presumed rank order of race, culture, and legal status. No free man could accept the orders of a slave. Whites and light-skinned castas presumed their superiority to blacks and Indians. Conflict along these colonial fault lines was necessarily charged with the potential for violence.

At least a third of the city's artisans and laborers were of African descent, and free blacks and slaves were found in every working-class occupation. Nearly all the city's workplaces were integrated by both race and legal status. Slaves and free men, Europeans, creoles, and castas all lived and worked together in diverse and unpredictable ways.[18] Although not common, it was not unknown for black (*moreno*) master craftsmen to employ both casta and white apprentices. Journeymen were the most integrated cohort of this larger class. It is nearly impossible to find evidence of racially segregated housing, work, or social arrangements among journeymen in any of the skilled trades. Yet race was a central component of social identity, and prejudice and discrimination were common. This combination of pervasive integration in work, housing, and social life and the hierarchical social ideal expressed in the *régimen de castas* (system of racial classes) led inexorably to conflicts, as plebeians struggled to sort out their sense of proper order.

In the surviving criminal records for the period 1776 to 1810, there are only a few homicides where the victim was white and the perpetrator black. There are even fewer cases where a white took the life of a black in a private quarrel. Generally speaking homicides and assaults in Buenos Aires linked perpetrators and victims from the same or proximate racial and class categories. In fact the majority of both homicides and assaults involved castas or blacks. Inhibited from freely protecting their honor from the taunts and insults of whites, young black freemen often vented their anger and frustration on targets less comprehensively protected by law and custom—slaves.

It is among these marginalized groups that the interplay of masculine values and anxiety about status produced its most dangerous manifestation, what Sigmund Freud called the "narcissism of minor difference."[19] Free blacks (both pardos and morenos) and other castas operated within the same system of masculine values as their white peers; that is, a masculine culture of honor derived largely from Mediterranean Europe. Even male slaves sought to achieve some approximation of this ideal. Yet in their daily lives, black and casta males, free and especially slave, were compelled to accept a set of legal restraints and social

Figure 20. Because slaves were prevented from taking revenge on those who beat or tormented them, most colonial residents believed that they could not have honor. Fear that they would be seen as slavelike was the reason that black freedmen sometimes lashed out when a slave failed to treat them with respect. (Jean Baptiste Debret, Albúm de aquarelas da região meridional do Brasil datadas de 1827, Inéditas, Coleção Conde de Bonneval, São Paulo.)

presumptions that conflicted with their need to protect personal honor against insults and physical challenge. The position of a free black male or male slave in this social system was nearly intolerable, since neither was sanctioned to assert unambiguously the pride and aggressiveness that were at the center of male culture.

The colonial courts provided some limited protection for slaves in cases where they were ruthlessly abused by their owners. At the same time harsh penalties were reserved for slaves who struck back when mistreated. Free blacks and other castas had greater freedom than slaves, but they were still burdened with the society's racist presumption that they had, and should have, a position inferior to whites. Although there was no legal protection for free blacks when they confronted economic or social discrimination or were subjected to the open expression of racial prejudice, they were granted a higher status and greater autonomy than slaves. These small differences and advantages were fiercely defended. Free black males struggled to separate themselves from what the masculine culture saw as the debased condition of male slaves, who were incapable of asserting honor or protecting the reputation of their families. When slaves resisted these efforts to maintain social distance by treating black freemen as equals, violence was likely.

In November 1790 a group of young slaves playing in the street precipitated a violent confrontation by throwing stones at the shop of José Juanis, a pardo master barber, during the afternoon siesta. Furious, Juanis raced into the street and grabbed Eusebio, the twelve-year-old slave of don Mateo Masa, before he could escape. Juanis then severely beat the youngster with a large iron key, cutting him on his hands and face.[20] With blood streaming from his wounds, the victim took refuge in a neighbor's house until the authorities arrived. Here again the response seems disproportionate to the provocation, given the absence of any evidence of earlier contacts between the barber and his victim. Juanis expressed anger, when questioned, that a moreno slave would act in such an insulting manner. This difference in status was reinforced by the apparent failure of the youngsters to grant proper respect to an older man. Juanis's rage originated in what he took to be an assault on the hierarchies of color, legal status, and age. Could a man permit children to make him a victim and retain the respect of other men?

Shoemaking was the most completely integrated artisan occupation in colonial Buenos Aires. At the time of the creation of the Viceroyalty of Río de la Plata in 1776, there were already a large number of successful black masters in this trade. The shop of the pardo master shoemaker José Antonio Orrega was not unusual: he employed five journeymen, two apprentices, and a slave helper. This group included two whites, four free pardos, a mestizo, and the moreno slave owned by someone else.[21] Testimony later provided to investigators makes clear that few of the workers knew each other well. Almost no one could provide the last name or birthplace of any workmate. Still, it seems clear that José Antonio Orrega's shop was an easygoing workplace, characterized by constant banter and playful jests. On October 30, 1777, the journeyman Matheo Troncoso's repeated taunts provoked the moreno slave Casimiro Falcón to respond in kind. As the exchange heated up, insults flew. When Troncoso, a free pardo, threw a shoe, the slave Casimiro grabbed a stool and a sharp tool. Troncoso then pulled his knife and stabbed the slave twice, nearly killing him. Following the investigation Troncoso agreed to pay Casimiro's owner for lost wages, medical costs, and court fees.

This pattern was also present in two similar incidents. In 1780 José, slave of the master carpenter Domingo Garay, was seriously wounded by his owner's journeyman, the free pardo Terbacio. Again the attack was preceded by what appeared to be jests and harmless taunts. As was customary the slave had prepared *mate*, Paraguayan tea, for his master's employees at midmorning. On this day he asked Terbacio for an unfinished board he was working on to use as a serving tray. When Terbacio refused this request, the slave continued to tease and importune his workmate. Finally insults were exchanged. Enraged by what he took to be the presumption of a slave, the free pardo journeyman used the chisel he was working with to strike a nearly mortal blow.[22] As in the previous case, the perpetrator and victim were workmates who saw each other on a daily basis, even sleeping in the same room. These living conditions tended to cloud social boundaries and undermine the conventions of the larger society that granted higher status to free blacks. Within the culture of masculine honor, Terbacio could no more allow a slave to command him than the barber José Juanis could allow children to throw stones at his shop. Despite the society's use of laws and less formal devices to define and enforce hierarchies of race and status, the everyday understanding of hierarchy among plebeian men—the ability of one man to compel the subordination of another—was forged dialectically in contests of strength and will.

In 1795 the slave Antonio García was killed by the sixteen-year-old free moreno Eusebio Tonson. Tonson was an unskilled laborer who sought daily employment among the artisan shops and small manufacturers of the city. By midmorning on March 31, he had begun drinking as he wandered the streets asking for work. His requests at the door of a tailor's shop owned by a Spanish immigrant brought insults and taunts. His ineffective efforts to verbally defend himself encouraged the journeymen at a neighboring shoemaker's shop to join in. Outnumbered and thick-tongued from drink, he flew into a rage. As this scene of apparent hilarity reached its climax, the slave Antonio García appeared in the street to deliver hides to the shop of the shoemaker. Tonson immediately focused all his anger on him. Although the slave attempted to hold off his attacker with the pole on which he was carrying the hides, Tonson was able to strike a fatal blow to his stomach with his knife.[23] Here the victim clearly served as proxy for the real targets of Tonson's violent rage.

HONOR AND SEXUAL POLITICS

Because the honor of men was intimately tied to the reputations and actions of their wives and female kin, the relations between men and women were charged with the potential for violence. Susan Socolow has explored the topic of violence against women in colonial Buenos Aires in an article published in the *Journal of Latin American Studies* in 1980.[24] It is worthwhile, however, to revisit this topic briefly in our efforts to discover plebeian concerns with individual honor. Colonial criminal records provide a distressing number of violent assaults on women. Many were sexual assaults, but the majority of surviving cases record the use of violence to humiliate or discipline them. These records suggest that plebeian women, like male slaves, often inherited the violent reactions of working class males frustrated in their efforts to assert claims to respect and autonomy among peers and employers.

In the plebeian culture of late colonial Buenos Aires, an overly assertive or combative wife was a threat to the reputation of any man. Men were expected to control or, perhaps more accurately, to appear to control their households, and no man could overcome the humiliation of being dominated by his wife. Males who were bullied or physically intimidated by women were objects of ridicule and were viewed, like cuckolds, as less than men.[25] In the contentious households of the lower classes, every argument or fight was likely to draw a crowd of hooting derisive neighbors into the street. Such public humiliation was likely to be a catalyst for violence, because in the culture of honor, "there was no self-respect independent of the respect of others."[26] Plebeian families enjoyed little privacy, and few conflicts between a husband and wife passed without comment. Given the expectation that a man should control his wife and family and the presumption that any failure to live up to this ideal indicated sexual inadequacy, many plebeians males tyrannically imposed their will on wives and families.

Any question about the sexual fidelity of a wife, in particular, had the potential to ignite verbal or physical assaults. Allegations of sexual promiscuity or infidelity leveled against female family members were received as a direct assault on the status and reputation of the male household head. Because these imputations were so difficult to refute once they had begun to circulate, each retelling multiplying the provocation, laborers and artisans often lashed out at wives and daughters, even when their innocence was obvious. Even a son-in-law might presume the right to discipline his wife's mother, if her behavior seemed to sully the family reputation. For example in 1797 Manuel Mallorca publicly called his mother-in-law "a whore and procurer" for not scrupulously protecting the reputation of her daughter.

The public shaming or humiliation of women believed to have offended sexual mores was also common. Haircutting was the most common form of retaliation. The poor women of colonial Buenos Aires commonly wore their hair in a single braid; when a woman was suspected of promiscuity, her husband or sometimes her neighbors might cut it off as a punishment.[27] The woman was then predictably subjected to endless insults and humiliations.[28] This brutal ritual was often public in nature and was commonly accompanied by a beating. Although it was nearly impossible to repair the reputation of a woman accused of immorality, a husband or father could protect himself from rough treatment by neighbors and workmates by enforcing the community's judgment in the street or another public place.

It is impossible to separate masculine concern with the sorting out of the male hierarchy and the defense of honor from the conscious and unconscious sexual energies that informed relationships between men and women. Rape and other forms of sexual assault are both sexual and political acts. They are also acts that contain a powerful symbolic component—the woman's family was assaulted along with the victim. In law as well as in the value system of masculine culture, a woman's male relatives were also understood to be victims of any sexual attack.[29] As a result it was common, if not universal, in colonial Buenos Aires for the male relatives of female victims to initiate legal action or seek revenge.

A criminal case from 1794 can be used to illustrate the complex ways in which a sexual assault could be connected to masculine concerns with hierarchy and honor. One morning the master baker don Benito Núñez awakened his foreman, Gabriel Gutiérrez y Cevallos, and ordered him to go to the nearby countryside to purchase wheat. Shortly after Gutiérrez y Cevallos left the bakery's enclosed compound with his cart, Núñez forced his way into the house he provided his foreman as partial compensation. After a brief struggle, he then raped the absent foreman's wife, Francisca Rodríguez. When the husband returned after nightfall, Núñez attacked him without warning. Armed with a heavy club, he beat the unprepared husband senseless, breaking his arm. After locking his battered foreman in a shed, Núñez returned to Gutiérrez y Cevallos's cottage a second time and raped the woman again. The following morning Núñez released the husband from the shed and offered to pay his medical expenses. He offered no apology or compensation for the terrible assault on Francisca Rodríguez.

A formal criminal complaint was not initiated until more than a month had passed. Action was then taken by Francisca Rodríguez's husband and father, who testified that Núñez had begun publicly to taunt them.[30] These actions suggest that Francisca's husband and father viewed the public taunts of the perpetrator as a more direct threat to their honor than the act itself, which was most assuredly a serious case of premeditated violent sexual assault. Neither the perpetrator nor any other individual interviewed by the authorities suggested that the woman had invited or provoked Núñez's violent attention. But the testimony also suggests that this violent rape and assault was an extreme example of the plebeian culture's often violent process of establishing male preeminence and domination. In this case both victims were castas and the perpetrator white. Moreover the foreman was the employee and dependent of the perpetrator, accepting his salary and living in a residence on his property. His position was understood to be subordinate. Testimony offered by other employees of the bakery stated that Gutiérrez y Cevallos and his employer had recently argued in front of them. Given the racial assumptions of the society and the masculine culture's understanding of the proper respect due one's superiors, even if in this case both men were poor and uneducated, Nuñez must have experienced the earlier argument as a challenge to his honor. His violent attack on both husband and wife were, to him, justifiable as the re-establishment of proper hierarchy and the respect due him as a social superior, based on his marginally higher status and wealth. The fact that the rape victim's husband and father sought a legal remedy, rather than revenge, suggests that they accepted, even if reluctantly, the essential logic of Núñez's claim to preeminence. They could not, however, accept the combination of his violent sexual assault on Francisca and subsequent efforts to humiliate them publicly.

This case reinforces the conclusions of Socolow, who pointed out that every legal action brought to avenge the rape of a married woman in colonial Buenos Aires was initiated by the husband. This pattern reflects the requirements of the Spanish legal system, since a wife could not appear in court without her husband's permission, as well as the presumption within masculine culture that it was the husband's loss of honor that required redress. Unmarried and unprotected women were particularly vulnerable. The testimony preserved in colonial criminal cases suggests that some plebeian men were sexual predators who believed that any woman not living under the protection of another man had invited sexual attention. In the eyes of many people, any woman who lived alone was presumed to be promiscuous. Even women whose husbands or fathers were merely absent due to the obligations of the labor market were routinely propositioned and, in many cases, verbally or physically assaulted when they rejected the unwanted attention. Neither the legal system nor the court of public opinion was sympathetic to the complaints of unattached single women living outside their parents' home. For many males of the plebeian class, the right to say no belonged to other males or to women whose unassailable respectability was guaranteed by wealth and family status. In fact plebeian victims of rapes were routinely required by the authorities as well as by their fathers and husbands to prove that they had not invited the attack. Violently asserting domination and precedence was expected by the culture and seldom punished by the courts.

CONCLUSIONS

Some general conclusions are possible, both about the place of honor in the relations among plebeian males and about the connections between honor and masculine violence. *Honor* was not a term commonly used by the artisans and laborers of the colony's plebeian class when they attempted to explain their conflicts to the authorities. Nevertheless the men of this class consistently acted in ways that demonstrated a fundamental concern with the values of the culture of honor and a willingness to defend their reputations against insult. They quickly and often violently reacted to words or deeds that challenged their place in society. When shamed or humiliated by peers, they attempted to rehabilitate their reputations by seeking physical revenge. When threatened by the actions of wealthier and more powerful men, they turned to the courts. In the culture of honor, a man's self-respect depended on his reputation among neighbors, fellow workers, and leisure-time acquaintances. Any man who would accept an insult or allow himself to be bullied or dominated squandered his essential capital, his reputation, within the community of men.

When violence occurred, it was likely that victims and assailants knew each other at least casually. However, only a tiny minority of criminal prosecutions for violence in colonial Buenos Aires involved marriage partners, other family members, and close friends. It was among workmates and neighbors or among casual acquaintances in pulperías that presumption and aggression led to violent conflict. The nature of employment and housing in colonial Buenos Aires contributed to the likelihood that misunderstandings among men would lead to violence by inhibiting the development of long-term, personal connections among male plebeians. Few men found steady employment with a single employer or lived continuously in one residence for any length of time. The fluid nature of employment, leisure, and housing among plebeians therefore promoted a multiplicity of superficial acquaintances rather than the deeper, more constraining patterns of association found in more settled places.

The built environment, the city's physical layout and architecture, also contributed to the violent resolution of questions of honor. Because Buenos Aires maintained its small-town character until the end of the colonial period, the city's small scale, numerous plazas and small markets, narrow streets, and residential architecture focused and channeled social and economic life within compact patterns of pedestrian movement that reinforced the proliferation of casual social contacts imposed by the city's labor and housing markets. The shortage of affordable housing was experienced most acutely by young working-class males, but nearly all the city's poor were denied privacy. Most laborers and unmarried artisans shared primitive living arrangements at the back of workplaces, in the patios and hallways of tenements, or in ramshackle huts on the city's periphery. There were very few opportunities to escape from intrusive or assertive neighbors; nearly every conflict, therefore, was conducted in front of an audience ready to condemn any failure of courage. These difficult living conditions exacerbated racial and class tensions by throwing together men who sought to maintain the often petty hierarchies that divided the plebeian class. They provided an ideal environment for the discovery of grievance and the manufacture of revenge.

Other large-scale forces played a contributory role as well. Even in the late eighteenth century, Buenos Aires was an immigrant city. The working class was fluid in nature, with large numbers of young men entering the city's labor force for brief periods on their way to other colonial cities, the agricultural frontier, or the Atlantic trade system. This diverse class encompassed large numbers of free European immigrants, including Portuguese and Italians in addition to Spaniards, and after 1790, substantial numbers of African slaves. Males of the plebeian class were divided by ethnicity, language, and culture but shared a desire to protect themselves from insult and intimidation. Because the labor market of colonial Buenos Aires depended so heavily on immigration and the slave trade, there were relatively few older experienced men to restrain the passion and aggressiveness of young apprentices and laborers. Moreover the unpredictable nature of employment and the high cost of housing suitable for family life ensured that only a minority of these manual workers married before their thirties. Surrounded by strangers, lacking privacy, and unconstrained by family obligations, young men found the burden of defending their honor heavy indeed.

These features of the *porteño* economic and social structure influenced in fundamental ways the transmission and adaptation of Spanish masculine cultural values. The assumed hierarchies of colonial law and metropolitan prejudice were only imperfectly realized in society. European whites of the working class commonly demanded, but seldom automatically received, deferential treatment from their American-born casta and black workmates and neighbors. Similar social realities blurred the distinction between journeymen and masters and even obscured the boundary between slaves and free men. Rigidly formulated ideals of masculine social hierarchy and individual honor were constantly challenged by the city's fluid social makeup. In this environment the working poor could only imprecisely assert and clumsily defend their understandings of the traditional masculine values of autonomy, respect, and honor.

NOTES

1. Archivo General de la Nación (hereafter AGN) Criminales, año 1782, legajo 34–1–11.

2. William Ian Miller, *Humiliation* (Ithaca: Cornell University Press, 1993), 84.

3. This is not an appropriate place for a thorough review of this literature, but a brief citation of some of the more important studies might be useful to the reader. See Julian Pitt-Rivers, *The Fate of Shechem or the Politics of Sex: Essays in the Anthropology of the Mediterranean* (Cambridge: Cambridge University Press, 1977); J. K. Campbell, *Honour, Family, and Patronage: A Study of Institutions and Moral Values in a Greek Mountain Community* (Oxford: Clarendon Press, 1964); Carol Delaney, "Seeds of Honor, Fields of Shame," in *Honor and Shame and the Unity of the Mediterranean,* ed. David D. Gilmore (Washington, DC: American Anthropological Association, 1987), 35–48. I also find Stanley Brandes, *Metaphors of Masculinity: Sex and Status in Andalusian Folklore* (Philadelphia: University of Pennsylvania Press, 1980) to be very helpful.

4. Among the many useful studies of crime see Colin MacLachlan, *Criminal Justice in Eighteenth Century Mexico: A Study of the Tribunal of the Acordada* (Berkeley: University of California Press, 1974); William B. Taylor, *Drinking, Homicide and Rebellion in Colonial Mexican Villages* (Stanford, CA: Stanford University Press, 1979); Patricia Ann Aufderheide, "Order and Violence: Social Deviance and Social Control in Brazil, 1780–1840" (Ph.D. diss., University of Minnesota, 1976); and Susan Midgen Socolow, "Women and Crime: Buenos Aires, 1757–97," *Journal of Latin American Studies* 12 (1980): 39–54.

5. Typical of the city's small number of cases of premeditated murder is the trial of a woman and her lover in AGN, Archivo del Cabildo 1789, folios 269–70. In this case the lover was garroted and then beheaded. His head and right hand were subsequently displayed in the town where the murder had occurred.

6. Archivo de la Provincia de Buenos Aires (hereafter APBA), Criminales, leg. 34–1–12.

7. APBA, Criminales, leg. 34–1–9.

8. APBA, Criminales, leg. 34–1–18.

9. AGN, Criminales, año 1794, leg. 34–1–19.

10. Miller, *Humiliation*, 116.

11. AGN, Criminales, año 1783, leg. 34–1–12.

12. APBA, leg. 34–1–18. See also APBA, Criminales, leg. 34–1–10, for a similar case.

13. APBA, Criminales, leg. 34–1–19.

14. APBA, Criminales, leg. 34–1–13.

15. APBA, Criminales, leg. 34–1–10.

16. See examples in APBA, Criminales, legs. 34–1–10, 34–1–20, and 34–1–35.

17. APBA, Criminales, leg. 34–1–22.

18. See Lyman L. Johnson, "Artisans," in *Cities and Society in Colonial Latin America,* ed. Louisa Schell Hoberman and Susan Migden Socolow (Albuquerque: University of New Mexico Press, 1986), 227–50, and "The Impact of Racial Discrimination on Black Artisans in Colonial Buenos Aires," *Social History* 6(3) (October 1981): 301–16.

19. Sigmund Freud, *Civilization and Its Discontents*, trans. and ed. James Strachey (New York: Norton, 1961), 61.

20. APBA, Criminales, leg. 34–1–16.

21. APBA, Criminales, leg. 34–1–19.

22. APBA, Criminales, leg. 34–1–10.

23. APBA, Criminales, leg. 34–1–20.

24. Socolow, "Women and Crime," especially 44–51.

25. APBA, Criminales, leg. 34–1–19, for a case of a man wounded by his dominating wife.

26. Miller, *Humiliation*, 116.

27. APBA, Criminales, leg. 34–1–19, provides one of many examples of haircutting. In one case the bundle of documents contained both the victim's single braid and a tracing of the knife used by her assailants.

28. See APBA, Criminales, leg. 34–1–20, for a criminal prosecution of verbal abuse brought by a widow against a young man who had impugned her reputation publicly.

29. See APBA, Criminales, leg. 34–1–21, for an excellent statement of this legal principle.

30. APBA, Criminales, leg. 34–1–19.

CHAPTER SIX

HONOR AMONG PLEBEIANS
Mala Sangre and Social Reputation

RICHARD BOYER

Honor in the Hispanic world turns on issues of seduction and revenge.[1] Or so the stories go. A donjuanian protagonist typically seduces or rapes another man's wife, deflowers his daughter, or forms an 'illicit friendship' with his servant. The husband, father, brother, or master has thus been dishonored. The woman, whether assenting or assaulted, counted only indirectly in a masculine drama that made her the occasion for male dishonor rather than the subject of her own. If defended at all, she would be portrayed as deceived—most likely by a promise of marriage—or overpowered, not as having consented to a pre- or extramarital sexual liaison; her partner, on the other hand, would portray her as a 'woman of the world' who had invited his attentions or, if she were unmarried, as a scheming woman who had 'extracted' the promise to marry while seducing him.

Colonial courts found such defenses plausible, for they viewed complaints of sexual assault with suspicion. Women who accused men of assault, judges reasoned, had probably provoked them. Justice represented, in Jean-Clément Martin's words, "more a male than a 'moral' order";[2] the outcome of assault claims hinged more on family and clientele connections (networks of friends and dependents) than the merits of cases. And just as the uncertain reception of complaints inhibited the lodging of them, so too did the notoriety that came from airing them publicly. Litigation fueled the gossip network, adding insults to injuries and thus bringing dishonor; for honor, after all, was a thing of appearances. True, reputation could be repaired, or so the convention went, and manhood affirmed by vengeance or by forced marriages. Yet marriage as a solution to rape or seduction assumed the social equality of the contracting parties (implicit in custom from early times and explicit in Spanish marriage laws of the late eighteenth century). Women of lower standing therefore had to settle for a small monetary settlement—in theory a kind of 'dowry' that allowed a nonvirginal commoner to compete in the marriage market at about the level she would have, had she retained her virginity. Often, however, she might have to settle for nothing at all.

In this essay I argue that our view of the honor complex draws too much from the playhouse and too little from the public house, too much from *comedias* staged to entertain and too little from everyday commerce. Thus a single variant—dramas of seduction and intrigue set in the court and country houses of nobility—has been assumed to represent the entire complex. It is nevertheless of interest that such dramas struck a responsive chord. Seventeenth-century Spain, let us remember, gave birth to the don Juan legend. And donjuanian types ever afterward captivated audiences as protagonists of sexualized honor dramas. The formula was perfect: it entertained audiences, but also supposedly edified them with the message that living life as an honor drama was foolish.

Lope de Vega himself said this most clearly 'offstage' in referring to his play *Wise Vengeance* as "absurd . . . because all revenge is unwise and unlawful."[3] His *Punishment without Vengeance,* ironic in the same way, dramatizes 'punishment' that springs *only* from vengeance. Audiences watched a protagonist compromised by turpitude and hypocrisy, in this case a duke who neglected his wife while prowling the streets in search of prostitutes. He then kills her and his son when they become lovers. Lope separated entertainment from life, but he also underscored the absurdity of the honor complex to detach it from life as it should be lived. "I have *always* thought," he wrote in a letter, "that the stain of dishonor of the offended cannot be washed with the blood of the offender, for what has happened cannot cease to be and it is folly to believe that it can by killing the offender."[4]

Lope's comments matter, for they show that he distanced himself from his plots. Honor dramas, he seems to say, must exaggerate rather than imitate life in order to place emphasis on their folly. Of course all theater, as Father Rincón, censor of the Mexican theater argued in 1790, must obey rules of verisimilitude, otherwise they are "monstrosities . . . that only corrupt [public] taste." Thus it was a matter of emphasis. Lope thought of plays as entertainments that moralize; Rincón, as morals that entertain. The theater, Rincón said, should be "convert[ed] . . . into an entertaining school of private and public virtues."[5]

However different their perspectives on the theater, Father Rincón and Lope de Vega deny its correspondence to life. Father Rincón, perhaps accustomed to captive audiences attending the mass, may not have understood as Lope did that playwrights had to exaggerate to attract audiences "noisy, undisciplined, and tyrannical,"[6] who paid to be entertained. And what better way to engage them than with stories of "sexual aggression, sexual jealousy, or sexual threat," which, as Melveena McKendrick points out, monopolize every portrayal of honor issues in the Golden Age theater.[7] And the same stories continued to do so in theaters of Mexico, Lima, and Madrid throughout the eighteenth century, as audiences on both sides of the Atlantic "craved," in Irving Leonard's words, a steady diet of "action, intrigue, and excitement."[8] Theater imitated taste, not life.

And so did the chronicle, a genre of colonial writing explicitly concerned with 'real' events. Why then did the chronicler of Potosí, Bartolomé Arzáns de Orsúa y Vela (1676–1736), crowd his history with so many "stories of passion, seduction and revenge, in which the impulses of lust and honour drove men and women to destruction?"[9] Did they happen? Surely not, for Arzáns took his stories from the theater, not from the archives. He retold them as if they had actually happened, to decry their bad example in the exemplary way of a moralist. They were stories with true lessons, not true stories. They demonstrated, he thought with Lope, that living life as an honor code was unwise and unlawful, by overstating extreme behaviors, not by depicting ordinary ones. The difference lay, perhaps, only in the explicitness of the moral.

So comedy and chronicle, just as the romances of chivalry so much the rage in sixteenth-century Spain, could be believable if not true. However exaggerated they had a quality of verisimilitude, but at the same time they rose above everyday drudgeries by portraying dramatic and exemplary incidents. Perhaps the romances of chivalry, denounced by Luis Vives and others in the sixteenth century and supposedly killed as a genre by Cervantes, mutated into the honor theater and chronicle. Public taste demanded them; audiences clamored for the same old plots right to the end of the colonial period and beyond.

Unlike playwrights and chroniclers, historians deal with ordinary life and events that actually happened. They try to account for the whole range of what was said and done and work from archives filled only with fragments of lives. Brief glimpses of the ordinary and mediocre hardly count as 'important' texts and have largely been bypassed by students of literature. In this essay I shall sample documents of no canonical status or official literary value, in search of some manifestations of honor dynamics in mundane, not necessarily sexual, transactions among plebeian people of colonial Mexico.

MALA RAZA, PLEBEIAN SOCIETY, AND HONOR

Why *plebeians,* a term which here refers in a general way to the lower orders? Because as *indios, negros,* and *castas,* Spaniards considered them people of *mala sangre* or *mala raza,* by definition people without honor. This view stems from Spanish preoccupation with pure lineage (*limpieza de sangre*) that goes back at least to the fourteenth century, when Spaniards labeled people of known or suspected Moorish or Jewish ancestry "New Christians" and therefore inferior to Old Christians. A few Spaniards—fray Augustín Salucio was one—recognized the absurdity of the cult of pure lineage. Over twenty generations (six hundred years), he pointed out in 1600, one would have had more than a million ancestors.[10] Obviously so many could never be known, much less certified untainted. Given the nature of the middle ages on the Iberian peninsula, long centuries of frontier skirmishes and *convivencia*—the latter involving the intermixing and collaboration of Christian, Jew, and Moor—it stretches one's credulity to believe any Spaniard living in 1600 'pure' in the sense called for by the purity cult.

But Spaniards nevertheless invoked it. And in the Americas they applied the notion of mala raza to people of Indian and African descent and to their racial admixtures with one another and with Spaniards, all of whom they called castas (castes).[11] Terminology specifying a range of *casta* categories crops up in every possible context to describe and classify people. For our purposes, however, a revealing one is the conventional petition to be exempted from vile or illegitimate birth or from having to prove the absence of such descent. The latter had become a problem for the licentiate don Basilio José Arrillaga in 1814, for example, because it prevented him from entering law school (*colegio de abogados*) in Mexico City. He lacked proof of untainted birth because his mother had been raised a foundling; thus he had no knowledge of, and lacked baptismal certificates for, his maternal grandparents. "I am [un]able to prove (*acreditar*) that my maternal grandparents were Old Christians free of all mala raza of Moors, Jews, mulattoes, or those recently converted to our holy faith."[12] It is notable that in the colonial context, he specifies mulattoes along with the traditionally formulaic Moors and Jews and also uses the catch-all category "recent converts," which surely applied to Indians and Africans.

As noted above by Mark Burkholder and Ann Twinam, for a fee in the late colony, petitioners such as don José could be exempted from proving the pure descent required for the training he sought. He had an advantage in being clearly in the Spanish strata in culture, appearance, and connections. For most of the colonial period, however, white Spaniards viewed the "subordinate [casta] classifications" as, in Charles Gibson's words, "fundamental, assumed, [and] unchanging.¹³ In other words they presumed them fixed in the natural order, while they bickered among themselves over less obvious distinctions between peninsulars and *criollos*. The great divide separating Spaniards and Indians or castas of all sorts, let us repeat, was simply assumed. This must be underscored, for it shows us that the complex range of casta distinctions rested on a fundamental two-tiered division.

Thus Spaniards failed to see, or failed to see the importance of, the complex patterns of social interaction among the lower orders. Plebeians of mixed race, however, knew that a single person could claim a range of casta classifications, for phenotype alone did not define worth. The point is crucial, for 'worth'— which I define as the public recognition of reputation and character—was the axis on which an honor complex played out. Given a rough equivalence of the gradation in skin coloration, these became the issues for claiming (or awarding) precedence.

My first point then is to underline the argument made also by Lyman Johnson in the previous essay: plebeians viewed themselves as possessing honor and competing for it. Much as did elites, they thought of honor as concerned with reputation and character. Reputation was the social self, the persona of lineage/family, position, influence, wealth, and connections; character was personal, the individual whose word could be counted on, who suitably dominated wife, children, and dependents as family patriarch, who reciprocated favors and loyalties in clienteles.¹⁴ Both reputation and character required social validation in a process demanding a degree of self-promotion and self-presentation. In combination they established standing in the pecking order, degree of influence, and access to rights and recognition. These could be quite minimal, however, as we shall see in reviewing claims to rights following from marriage, from being Indian, or from the condition of being a 'humble and lowly person.'

If honor had to do with reputation and character, it also had to do with rights. The first two comprised the content, while the third comprised the treatment or recognition that corresponded to, and therefore validated, worth. Yet because worth was not always self-evident, plebeians suffered slurs, snubs, and slights that sometimes clashed with their self-assessments. The source of such slights mattered. If from the neighbors and cronies of one's own community, they attacked a settled view of the self; they therefore had to be resisted and rebutted. The fights and feuds within communities could be a cause as well as the result of individual slights. Challenges to reputation, character, and placement of individuals inevitably mobilized clienteles, friends, and families. If challenges came from outsiders, they took the form of racial labels, broad-

Figure 21. This street scene provides an interesting contrast with the elite members shown in previous illustrations. The man wears patched clothes and is barefoot; his long hair signifies his indigenous status. His near nakedness marks him as poor and powerless. (Claudio Linati, Costumes civils, militaires et religieux de Mexique *. . . [Brussels: Ch. Sattanino, 1828].)*

Figure 22. Gambling drew men to public places where they met workmates and neighbors, initiated friendships, and sometimes provoked violent quarrels. (Claudio Linati, Costumes civils, militaires et religieux de Mexique . . . *[Brussels: Ch. Sattanino, 1828].)*

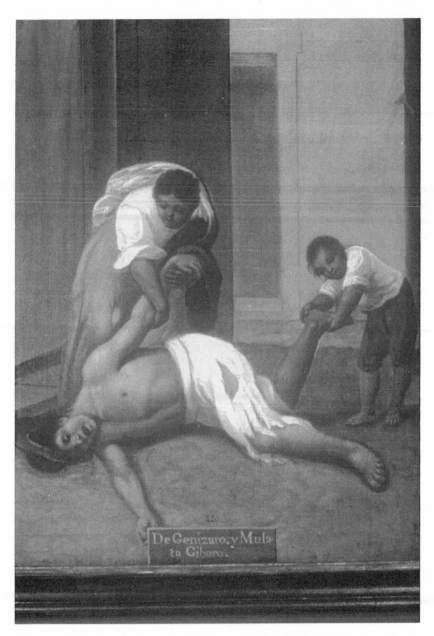

De Genizaro, y Mula-
ta Cibaro.

Figure 23. When lower-class men drank to excess, they fulfilled all the stereotypes the elite held of them. Here this man is passed out and is practically nude, which may indicate that he has pawned his clothes for drink. His wife and child are trying to help him, but his condition would make it difficult for them to live a life in which they could aspire to honor. (Painting by Francisco Clapera, active 1770–1810, courtesy Denver Art Museum, Jan and Frederick Mayer Collection.)

Marchand de Volailles.   Marchand de Graisses.   Marchande de Bonbons.

Figure 24. Men and women of the plebeian class spent much of their lives outdoors. the markets of colonial cities and towns served as social arenas as well as commercial centers. Here a woman selling sweets crosses paths with a rural resident bringing chickens to market. (Claudio Linati, Costumes civils, militaires et religieux de Mexique . . . [Brussels: Ch. Sattatino, 1828].)

brush strokes of stereotype meant to denote *calidad,* or general worth. But outside judgments wounded or validated differently from inside ones and called for contestation by different strategies.[15]

THE HONOR OF SLAVES

Standard classifications put María Negra—a slave, a black, and a female— among the lowest of the low in the status-conscious society of a colonial Mexico informed by the purity cult.[16] With a racial marker "black" for a surname and the conventional and unadorned "María" for a Christian name, her society knew her stereotypically, a black María interchangeable with count- less others. Yet however lowly, she clung to a place in her society as a Christian woman baptized and married by the holy mother church, albeit to a slave of equally low station, Nicolás Negro.

María thus claimed the individualizing markers 'Christian' and 'wife'— attested and documented in rites of baptism and matrimony as certified by a priest and witnesses in a given time and place—just as she was labeled with generic ones, 'black' and 'slave,' that came by accident of birth.[17] The latter barred her from respectability in the community, the former allowed for it. 'Christian' and 'wife' therefore implied that she had rights. What were they? We have no listing, of course, but a short document shows us at least part of what she thought she had a right to. In 1633 she stood before the corregidor of Mexico City and complained that the baker Alonso Bueno, owner of Nicolás, had for no reason whipped and punched him nearly to death. And now she feared for his life. "Unfortunate and humble persons" (*personas desventuradas y humildes*), she reminded the magistrate, had no protector but him. "I beg you to send a bailiff to Alonso Bueno's house and bring my husband here before your honor to see [the evidence of] his mistreatment."

The magistrate asked Alonso to reply to the charge. He said he had whipped Nicolás for running away and had thus corrected a truant rather than abused an innocent. At issue here was reputation, the outer man of a given calidad, and the inner one, of supposed moral qualities. Of course the judge would not have distinguished the two so schematically. In fact without overwhelming evidence to the contrary, he surely would have assumed that the former corre- sponded to the latter. He, like other officials, worked with conventional stereo- types that in this case supposed masters more honorable (and more reliable witnesses) than slaves, just as in other circumstances they supposed men more honorable than women, elders more than youths, clergy more than laymen, and Spaniards more than castas.

As well as two versions of Nicolás's character, the magistrate had two versions of Alonso Bueno's, which as a free man, a baker, and probably a white, automatically weighed his testimony as more likely 'true' than María's. In fact 'truth' was less at stake here than the continuing need to reaffirm a colonial order in which some people were naturally vile and others inherently respectable. This is why María urged the magistrate to personally examine Nicolás. She understood, I think, that the indisputable evidence of Alonso's battered body was her only chance to overcome a presumption of Alonso's blamelessness. The two explanations for Nicolás's distress, then, hinged on the judge's assessment of the character of the two men (and a woman) of different worth. Had the baker been cruel or the slave wayward? Or in different terms, should white masters be presumed to be acting justly in punishing their African slaves? Whatever the judgment—it is not recorded—it matters less for our immediate purposes than María's challenge of convention. That she did so tells us that being of "unfortunate and humble" station was entirely compatible with the possession of rights. María had no doubt that even servile persons such as Nicolás had the right to live without excessive and arbitrary brutality and believed that a magistrate would agree. And Alonso Bueno, perhaps unwittingly, agreed in insisting that he had merely punished, not abused, Nicolás.

Many dominated people sought no paternalistic intervention, and many who did failed to obtain it. Yet a good deal of evidence in colonial archives points to the litigiousness of Indians, Spaniards, and castas. María, apparently unconcerned by generic categories, seems quite at home lodging her complaint. We can well imagine her motive for making it: the bond between wife and husband. Brutal treatment of a husband, as if he were a mere animal, also dishonored a wife. Yet marital bonds were not only personal and sentimental; they were contracts linking people to the moral economy of society. This is why her complaint had to be taken seriously and why she made it unflinchingly in terms of beliefs held by everyone. Slaves, perhaps the most powerless people in Mexican society, were not only slaves; they were Christians, wives, and husbands.[18]

Here are two additional examples of slaves claiming a right, in this case to married life. In 1610 Gerónima Negra said, "I am married, and blessed according to the law of the Holy Mother Church, with Luis Negro, slave of Baltasar de Pastraña, who for seven years hasn't let us live a married life; *he therefore mistreated us.*" In the same year Luisa Negra said much the same thing: "my master doesn't let me live with my husband, *thus mistreating me* and giving me a very bad life (*mala vida*) by preventing us our marriage" (emphasis added in both cases). Both of these young slave women confidently termed a master's actions mistreatment. How did they 'learn' this? Why did they think they had the 'right' to judge their betters on such an issue? The answer, I think, has to do with their sense of honor, with their sense of themselves as people who, while easily abused, nevertheless were part of a moral order. Caste ascriptions, even lowly ones, included people in the social contract; Christian marriage attached every station of people to rights meant to be universal. This was not radicalism, not a form of leveling, but part of an organic vision presuming that the lower orders complemented the upper ones in performing useful, if not particularly honorable, functions. Those of lower station thus had the leverage of a common vision of the whole and the strategy of appealing to patron-protectors on the basis of their inclusion in it.

Returning here to reputation, character, and rights, let us remember that the slaves we have discussed would have been considered vile. But that was only one dimension of their identity. They could and did pass over the reputational stereotype implied by the category 'black slave' to insist on rights associated with another category, 'married person.' And Gerónima's and Luisa's claims were vindicated, for on February 26, 1610, the ecclesiastical judge, Dr. don Juan de Salamanca, ordered their masters to allow them "weekly cohabitations" (which meant leave to spend Saturday nights with their husbands) within three days, on pain of excommunication. Gerónima and Luisa, like María and Nicolás, thus presented themselves as powerless to harm others while, at the same time, suffering harmful treatment. They said nothing of their caste, nothing of their race. Both would have been evident, neither would have been an advantage. Instead María called herself and Nicolás "humble and unfortunate"—in effect the *miserables* of Hispanic jurisprudence—in order to claim the weak person's protection of last resort.

The 'rights' of the weak may seem trivial, a given by virtue of being human. Yet they were not simply given, for ascribing vileness and mala raza to people of servile status implied 'less than human.' Plebeians and peasants therefore had to claim rights, to fight for them sometimes, as others withheld them. Moreover the way they claimed them mattered. Josepha Delgado, complaining to the magistrate of Xochimilco (in 1749), said that her husband regularly slapped, kicked, punched, and insulted her, had wounded her twice with a chisel, and had cut off her hair.[19] This "isn't a life," she said, "but a continual martyrdom." Pairing "life" with "martyrdom" tells us a great deal. Some women, she well knew, might have acquiesced in such treatment as an identification with the saints, as did Esperanza Hernández, a woman of contemporary Mexico who suffered at the hands of her husband much as Josepha did. Esperanza took as "a key model," in the words of Ruth Behar, "the Christian narrative as a story of suffering . . . as a vehicle for the release of spirit and divinity."[20] Josepha explicitly rejects such an association. If she could not have a few comforts and some affection from her husband, something like a 'normal' life, at least the open warfare might be stopped.

HONOR AMONG INDIAN *PEONES*

Slave women of lowly status refused to accept as right violent beatings, separations from spouses, or extreme abuse. They appealed, firmly but almost formulaically, to religio-legal norms that included them in society. A more complicated case gives us a glimpse of Indian peons claiming rights in response to the abusive treatment of an hacienda *mayordomo* (foreman of a large estate). In making their appeal, they presented themselves as people of character and reputation, thus showing us something of what they valued about themselves and how they placed themselves in their social world.

In 1785 Simón de los Santos, an Indian of Pueblo San Estevan Tepetlixpa (jurisdiction of Ozumba?) working as a *gañán jornalero* (resident worker) at hacienda Atocpam, complained that his wife, Antonia Manuela, had been mistreated.[21] She had taken his midday meal to the wheat fields, Simón said, where he was working with a crew harvesting the grain. Returning to their hut, she crossed a newly harvested field with other wives who had come on the same errand, and the women began to glean uncollected grains lying on the ground. Seeing them, Pedro Carmona, the mayordomo of the hacienda, rushed over, called them robbers, and in order to identify them later, snatched their shawls (*reboso*). But Antonia resisted. Picking up the fallen grains "did no harm to the patrón," she protested, "for the sickles had already passed." Meanwhile she held her reboso tightly, and Carmona tore it in wrenching it from her grasp. By then he was so angry that he threw it to the ground and stamped on it and then punched and kicked Antonia. He injured her leg badly enough that she had trouble walking and took to her bed to allow it to heal.

This is what happened according to Simón. Although an apparently trivial incident, it was not trivial to him, to Antonia, or to Carmona. It interests us because it documents a rupture in 'normal' patterns of behavior. The force of Carmona's reaction tells us much. That a woman and an Indian, the wife of a mere gañan, should have challenged him was bad enough; that she did it before an audience of her peers was humiliating. Yet she did it cleverly, in the time-honored way of subordinate people, by playing off an intermediate authority against his superior. This had the effect of undercutting, at least temporarily, Carmona's standing as boss and superior by virtue of his position but also as presumed by calidad and gender. That Antonia rebuked Carmona instead of deferring to him explains his rage, which arose so quickly and uncontrollably.

Simón's arguments tell us as much as Carmona's behavior. The foreman, Simón said, had not given Antonia the respect due a married woman. "Although an Indian, she is a married woman." His statement implies that marriage conferred rights that transcended ethnicity. It also included him, as Antonia's husband, in the mistreatment. His juxtaposition of ethnic and civil status amounted to a rhetorical question: did the former cancel the latter? The answer was 'no,' for the king's cédulas had ordered "people of reason" not to vilify Indians, "people without reason."

If the crown urged paternalism in the treatment of 'lesser' peoples, if the church insisted on respect for women of married state, a more down-to-earth reason could also be advanced for good treatment. "People of reason in our pueblos," Simón said, "always treat us uncharitably, even though they get money from our work. Having us from sunup to sundown for only a real and a half isn't enough; they mistreat us and even say we owe money as presently they say I owe 25 pesos [to the hacienda] when I do not." With a weekly wage of nine reales, Simón explained, he had been underpaid four reales per week for three years . (Payment of two reales in silver and three in maize rations over three years would leave a balance of 78 pesos still owed Simón.) Until the incident with Carmona, Simón said, he had overlooked his underpayment, but "the mistreatment they give us" changed his mind. Having left the hacienda to live in his pueblo, he asked the judge to protect him from mayordomos who might take him away by force to work on the hacienda.

Simón's experience at the hacienda did not pull him irrevocably into the Hispanic world of wage labor, regimented work routines, and consumption through debt. Quite the contrary, he spurned that immoral economy of mistreatment and fraud. Mistreatment loomed largest, for it unmasked paternalism as a system of mere "gestures and postures," in E. P. Thompson's words, rather than one of "actual responsibilities."[22] Simón had thus retreated to his little plot (*tierritas*) in the village, where "with more peace," he said, he could earn "enough for the royal tribute" and for pueblo expenses. This succinct summary of his material needs may also suggest his view of his 'identity': a man taking refuge in his pueblo with no intention of disavowing his duty to the crown. His reference to the king's cédulas tells us, in fact, that he thought of the crown as a guarantor of his 'identity' against the likes of the *hacendados*.

THE STABBING OF PAULA MARÍA: HONOR AND RESPECT

The pummeling of Antonia by a mayordomo brings into relief the divide between native peoples and Spaniards, between workers and managers, between the fiction of paternalism and the reality of petty (and arbitrary) authoritarianism in out-of-the-way places. A sudden flare-up of tempers in an equally out-of-the-way place, resulting in the stabbing and death of Paula María, gives us a view of the internal tensions and dynamics between people of similar status.

The incident occurred in the arid hill country near the mining camp of Cimapan (today Zimapán, Hidalgo state), at Tablón, a rancho growing the maguey plant and processing its products.[23] Shortly after noon on March 28, 1809, an Indian worker named Marcos Antonio, age thirty, took a break from collecting sap (*aguamiel*) and preparing fiber to stop by Paula María's house. Apparently he intended to visit for a while with Paula's son, Juan Nepomuceno (Indian, age twenty-five), an unmarried man roughly his own age; then he would be off to eat his midday meal at his own house a short walk away, where his wife awaited him. Marcos's uncle, Juan Ygnacio (Indian, age forty-eight), passing by on his regular Monday rounds to collect rents from tenants of the rancho, joined the younger men. Deciding "to drink a little pulque," Juan Ygnacio said later, they sent Juan Nepomuceno to get it at the master's *taberna*, "not very far away." Nepomuceno was the logical one to fetch the pulque, for he was the youngest of the three and, because it was his mother's house, he acted as a kind of host. The layout of the rancho thus suggests the appearance of a small hamlet: a nucleus of small houses inhabited by workers stood bunched together; the master's house, with its tavern-store, stood apart but close enough for easy access; the fields of maguey, worked or leased by tenants, surrounded the buildings.

At about three o'clock, the routine socializing of working men began to go wrong. Juan Ygnacio, in his role as a kind of rancho supervisor, turned to his nephew Marcos Antonio and said, as Marcos remembered it, "it was getting late and he should go collect his aguamiel or prepare his henequen fiber, and shouldn't keep drinking pulque because his master don Miguel Labra would become angry." These words angered Marcos. "Get out," he remembered shouting, "who was going to stop him [from drinking]," "he would rasp his henequen leaves when he felt like it and nobody was going to order him around," and "stop bothering him." Astonished by this shameless outburst, Juan Nepomuceno jumped in: "why are you speaking this way to your uncle?"

At this point Paula María returned to her house—she had stepped out to collect two reales owed her—and, hearing at least part of the angry words, rushed at Marcos, slapping and pushing him while shouting that she wasn't going to have fighting (*bullas*) in her house. Marcos grabbed the *cachicuerno* (work knife) from his pocket, and stabbed Paula in the stomach. This was Marcos's version; Paula María's was different. She ran at Marcos, she said, only after he threatened Juan Ygnacio with his knife. Trying with her son to separate

PL 38.

XIX.ᵉ Siècle

COSTUMES MEXICAINS.

Extraction du Pulque du Maguey (Aloes) au moyen d'une longue Calebasse avec
laquelle on l'aspire.

*Figure 25. A rural worker extracts the juice of the maguey plant. This juice would
then be fermented to produce pulque, colonial Mexico's most popular alcoholic
beverage. (Claudio Linati,* Costumes civils, militaires et religieux de Mexique
... [Brussels: Ch. Sattanino, 1828].)

the two men, she received the stab wound. Paula's version answers two other-wise puzzling questions: why did Paula react so fiercely, and why did Juan Ygnacio fail to react at all? To address the first, an already-drawn knife com-pelled an urgent reaction, for the house was Paula's space, and a drunken brawl would dishonor her as much as it threatened Juan. To address the second, Marcos's words, in combination with a threatened attack, evidently stunned and immobilized the older man. It was almost unimaginable that an elder would be attacked in this way, and Juan Ygnacio, "surprised and filled with fear," he said, stood transfixed and immobilized even after the stabbing. Mar-cos had indeed overstepped the bounds of custom and propriety; even his stabbing of Paula failed to bring him to his senses, for he fiercely resisted attempts to subdue him and tie him up, even to the point of cutting his own leg as he thrashed about.

When stabbed Paula shouted "Ave María purísima, this man has wounded me" and called to the others to catch Marcos and tie him up. Juan Nepomu-ceno, helped by José Martín, a sixty-year-old Indian just then passing by, did so, but not before Juan received a nasty cut on the hand from Marcos's knife. Juan Ygnacio, as we have noted, simply watched, dumbfounded. Paula María, in the meantime, slumped to the floor holding her stomach, from which Juan and the others could see her guts (*las tripas*) hanging out. Paula's sons, Juan Nepomuceno and Antonio Trinidad—the latter five to seven years younger than Juan, Indian, unmarried, native to and sharecropper on Rancho Tablón—carried her to the courthouse of Cimapan and placed her on the jailer's bed for medical treatment. Probably that evening don Victoriano Cuellar, a surgeon, examined her and in a statement recorded by a notary the following day pronounced: "[Paula María] has a mortal wound in the left side of the stomach beginning above the bowel which it did not penetrate, although it did cut the peritoneum in several places. The wound is diagonal and about three fingers across, it is very sufficient to allow the intestines to come out, which this witness found and put back in, and it is a mortal wound as he has said."

Don Victoriano's prognosis proved correct. Paula, knowing she was dying, gave her statement on March 29 and also most likely received the last rites of the church, although this is not recorded. That same afternoon the jailer, Calixtro Labra, no doubt a relative of the owner of the rancho, don Miguel Labra, found her dead. He ran to tell the magistrate, don Santiago Martínez, who, in the absence of a notary, certified the death: "I went immediately to the room that serves as an infirmary in these royal houses where I found the body of the said Paula María stretched out face upward; recognizing and inspecting it, I observed no movement, only that it is now an inert cadaver."

The investigation into Paula María's sudden and tragic end gives us a view of ordinary life on a rancho; it also gives us a glimpse of the honor complex as Marcos and his neighbors lived it. Let us see how Marcos explained his actions in the confession he gave about four months after the stabbing, which had taken place on July 20, 1809. This was the second time Marcos testified. The first time had been to make a preliminary statement (*declaración preparatoria*) on April 5, 1809, about a week after he stabbed Paula. Having become drunk with pulque, Marcos said, and burning from Paula María's *bofetón,* or slap, he became *perturbado,* a term implying (temporary) insanity: "blind with rage, he grabbed his knife and stabbed Paula, not with premeditation, nor with intent to kill, but only to vent his anger in a primal act."

Marcos stressed his previously friendly relations with Paula María, thus underscoring the instinctive, unpremeditated nature of his reaction. This later became an argument to blame the victim: she surely should have realized, given the "miserable state that she found Marcos in," given that he was "incapable of any understanding (*conocimiento*), incapable of respect (*consideración*) for the people dealing with him," that slapping, pushing, and screaming at him was foolhardy. So argued don José García (on December 10, 1809), a lawyer appointed by the court to defend Marcos. "She provoked [the act]," he stressed, "and caused her own misfortune."

This argument merits close attention, because it relates to our central concern, identity and honor. Paula María, don José stresses, should have used more "prudent means," however understandable her urgency to break up a fight in her own home. In fact she was defending her honor and the reputation of her person and family. It was her space, not Marcos's. Yet the evidence is clear, from the testimony of Marcos and from that of Marcos's wife, María Inés, who said Marcos was "very drunk" (*bastante ébrio*).[24] Don José therefore characterized Marcos's condition correctly. María Inés, hearing the uproar from her house, ran to Paula's house to see what had happened. She found her husband pinned to the ground and Paula sitting bent over, holding her stomach. She said she did not even bother asking her husband what had happened, because she could see he was incapable of answering, and so she turned to Paula.

Paula should have realized, so don José continued, that Marcos was 'completely gone' (*a el último grado*) by the way he spoke to his uncle. However outrageous his words, however offensive his violation of Paula's space, Marco's disrespect for his uncle shamed him, not her. This was underscored in the aftermath, as discussion centered on his central sin: Marcos had breached a central norm of patriarchy, that younger men should respect their elders. "Whoever has dealt with the Indians [don José noted approvingly] will have noted that kinship, even a tie as immediate as between Marcos Ygnacio and Juan Ygnacio, does not in itself imply mutual respect, but young people *always* treat their elders with a courtesy and respect that is exemplary" (emphasis added). "Who could possibly believe," he concluded with a flourish, "that an uncle's advice, so judicious and appropriate, could cause such insulting words to burst forth if [Marcos] had not himself been insane with drunkenness?"

The argument, let us note, transformed the stabbing of Paula into an afterthought by making Marcos's disgraceful conduct toward an elder the primary issue. If both could be blamed on his drunkenness, the stabbing had been provoked whereas the insults to Juan Ygnacio had been gratuitous. So the argument went, for normally, don José said, Marcos treated his uncle with "veneration" and would not have answered friendly advice with taunts and insults. In the gendered world of rancho life, a woman's right to defend her honor and the decorum of her house was relative, the respect owed an elder male less so. Paula should have given up her rights rather than 'provoke' the attack; Juan Ygnacio, the target only of a verbal attack, had also 'provoked' it but unwittingly, by speaking as he normally did to his nephew. Paula's 'normal' behaviors should have been modified by the variable of drink; in his drunken state Juan Ygnacio could not possibly have spoken to Marcos except as he did.

And indeed we must not forget how shocking Marcos's words had been at the time to Juan Ygnacio, to judge by his immobilized and fearful figure at the scene of the crime. In his words, as we have noted, he was "surprised and filled with fear" at his nephew's unexpected and harsh outburst. And if the older man was mute, Juan Nepomuceno blurted out his disapproval just as Paula too had been provoked beyond her ability to control herself. Don José, perhaps, had a point in saying that she should have acted more prudently. That she had not, and possibly could not, but instead threw herself at Marcos to remove him from her house, tells us how shocking and disturbing the breech of decorum of her house and name had been. Moreover, as we have noted, she had not been alone, for her son Juan also challenged Marcos spontaneously and immediately. The three reactions—shock and fear, disapproval, and near hysteria—should have told Marcos that he had disgraced himself. They matter because honor dramas required audiences; in this one Marcos's reputation and character stood as impugned. Before he grabbed his knife and plunged it into Paula, he, however drunk, had been shamed and dishonored because he had transgressed the rules of order and respect of his community. These, let us note, had been most vigorously upheld by a woman, but on her own terms. She had intervened in a man-to-man exchange, but in doing so had ranked the disrespect to herself and her house as the primary event. For Paula, then, the event was an inversion of don José's later argument, which placed central emphasis on the dishonoring of Juan Ygnacio. Her intervention, I think, added humiliation to the shame faced by a Marcos befogged by alcohol. The stabbing of

Paula, therefore, represented a gendered disagreement over the values in a culture, and Paula paid for her stand with a violent death. Don José's retelling submerges her voice by dismissing her behavior as mistakenly imprudent rather than deeply grounded in her own sense of honor.

THE ALLEGED DEFLOWERING OF CATARINA MARÍA

Disputes over sexual transactions, just as disputes over conventions of propriety and respect, also turned on reputation and character, on who people were or who they were trying to be in their community. Although the protagonists in the case involving Catarina are Indians, they repeat arguments Patricia Seed has analyzed in comparable disputes involving more 'respectable' Spaniards. Seed characterizes these as male "strategies," cynical in nature, to avoid the contract implied by the promise to marry.[25]

But if the cynical discourse she has identified was well-entrenched, women too might seek to use it to advantage, as did Catarina María, an *india* of Malinalco (now in the state of Mexico). On August 20, 1696, Catarina complained to the local magistrate (*justicia maior*), Capitán don Luis de Alipo, that Juan Telloa, Indian, about twenty and native to the pueblo, had deflowered (*estuprado*) her.[26] "Juan caught me yesterday next to the house of an india Magdalena," she said, "and forced me, taking away my virginity." He should be put in the public jail and "forced to pay for it," she added. Don Luis arrested Juan, put him in jail, and questioned him.

Under oath Juan explained that Catarina "had sent him many love messages" (*recados en materias de amor*) through his sister, the india Magdalena mentioned in Catarina's original complaint. He had ignored them, he said, but she continued, even to the point of writing that he "wasn't a man, nor did he know how to do anything because he didn't answer her call." When Juan ran into Catarina "yesterday" near Magdalena's house, she "began to tempt him as a seductress (*le empezó a provocar con amores*) and, in fact, lured him inside where she threw herself on the floor for the witness and he deflowered her (*la estrupó*), after which she said 'look at what you've done, don't treat me badly, I love you very much.'"

A second account of the deflowering comes from Juan's sister Magdalena María, about twenty-eight, married, resident of the pueblo. Through an interpreter she recalled that "on five or six occasions Catarina gave her love messages for Juan," and she also remembered a particularly provocative one telling Juan that "it seems he was afraid and not a man." After giving Juan that note, Catarina had gone into Magdalena's house and called for Juan to come in.

Magdalena, about to run some errands, saw them no more until she returned and "found them very happy (*muy contentos*) together and they said that Juan had had her virginity."

So far, then, the testimony establishes that a deflowering may have occurred, but not a rape. From Magdalena's picture of the contented couple following sexual intercourse, and from Juan's report of Catarina's amorous words, it is reasonable to think that she hoped to marry Juan. On August 25, however, Juan and Catarina appeared jointly before the magistrate in a *careamento*, a face-to-face meeting to speak and respond to one another for the record. Each added a point or two: Juan said that "in his view Catarina was not a virgin," and Catarina, that she wanted damages for the loss of her virginity but did not want to marry Juan. Following this hearing she was "deposited" in a respectable house, in the custody of doña Bernabela Vargas, a resident of the pueblo.

On September 4 Juan again tried to counter Catarina's charge. Denying that he had "ruined her by force [and] with trickery," he repeated that Catarina had sent the love notes to him, not he to her. Curiously this is the first time Juan refers to Magdalena as his sister. (The reason, surely, was that in the pueblo everyone knew this already, and therefore it only comes out in the testimony as an aside. It is nevertheless an important piece of information, because it explains why Catarina chose Magdalena as an intermediary.) Marcos also said he would pay whatever damages the magistrate ordered, to avoid marrying Catarina. So while denying that Catarina had been a virgin, Juan nevertheless agreed to a settlement as if she had.

With Catarina's honor commuted to a cash settlement, her three legitimate brothers, also indios of Malinalco, now tried to make the most of it. In a petition to the General Indian Court dated October 6—the petition had more force coming from a family constituted and recognized by law and custom and therefore honorable—they portrayed Juan as having betrayed Catarina. Their embellished version of the story had it that Juan "grabbed" Catarina, a virgin (*doncella*), "under cover of darkness, . . . took her by deceiving her to an empty house, and deflowered her after promising to marry her." Their petition invoked all the right elements common to pleas for damages: stealth, treachery, force, deflowering, and most importantly, the cynical use of a promise to marry, which was binding whether witnesses heard it or not. Marriage or a cash settlement would normally have settled the dispute, but the latter seems to have been what they really had in mind, for they noted that Juan had enough property (*caudal*) to pay.

After some consulting between officials in Mexico City and Malinalco, Juan once again appears in the record, on October 26. As before Capitán don Luis de Alipo, justicia maior of the district, presides, and no notary is available;

Francisco de Herrera, Juan's lawyer, is present, as is Juan de Medina, the interpreter. As in his other depositions, Juan identifies himself as unmarried, an *indio,* and a gañán; he does not know his age, but don Luis notes that he appears to be about twenty.

The transcript of Juan's "confession" is worth our close attention, because it proceeds as a dialogue, with Juan's interlocutor sometimes pushing him to elaborate or explain his answers. When asked to state the cause of his imprisonment, for example, Juan answered laconically, "because of a woman." That clearly did not satisfy his questioner, don Luis, who reminded him that he had been charged with "violently deflowering an india named Catarina María." In response to this more detailed charge, Juan repeated that "it seemed to him she had not been a virgin." But how could this be, don Luis asked, if Juan had already confessed to "ruining" Catarina. Juan asked (possibly on the advice of his lawyer, though this is not mentioned) that the transcript of his earlier statement be read, and on hearing it, said it was correct, repeating that his uncertainty about Catarina's virginity stemmed from the fact that it had been "the first time he had known a woman and he had been inexperienced in such acts and had been beguiled by the messages Catarina sent through Magdalena María."

Don Luis then asked Juan if he had other evidence that Catarina was not a virgin. Juan spoke again of his inexperience, but then recounted a brief encounter with Mateo Clemente, an indio of the pueblo. "Watch what you're doing," he recalled Mateo saying, "don't get mixed up with Catarina María in anything, and if she wants to marry you, you don't want to because I know she isn't a virgin." Two other witnesses speaking on behalf of Juan said the same. Lucas de la Cruz, married, a hatmaker, about forty, said it was generally known in barrio San Nicolás Malinalco that Catarina was "a public and worldly woman" (*muger pública y mundana*), and "he is certain that Juan did not ruin her." Baltasar de los Reyes, indio, about thirty, married, and a painter, had known Juan and Catarina for ten years. Catarina was known by reputation in the whole barrio, he said, as not a virgin, and he knew that she had enticed Juan with love notes with which, "as a *muchacho,*" Juan had not wanted to comply.

Juan's testimony and that of the defense witnesses, as summarized by Juan's lawyer don José García, emphasize two points. First, Juan was an unlikely candidate for such a crime. He was "a mere boy," "an indio without understanding," and quite "timid." Moreover he still lived under the tutelage of his father's "*patria potestad*" in a "family fearful of God and their consciences." Second, Juan should not be punished for deflowering Catarina, because she had "incited" him and even "spread herself on the ground, so this was not an abduction (*rapto*) or an act of violence but properly speaking a simple fornication." Catarina, not Juan, should therefore be punished.

Don José's argument more or less matched that of the audiencia judge, Dr. don Joseph de Morales, which normally would have been acceptable to the viceroy. Don Joseph, in the last document of this file, received the case on November 7 and presumably made his assessment immediately. He condemned Juan to pay 12 pesos, after which he was to be released from jail and acquitted of all demands arising from the charge. As for Catarina, he warned her not to "solicit" Juan or anybody else again and not to "tempt" men, on pain of placement in a home for wayward women in Mexico City for six years. "Live virtuously," he ordered, "or get married."

I, like don Joseph, have read the case of Juan and Catarina as if Juan, his sister Magdalena, and his acquaintances Lucas and Baltasar told the truth. They could have lied; Catarina might have been a deflowered virgin, as she and her brothers claimed. In any event she was at a disadvantage. The circumstances of the case made her vulnerable to the conventional defamation that she was not a virgin. She was after all a woman who moved about freely and passed notes to a young man who appealed to her either as a sexual or marriage partner. The presumption about such behavior—as reflected by the hearsay of witnesses, in turn a reflection of community gossip—was that only 'women of the world' engaged in it. Juan and Magdalena's vivid account of her sexual aggressiveness seemed to support that view. And in the end the judge accepted this compromised view of Catarina as a person (his fining of Juan, apparently, was not to secure a settlement for Catarina but to extract a fee for 'the court,' that is, himself). The remedy for her honor and reputation, to live virtuously or get married, refers us back to the claims for rights made by slave women. Marriage conferred rights for women, it seems, more than for men. Her unmarried condition and apparently immodest behavior worked against her. The preferred solution seemed to be her disciplining by a husband-patriarch.

But given the postcoital contentment of Juan and Catarina as viewed by Magdalena and Catarina's submissive request for good treatment, why should we believe Juan to be such an innocent? Might this not be yet another instance of sexual predation by a young male? Possibly, but we see an embarrassing departure from macho masculinity in Juan stressing his own virginity and lack of experience. Why embarrassing? Because Catarina herself taunted him about it. Moreover her ridicule proved irresistible. She overcame Juan's inhibitions by measuring his manhood against a model of male sexuality that presumed boldness not timidity, experience not virginity, virility not passivity. Had Juan, even though a muchacho, run from such taunts his reputation would have been forever tarnished.

Catarina, at least in her retelling, had played the part of the virgin deceived and deflowered and now was suing for damages or marriage. Unlike the virginal muchacho, the virginal muchacha fit formulaically an ideal type of female sexuality that, if we believe Juan's account, was a brazen misrepresentation of what actually happened. To resolve the case the judge had to think about the character and reputation of both Juan and Catarina. And from his perspective Juan had the better case: two witnesses repeated gossip that Catarina was not a virgin, Juan's sister corroborated his account of Catarina's aggressive solicitation, and his admission of his timidity and inexperience all made Catarina's charge seem out of character.

Both for Catarina and for Juan, the drama of her alleged deflowering involved a question of honor as their characters and reputations came under scrutiny. Juan had to disavow conventional claims to manliness in order to defend himself against Catarina's charge, while Catarina through her brothers, without corroborating testimony, presented herself formulaically as a virgin deceived. Yet Juan's unflattering portrayal of himself would only be a modest setback, for he had been only a muchacho, as one of his witnesses stressed, and he did in the end perform the sexual act and thus had graduated, so to speak, to manhood. Catarina, on the other hand, was put on probation and lost at least some of the freedom she had previously enjoyed to move about more or less as she pleased in the village. Her reputation in the future would be tarnished by her unsuccessful suit against Juan, and improving it, if that was possible in the face of village memory, would depend on finding a husband or living in a more 'virtuous' way.

HONOR AND IDENTITY

From the conflicts and complaints of ordinary people, we can see, then, that plebeian honor was a complex and not altogether stable negotiation between self and society. Our cases come from judicial sources, by definition documenting moments of confrontation. But we can view these as ruptures in the flow of everyday life, when behaviors or words exceeded acceptable limits, and judges were called on to intervene. I am interested in the ruptures because how and why they came about and how they were perceived by actors and witnesses tell us a good deal about 'normal' interactions. And if age, gender, rank, setting, and audience helped decide what to do when a self-definition was debased, the constant remains: lowering the reputation-honor of another set in motion a response to defend it.

I have used the records of these disputes, therefore, to think about how ordinary Mexicans placed themselves in relation to others and to society. The cases, as we have seen, involved slaves, hacienda peons, villagers, and rancho tenants. Except for the slaves, most are termed indios; most give testimony through an interpreter. They inhabit, at least in part, a Hispanic world of production, commerce, consumption, tax payments, invocations to crown authority, and litigation, at the same time that they continue to speak indigenous languages, fall back on village life, and recognize, even in the breach, traditional values such as respect for elders. My ordering of them in this essay moves, in rough terms, from simpler to more complex dramas. By complex I refer to the amount of detail available for recreating the settings and processes of conflict so the actions of protagonists can be seen as coherent in their own terms.

Plebeian honor dramas never captured the imagination of playwrights or their audiences. Writers of talent and genius never stylized them into a genre, a well-rehearsed structure of plot and characterization, in Joyce Carol Oates's words, combining "element[s] of the parable, the fairy tale, even the ritual."[26] Genre implies a contract between reader and writer, between audience and actor, to satisfy convention. Without audiences demanding plebeian honor dramas, great writers ignored them. And so to this day they lie scattered in archives in artless scraps of testimony recorded by notaries and magistrates. Historians who read them will find them reflective of life, not art. I confess I much prefer them to the theater's repetitive conflations of sexual intrigue with honor. But that, I suppose, is a matter of taste.

NOTES

1. I am grateful to the Social Sciences and Humanities Research Council of Canada for a grant that supported the research on which this essay is based. Antonio Gómez Moriana and Lidia Ernestina Gómez-García read an earlier draft and offered comments and criticism.

2. Jean-Clément Martin, "Violences sexuelles, étude des archives, pratiques de l'histoire," *Annales: Histoire, Sciences Sociales* 51(3) (May-June 1996): 647.

3. Quoted in George Ticknor, *History of Spanish Literature* (New York: Gordian Press, Inc., 1965) 2:308.

4. Lope de Vega, *Novelas a Marcia Leonarda,* ed. Francisco Rico (Madrid: Alianza, 1968), 141, quoted in Antonio Carreño, "La 'Sin Venganza' como violencia: *El castigo sin venganza* de Lope de Vega," *Hispanic Review* 59 (1991): 384–85, n.5.

5. Enrique de Olavarría y Ferrari, *Reseña histórica del teatro en México, 1538–1911,* 3d ed. (Mexico City: Editorial Porrua, 1961)1:78, 80.

6. Charles V. Aubrun, *La comedia española (1600–1680),* 2d ed. (Madrid, Taurus Ediciones, 1981), 68 n.1.

7. Melveena McKendrick, "Honour/Vengeance in the Spanish 'Comedia': A Case of Mimetic Transference?" *The Modern Language Review* 79(2) (April 1984): 332.

8. Irving Leonard, "The 1790 Theater Season of the Mexico City Coliseo," *Hispanic Review* 19 (1951): 110, 113.

9. D. A. Brading, *The First America: The Spanish Monarchy, Creole Patriots, and the Liberal State, 1492–1867* (Cambridge: Cambridge University Press, 1991), 399–409; quotation from 403.

10. Fray Agustín's calculation was purposely conservative. He inflated the age of maternity to thirty with full knowledge that women more commonly gave birth to children in their twenties or teens. His figure stands as a minimum, therefore, to give more force to his argument. Fray Agustín Salucio, *Discurso sobre los estatutos de limpieza de sangre* (Cieza: A. Pérez y Gómez, 1975 [1600?]), 1r–31r.

11. Angel Rosenblat, *La población indígena y el mestizaje en América*, 2 vols. (Buenos Aires: Editorial Nova, 1954) 2:133–87.

12. AGI, Indiferente, 1535.

13. Charles Gibson, *Spain in America* (New York: Harper & Row, 1966), 130.

14. In the remainder of this paragraph I draw on Frank Henderson Stewart's discussion of definitions in *Honor* (Chicago and London: University of Chicago Press, 1994), 30–63. Stewart says that "between roughly the twelfth and the nineteenth century . . . honor comes increasingly to be based on moral virtues" (p. 46). If there is general agreement on this point, as Stewart claims, such a transition in Latin America of the colonial period has not been established, to put it mildly. My reading of the cases, as we shall see, suggests that both tendencies coexisted, probably with reputation more important than character.

15. I will not be able to develop the outside-inside distinction in this essay, but an initial treatment can be found in Richard Boyer, "Caste and Identity in Colonial Mexico: A Proposal and an Example," in *Explorations in the Political Culture of Latin America: Essays in Honor of Hugh M. Hamill, Jr.* (Storrs: University of Connecticut Latin American Center, 1997). I continue to think of Robert McCaa's "Calidad, Clase, and Marriage in Colonial Mexico: The Case of Parral, 1788–90," *Hispanic American Historical Review* 64(3) (August 1984): 477–501, as a crucial piece of the puzzle. In my "Caste and Identity" I present evidence for viewing caste labels as political, not merely descriptive; with McCaa I think of calidad as a central category, a composite of reputation and character, as discussed above.

16. Archivo Judicial Tribunal [Mexico City], Penales, legajo labeled "Varios años, 1633–1635," "4/8/1633, María Negra como mujer de Nicolás Negro su marido contra Alonso Bueno panadero sobre hacerle malos tratamientos" (hereafter AJT). Some items in the bundle are numbered, but this one, according to my notes, was not.

17. Persons referred to as "the slave of so and so" received an individualizing modifier to the generic category slave. Plebeians in general, not only slaves, would have commonly identified themselves or been identified by others by their master. The difference between slaves and free men, however, was the former's inability to change masters at will. See Boyer, "Caste and Identity," for additional discussion.

18. A group of petitions of the type I have just analyzed can be found in Mexico's Archivo General de la Nación, Matrimonios, caja 135. The two examples that follow, not numbered separately, come from this group of documents.

19. AJT, Penales, leg. 2 (1719–46, exp. 64: "Contra Joseph García alias Rapia a pedimento

de Josepha Delgado su muger, Xochimilco, 13 de abril 1749"). Other witnesses collaborated Josepha's complaint.

20. Ruth Behar, *Translated Woman: Crossing the Border with Esperanza's Story* (Boston: Beacon Press, 1993), 11.

21. AGN, Criminal, vol. 91, fols. 1–4v. The case was adjudicated in the General Indian Court. Simón's deposition provides us with a rare instance of a man defining his own categories when he explains that gañán jornalero "es el título que tenemos los que trabajamos y vivimos de asiento en las haciendas de esta provincia" (fol. 1r). Antonia, like Simón, defined herself as an Indian from Tepetlixpa. I have drawn the following account from Simón's testimony. I am grateful to Sonya Lipsett-Rivera for arranging the photocopying of this document.

22. E. P. Thompson, *Customs in Common: Studies in Traditional Popular Culture* (New York: The New Press, 1993), 46.

23. AGN, Criminal, 256, exp. 7, fols. 311r–65v. The documents in this file fall within the period from March 28 to December 10, 1809.

24. María Inés testified on May 2, 1809; her statement can be found on fols. 326r–27r.

25. Patricia Seed, "Marriage Promises and the Value of a Woman's Testimony in Colonial Mexico," *Signs: Journal of Women in Culture and Society* 13(2) (1988): 265.

26. AGN, Criminal 139, exp. 24, fols. 363–76. More precisely, both Juan and Catarina are from the pueblo of San Nicolás, a barrio of Malinalco. The case went to the General Indian Court, for which Dr. don Joseph Morales, a lawyer attached to the audiencia, provided the legal opinion that Viceroy-Archbishop Juan de Ortega Montañés pronounced. The documents for this case date from August 20, 1696, to the end of October. A translation of this document will appear in *Colonial Lives: Documents on Latin American History* Richard Boyer and Geoffrey Spurling eds. (New York: Oxford University Press, forthcoming).

27. Joyce Carol Oates, "The Simple Art of Murder," *New York Review of Books* 42(20) (December 21, 1995), 32.

CHAPTER SEVEN

A SLAP IN THE FACE OF HONOR
Social Transgression and Women in Late-Colonial Mexico

SONYA LIPSETT-RIVERA

Fire, Water, and Honor joined together for a time. Fire could not stay still; Water also had to be in continual movement, and so Water and Fire insisted that Honor should travel with them. Before setting off on their trip, they agreed to give each other some signs by which they could find each other in case one got lost. "If, by any chance, I am separated from you," said Fire, "look for smoke and there you will find me, because that is my sign." "If you lose sight of me," said Water, "don't look for me in arid or cracked ground, but rather where there are willows, poplars, swampland plants, or grasses that are very green and tall, there you will find me." "As for me" said Honor, "watch me carefully and never let go of my hand for a moment. Because if by some bad fortune I leave the road and you lose me, you will never find me again.[1]

This tale was printed in a magazine for Mexican ladies as a reminder of the ease with which honor could be lost. From the perspective of their class it was understood that elite Mexican women had honor to protect and that they grasped the social expectations associated with its retention. They upheld their family honor not only by remaining chaste throughout their lives, but by acting only in a reputable manner so that their conduct would reflect favorably upon their families. For women honor was intimately bound first to their virginity before marriage, then to fidelity to their husbands, and finally to their chasteness as widows. Their sexual behavior (or rather lack of it) reflected upon the men associated with them. Thus a woman who defied these rules not only stained her own honor but also that of her father, her brother, and her husband.

But honor was also related to a sense of social superiority, and therefore when women struggled to protect their honor they were also inherently trying to safeguard their social position. Upper-class women were born with honor through their status, but the loss of the virtuous part of their honor could sully their social position. The two faces of honor—status and virtue—were intimately bound together.

Yet, this sense of hierarchy, so integral to colonial societies, was not just the perception of creole and peninsular elites but also of members of classes deemed inferior by these elites.[2] Honor was relative, so that in a small Mexican village, those belonging to the local elite felt as imbued with honor as did the nobility of Mexico City; yet when the village gentry traveled to Mexico City, their honor would be overshadowed by the aristocracy of the capital. And although a wealthy Spanish noblewoman would not recognize the capacity for honor of the mulatto wife of an artisan, the former would indeed see herself as superior to many around her, not only because of skin color or wealth but also her public behavior. In other words honor was self-defined within a certain context. For Mexican women as a group, personal honor manifested itself most obviously through conduct but also was a key element in the definition of hierarchies.

WOMEN AS DEFENDERS OF HONOR

The defense of personal or family honor has often been seen through the experiences of men; the duels fought by gallants or the lawsuits launched by husbands were often the most visible public face of this battle. Yet women were not totally passive in the protection of their own reputation and social standing. They acted to hide infractions, and they attacked those who insulted them and their families. They tried to maintain a public face that smoothed over the stains on their personal and family honor, and they censured those who were their inferiors in order to maintain the status that honor conferred. The documents usually contain records of the most flamboyant or obvious actions, but they do reflect the strategies chosen by women to stop the transgressions affecting accepted rankings and understandings of virtue and modesty. Women chose different types of strategies to engage in this struggle, but all saw themselves as having honor not only as virtue but also as social status.

Women suffered damage to their honor primarily through accusations of sexual indiscretions, the results of which they made every effort to conceal (see the discussions by Ann Twinam and Muriel Nazarri in chapters three and four, above). But once these blots on their reputation became known through whatever means, common knowledge of an infidelity, an illegitimate pregnancy, or a rape could lead to gossip and public insults. Most of these slights involved sexual purity or chastity, but the discussion of these problems reveals an undercurrent of concern with the maintenance of social position even among people generally considered to be of the lower classes. Members of the colonial elite developed ways to stave off threats to their family honor and status, either through manipulation of the courts or through the use of physical intimidation. But in many instances women of both the upper and lower classes did not hesitate to use violence to correct an insulting remark, to punish a slandering gossip or especially to protect their sexual honor. Concern over family or individual honor was neither the unique preserve of the elite nor an exclusively male rationale for the use of violence.

Because honor was a fragile quality, the appearance of honor was as important as the actual commodity. Public insults or slights were an extension of the struggle for social position and honor. Therefore individuals who considered themselves honorable had to respond to such acts. Mexicans frequently tried to force an apology from the aggressor through the intervention of officials. Don Alberto de Córdova, for example, sued doña Josefa Vila, who had spread the rumor that his wife, doña María Tomasa Lasaygne, had committed adultery with doña Josefa's husband. Don Alberto initiated the suit, following the traditional pattern in which male heads of families responded to insults to the honor of individuals within their households. But doña Josefa did not desist easily, and don Alberto finally declared his honor satisfied and left to work in the Philippines. Doña María, his wife, was left behind in the midst of this unresolved matter, with her reputation in tatters. Despite the perception that honorable wives should not engage in litigation, she vigorously defended her right to take up the suit abandoned by her husband and quite vociferously reiterated that she would not accept the insults of a woman of such low standing. Her resoluteness paid off; she won and doña Josefa Vila was sentenced.[3] This was a moral victory for doña María, no doubt, but one that was elusive and not totally satisfactory, since the original accusations could not be retracted entirely. But doña Maria insisted on a resolution, for to desist would be to acknowledge the fault. Only women who had honor could fight the slights that could stain their reputation.

HONOR AND GOSSIP

Gossip was a potent dishonoring tool and, as pointed out by Lyman Johnson in chapter five, above, could also provoke very severe and violent reactions.[4] Concern over hearsay motivated Rita Trinidad, a resident of Xochimilco (a town outside Mexico City) who was married to a muleteer, to attempt to put an end to rumors about herself. As the wife of a muleteer, who by the nature of

Figure 26. Because there were so few improved roads in the colonies, goods were most commonly carried by mules. Muleteers also served as a means of communication, carrying news, rumor, and sometimes lies from place to place. These informal sources of information could often determine the reputation of an individual or family. (Claudio Linati, Costumes civils, militaires et religieux de Mexique . . . [Brussels: Ch. Sattanino, 1828].)

his work was regularly absent, Rita's worries were not without foundation. Her husband, like most men whose work took them away from home, relied on the censure of his neighbors to keep his wife in line. Upon his return home, if he heard any whisper of scandal about Rita, it was quite likely that he would beat her. The damaging talk apparently originated with María (alias la Sincuenta), and so Rita decided to ask la Sincuenta's husband to control his wife's behavior. In the company of her aunt, she waited outside her house until Nicolás Padilla went by, and then she approached him to discuss this matter. But as she started to explain her concerns, la Sincuenta arrived on the scene and began to scold them. Nicolás Padilla hit la Sincuenta, and the matter was left unresolved except for the burning anger that hardened la Sincuenta's attitude toward Rita.

Retribution came swiftly. As Rita Trinidad left mass on this same day, a group of women accompanied la Sincuenta, and together they grabbed Rita Trinidad, cut off her braids, and wounded her in two places. In Mexico as

Figure 27. This mulatto woman defies elite conceptions by her lavish dress and luxurious jewels. Despite laws which attempted to bar black and casta women from wearing expensive clothes, the better off members of these groups continued to imitate elite styles. (Painting by Arellano, active 1690–1720, Collection of Jan and Frederick Mayer; photograph by James O. Milmoe.)

Figure 28. These two women are fighting in front of a tavern with a group of male onlookers. Such scenes were not particularly rare, as women fought to defend themselves against insults and gossip, as well as out of jealousy. (Claudio Linati, Costumes civils, militaires et religieux de Mexique . . . *[Brussels: Ch. Sattanino, 1828].)*

elsewhere, hair cutting for women was a gravely insulting, visible symbol of sexual and social dishonor.[5] Rita Trinidad's endeavor to control the scandal associated with her backfired in a very serious manner. A posse of women made clear to her that she could not escape the stigma of dishonor and perhaps punished her for approaching the husband of one of their group. Even with the presence of her aunt, this could also be interpreted as sexual laxity.[6] Yet the women on both sides of this conflict acted out of a concern for their honor. Rita Trinidad tried to influence the source of gossip by appealing to a male figure of authority—a husband. La Sincuenta, humiliated by the blow her husband gave her in public and angered by Rita Trinidad's insulting approach to her husband, went beyond gossip to physical attack.

HONOR, VIOLENCE, AND HIERARCHY

This level of violence may seem more appropriate for women of the lower classes, but women of the elite were not immune from such outbursts. At the end of mass in the small village of Teotihuacán, Josefa Cadena, a married mulatto, apparently brushed against doña Teresa Bravo, the wife of don Diego Fernández, an official with the Renta de Alcabalas y Pulques. Doña Teresa exploded and along with her daughter, a sister, and a *depositada* (woman in custody in an honorable household while awaiting an official decision regarding her) in her house, proceeded to hit Josefa repeatedly, even after she fell to the ground.[7] Josefa Cadena was six months pregnant, and the attack caused vaginal bleeding; both her husband and the doctors who examined her were worried about a possible miscarriage, although the outcome is not reported.[8] According to José de Alfaro, Josefa's husband, the attack was provoked solely by the act of brushing against her social better; the maintenance of rank and precedence was therefore the motivation for these elite women to respond so violently.[9] But José de Alfaro complained that the aggression was not only physical but also attacked the honor of his wife. The assailants called his wife a *puta negra* (black whore). He argued that there was no greater insult to a married woman "than to label her a black whore, insulting her fidelity and her quality, since her honor is well-known, and since she is not black but castiza."[10] José de Alfaro mediated two levels of honor; he referred explicitly to his wife's honra—that is, the status she derived from her birth and family heritage. His wife had potentially insulted the honor of an elite woman by her physical proximity, but this elite woman, in turn, had sullied his wife's honor by her words. The affront was twofold. On the one hand the term *puta* implied a lack of sexual morality or virtue and therefore attacked Josefa and, by extension, her husband. But the use of *negra,* on the other hand, suggested their inclusion a racial caste even lower than their self-identification. Thus in the eyes of the plaintiffs, the second aspect of the insult maligned their status. This perception, no doubt, was not shared by the Spaniards, who were not likely to recognize that Josefa and her husband did indeed possess any rank but the lowest. For the elite, the lower classes were for the most part a mass of relatively undifferentiated ruffians.

Indeed don Manuel Delfín, a Spaniard who was a witness to the brawl, gave a different account of the incident. He reported that before the attack, Josefa Cadena murmured to doña Teresa "that she was a whore and that no one had found her[Josefa's] friend under the bed."[11] These words implied that because of her virtue, Josefa's honor was superior to doña Teresa's. This rationale might seem like a suspiciously convenient excuse to justify doña Teresa's actions, but still it shows that punishment of gossips through such violence seemed acceptable and reasonable to him. Both parties to this fight portrayed it as an attack upon honor, although since their social perspectives were so different, their reasoning also varied. Don Manuel characterized it as an attack upon a superior's honor, which then became the primary motive for such violence. Although his account was not the same, José de Alfaro recognized that Josefa Cadena's intrusion upon doña Teresa's status sparked the assault. All were concerned with the words used to describe themselves and the stain upon their honor that could entail if unanswered. Doña Teresa and her female allies answered the insult directly, with violence, whereas Josefa Cadena and her husband responded through the legal system, most probably because they could see no other way to defend themselves.

No matter whether we accept the interpretation and explanation of don Manuel Delfín or that of José de Alfaro, the attack on Josefa revealed a preoccupation on the part of elite Mexican women with their rank within society and a willingness to act directly to maintain that status. For some elite women the temptation to lash out at their 'inferiors' seems to have been related to tensions within their own social circle that they could not act upon directly. María Cayetana Sandibar, a member of the elite society of the village of Xalatlaco, was angry when the local priest did not come to the village church to say mass one Sunday. Unable to malign the priest directly, she chose to insult his African servant, José Victoriano Millán, and to accuse him of a personal attack. She stated that he had threatened to kill her and that she had only escaped him by running into a house. Another member of the community gave a very different account. According to Pedro José Reynoso, as José Victoriano chatted with some young women in the street, María Cayetana passed by and insulted him. José Victoriano listed these insults: María Cayetana called him a *negro garrotero* (black armed robber), a pimp for the priest, and a *chivato* (an informer). The witness, Pedro José, concluded that her conduct toward José Victoriano was directly related to his status as the servant of the local priest.[12] María Cayetana could not attack a social equal or a man of status such as the priest, but she could make life impossible for a man who society categorized as her social inferior by his race, birth, and occupation.

Fear of the loss of social status and potential harm to family honor through harmful associations or attacks upon a person's rank reappears as a motive for violence in other incidents as well. Individuals who seemed to transgress the boundaries of social position were often harshly punished. Marta María and her husband Manuel Bartolomé, for example, described themselves as very poor Indians from a village near Teotihuacán. As they came into town to ask for credit to buy corn, Luciana, another Indian woman, came out of her house and laughed at them, calling Marta in particular an *otomita trapienta* (a ragged Otomí Indian). Marta María retorted that she was ragged because God had willed it, and that Luciana should go into her house and not judge other people. Luciana and her daughter assaulted Marta; between the two, they beat Marta on her face, head, and body all the while insulting her.[13] Although Marta's husband was present and later complained with her to the authorities, he does not seem to have intervened to assist his wife. Did he find it impossible to prevent this attack by a social superior? He is silent on this matter and so is Luciana, since she was not asked to testify. But it seems clear that Luciana believed she was within her rights to mock a poor woman and believed that Marta's transgression of those boundaries by talking back to her deserved a physical correction. In the eyes of elite Mexicans, both these women were of the same caste, but one was poor and the other was not, and they themselves did not conflate the categories. Luciana protected her status with the same tactic that doña Teresa chose to employ. While I am sure that doña Teresa would not want to be compared to an Otomí, their concerns and their reactions to a challenge to their honor were the same.

CUSTOMS AND CONVENTIONS

Gregoria Antonia, a tributary Indian of Tenango del Valle, reported a similar incident. She went to don Juan's store for some slaked lime—a product used to process corn for tortillas. The request or her presence apparently bothered the storeowner and his son. She stated that she asked several times for a little bit more of the lime, as was the local custom. Perhaps she asked one time too many, and the storeowners interpreted this repetition as an insult against their reputation and status. They insulted her and then when she left the store, the son caught up with her and beat her. She maintained that her request was well within the norms of local customs, but evidently the storeowner and his son felt that she had transgressed some social boundary.[14] Unfortunately the men were not called upon to explain their actions, so the document leaves some tantalizing gaps. But these men acted in a manner quite strikingly similar to that of doña Teresa and her cohorts when faced with an insult by Josefa Cadena; first they insulted their social inferior and then, when this was not satisfactory or did not seem to resolve the transgression, they used physical violence. Gregoria Antonia defended her actions as reasonable by complaining to the authorities. She did not claim that her social status was equal to that of the storeowner or his son but rather that she had behaved honorably within the customs of the town and deserved respect.

Deference to local conventions was vital in maintaining peaceful relations among the various levels of the social hierarchy. Members of the elite, as we have seen, reacted with fury when they believed that their social inferiors had crossed an invisible line to defame them. Yet these same plebeians were not quiescent. Social inferiors could also strike out if provoked. Joseph González, a *ministro de vara* in the town of Tacubaya, outside Mexico City, discovered this very fact. It was his job to collect a fee, usually in produce, from the Indian women who had stalls in the public market. But he did not realize (or conveniently forgot) that the fee applied only to those women who came from other towns. Manuela Peralta, a *cacica* (Indian official) of Tacubaya, objected when he tried to charge her sister the fee. Although to Joseph González Manuela Peralta might have looked like just another Indian, because of her official status any attack upon her was highly symbolic; it would also mean an insult to the town. Not surprisingly witnesses' and participants' accounts of the incident differ. According to Joseph González, Manuela Peralta called him a foreigner, a thief, and a pauper, among other affronts. Another witness elaborated on these insults. She told him to go charge his own people and that he was a *cornudo cabron* (a wretched cuckold). Quite clearly her words insulted his honor, but he had offended her by his assumption that she and her sister had no status within the market and the town. He said that he was about to give her a blow to the neck when she hit him and injured his face. He tried to take her prisoner, but the market women came to her aid; in the melee that followed, the crowd took away his staff of office.

This public attack, the mark on his face, and the loss of the symbol of his political office humiliated Joseph González. But the account given by the Indians was different. The local residents argued that González had carried a *garrote* (a big stick), not an official staff of office, but also that they had heard

De Españo. e India, o. e Mestiza.

Clapera

Figure 29. Women who worked in the market derived some status from their economic role. Just like this woman, they could be respectably dressed and insist on an orderly deportment. (Painting by Francisco Clapera, active 1770–1810, courtesy Denver Art Museum, Jan and Frederick Mayer Collection.)

him say publicly that "all the women of Tacubaya are complete whores." Manuela Peralta related a slightly different story. According to her, when González tried to charge her sister, she told him that natives did not pay the levy. He insulted her and hit her about the head and shoulders.[15] These conflicting accounts reveal some of the tensions in the concepts of honor according to social status. Joseph González believed that his rank and staff of office automatically conferred respect, but he did not recognize any status or honor among the women. For the market women his disdain of local practices negated any inherent rights conferred by race and political office. The women felt secure in their numbers and because in this small society they were accorded honor for which they were willing to fight. Witnesses who reported the insults on both sides gave as much weight to those hurled at Joseph González as to those with which he characterized the market women. But in the various testimonies, it is clear that the Indians believed that by hitting Manuela Peralta, Joseph González attacked the honor not just of this woman but of the entire populace. In fact when he called the women of Tacubaya "complete whores," he put into words what his actions had already made clear.

Joseph González made the mistake of underestimating the feelings of the townspeople regarding the status of a cacica. He also overestimated the status his race and office conferred as opposed to the fact that he was an outsider and to the Indians a foreigner. In other circumstances, however, the local population might have supported Joseph González. When local individuals claimed status and therefore honor that was not rightly theirs, the actions of officials like Joseph González were accepted.

Take the case of doña María Blasa y Velasco. At first glance she seemed to be part of the local elite of the small town of Tulancingo, in the Valley of Mexico. With the permission of her husband, she complained to the *subdelegado* (regional official) regarding the actions of the *alcalde* (town judicial official) don José Ochoa Ruiz. On the day of the archbishop's visit to confirm young children, such an enormous crowd waited to enter the church that no one could get through the doors, not even the archbishop himself. The alcalde was trying to make way for the prelate when, he said, doña María hit him in public. Doña María had of course perceived his actions differently. She accused him of trying to get his family into the church, to the detriment of others more deserving. She scolded him, asking him what he had that she did not, and then he hit her. In her account doña María left out any insulting words she may have shouted at the alcalde. One witness reported that she called don José a *gachupín de mierda* (shitty Spaniard) and that she scratched his face. Unlike the previous case, the witnesses called to testify were Spaniards, and their sympathies were clearly with the official. They denounced doña María not only for her rowdy behavior but also for trying to assume a rank that in their eyes she could not occupy. Don Mariano Ordóñez stated that she and her daughter "pass themselves off as doñas but they are not, nor do they deserve to be by any stretch since they are simply free mulattoes, the granddaughters or nieces of a cobbler whom this town called the Tejonejo Nillordejo or Claquachejo." He also described her husband as a freed slave.[16] Unlike Manuela Peralta, doña María could not successfully assert the status to which she aspired. When she tried to ensure that she and her family could enter the church in good time and therefore have a good position to witness her child being confirmed by the archbishop, she crossed the line. Although she tried to portray the alcalde as a foreigner by calling him a gachupín, she was in foreign territory herself, because she was asking that her assumed rank be respected.

HONOR AND MARRIAGE

Concern over social status was evidently not a question that preoccupied only the Hispanic elite, but was rather an issue that permeated a society profoundly concerned with the stratification of position and honor. Marriage could provoke anxiety since it brought into the family nucleus a new person, one who could either augment or detract from the family honor. The race and status of a prospective son-in-law or daughter-in-law might be considered, but the sexual conduct of a future daughter-in-law was of paramount concern.[17] In the village of Xochimilco, José Galicia announced his betrothal to doña María Manuela Morales—the woman with whom he had long had sexual relations and who was pregnant with his child. His parents hit the roof. It was not entirely unusual for couples even at the highest levels of society to engage in premarital intercourse once marriage was promised, nor was it unusual for parents to object to lower caste or class alliances.[18] The problem here, however, was not the classic case of Spanish parents objecting to a mulatto daughter-in-law. In fact doña María Manuela was described as Spanish, whereas the Galicia family identified themselves as Indians, although some members of the community suggested they were really mulattoes. But the Galicias were related to the governor of the town and as such may have considered that their status as leaders within the community outweighed doña María Manuela's race.[19] She was also described as a *soltera,* not a doncella (a single woman as opposed to a virgin), which may indicate that she was considered a loose woman.[20] The Galicia family objected to any association with her because of her alleged promiscuity; in other words, she was pregnant with their son's child before marriage and did not hide the fact. Her social status by race was not sufficient to overcome her lack of sexual honor. The actions of José Galicia's family demonstrate that they did not believe marriage could overcome this taint.

Tensions concerning the relationship between doña María Manuela and José Galicia seem to have started when they announced their marriage by celebrating their betrothal. At the fiesta of Tepepa, in front of a crowd, José Galicia's sister shouted at doña María Manuela: "You're here, you big whore? Here, are you so shameless? You came to show off the belly that my brother gave you? Did you get tired of fornicating?; but I promise you that I will take your child out in pieces." José Galicia's mother gave her the same treatment and also threatened her unborn child.[21] Doña María Manuela provoked the Galicias (intentionally or not) by showing herself in public, obviously pregnant, just after she had been linked to the family by her betrothal. The Galicia family, in fact, accused her of being a prostitute, although this charge seems to have been a metaphor for her open association with José Galicia.[22] Doña María Manuela's sexual honor did not measure up to theirs, even though she was a Spaniard and a doña.

Public insults were not enough to dissuade doña María Manuela from sullying the Galicia family's honor through marriage to their son, and neither she nor José called off the union. So from invective the Galicias passed to direct action, which entailed both an attack upon the offending woman and also an effort to abort her baby. One night at around midnight, the Galicia family—minus the son—broke into the Morales home. José Galicia's father pulled doña María Manuela from her bed and his mother began to hit her with a stick, while José's sister bit her all over and tried to tear her nearly full-term fetus out of her.[23] In this attack it was the mother and sister who were the most directly violent. It seems evident that the pregnancy had not been an issue earlier, when it might have been simpler to cause an abortion, but it became important with the celebration of the betrothal. It was one thing for José Galicia to have an illegitimate child with a Spanish woman of loose morals, but it was not acceptable to bring this woman and her sexual dishonor into the family. Once again women took an active and violent role in maintaining and protecting their status.

HONOR AND INFANTICIDE

Women of the elite could usually avoid the scandal associated with premarital pregnancies through their manipulation of the laws on bans but also (as Ann Twinam and Muriel Nazzari discuss in chapters three and four, above) by hiding their pregnancy and even their child, possibly later legitimating their offspring.[24] These manipulations and the actual seclusion needed to undertake such hidden pregnancies were not always available to the poor, of course, but lower-class women did at times feel strongly enough about their honor, or more frequently about the reputation of their family, to want to conceal their illegitimate offspring. This undertaking was much more difficult, given their lack of privacy, but many were able to give birth secretly—in some instances totally alone.[25] Some women then resorted to infanticide to conceal their shame and to protect their families.[26] The new mothers justified their actions in terms of preserving the honor of the house or the head of the household.

In 1819 on an hacienda in the region of Tepeapulco, María Jacoba gave birth in the middle of the night and then, apparently without the knowledge of her uncle (the only man in the house), her aunt ordered her sisters to get rid of the baby, which they did by burying it. After their act was denounced, none of the women involved tried to deny that they had killed the child, nor was this an issue. In fact the judge was more interested in the motivation for the infanticide. In his inquiry he asked María Jacoba why she did not give the baby away, since the hacienda was large and had many houses and people who might adopt the child. She replied "so that neither the masters nor the servants of this estate should know about her childbirth since it was against the honor of the house of the captain her uncle, and principally against his son José de Santiago, who was the one responsible."[27] Her aunt pleaded for a lenient sentence on the grounds that the pregnancy was an intolerable stain on her own honor:

> This order [to kill the baby] was not and could not have been premeditated but was rather the product of my rage at seeing that my niece had lacked respect for my house and exposed me to unpleasantness in my marriage: it was the product of the fear that my husband would find out and I would lose my honor among the people of the estate who would whisper that I am a procuress.[28]

It was clear to all the women involved as defendants in this case—all of lower class and caste—that their actions reflected the necessity to protect the honor of their household and of the male head of that household. The mother of the baby, even though she refused to carry out the infanticide, used the language of honor and understood the rationale behind the actions of her aunt and her sisters. Teresa Escobar y Bebolaza provided the same explanation for the abandonment of her child. When the Tula authorities asked her why she had gone to a deserted location to give birth totally alone, she replied that "because her natural modesty assisted her in this predicament and also to conserve the sacred respect for a house of honor and seclusion."[29] These women resorted to the violence of killing newborns to escape the social stigma of illegitimate births—not only for themselves but also for their house. If they had had access to the types of manipulation of public knowledge available to elite women, perhaps infanticide would not have been necessary.

RAPE

Since female honor was linked to chastity and modesty, rape was one of the ultimate affronts for women. Following the logic that defiled women had lost their honor, there were many instances when marriage to the rapist was deemed an acceptable resolution, since it covered up the rape and the loss of virginity.[30] Families of the victims often advocated this solution; it seems that the mortification of sexual dishonor—even if it was involuntary, as in the case of rape—was stronger than any desire to punish the rapist.[31] Leonarda Antonia, an Indian woman of Xochimilco, was working in her *milpa,* or cornfield, when three men grabbed her; two held her down while the third raped her. The assault was actually a clumsy attempt at forcing a marriage, since the rapist, in effect, wanted to marry her and she had previously resisted all his advances. He kept her prisoner in his parents' house overnight and in the morning set her free. She went to her sister who, when notified of the rape, whipped Leonarda and dragged her to see the priest in order to force her to marry her rapist. In the face of her sister's many threats, Leonarda temporarily assented to the marriage, and she was put in the custody of a prominent citizen. Shortly thereafter she escaped this confinement and reported the crime to the authorities. Rather than concealing the rape she wanted the rapist punished, and she was adamant that she still did not want to marry her attacker.[32] In this instance there was certainly no feminine solidarity and little sympathy for the victim from her sister. Taking the role traditionally associated with fathers and brothers, the sister seemed particularly anxious to hide the stain on their family's honor through a quick marriage; only the fortitude and insistence of Leonarda foiled the cover-up. It is clear in this instance that her sister believed she was defending her sister's and the family's honor.

The loss of virginity seems to be one of the major determinants in reporting rape; while virginity was often equated with honor, the two terms were not exactly synonyms. In fact the word *honor* is so capacious that it is defined in many different ways according to the context. Women, however, were often said to have lost their honor when they surrendered their virginity outside marriage.[33] The two concepts are equated in the phrase "He finally triumphed over my virginity honor" ("triunfó por fin de mi virginidad honor"). Both men and women used this language in their testimony. A man denied rape by saying "I do not owe her her honor" ("no le debo su honor"); a rape victim said of her attacker that he took her honor; Mariano Guadalupe was whipped "for not wanting to cover the honor" ("por no querer cubrir el honor") by marrying the cousin whom he had deflowered; and a woman accused her stepdaughter of having "direct complicity in her dishonor" ("directa complicidad en su desonra") after she revealed that her father had raped her.[34] It is at times difficult to determine whose words we are reading in the documents and what is the influence or interference of the notaries and judges in the recorded testimonies. But it is clear that for all concerned the basic equation of feminine honor with virginity held true for these women and that neither the women, the accused men, nor the officials involved found the use of such language farfetched.

Where this language is more interesting and less anticipated is in some of the few reports of the rape of married women. For a nonvirgin the decision to report a rape in this society was courageous; certainly these women could not expect the compensation or the support that a virgin could command. Since rape was usually defined as a deflowering, restitution was generally defined as a sum of money to form a dowry or as marriage to the rapist to cover the loss of virginity. Married women who reported rape could not expect nor want these forms of restitution, but neither could they realistically expect severe punishment of the rapists unless the accused was a serial rapist or had engaged in a gang rape or robbery or some other associated crime. Although officially the sentence for rape was death, any penalties actually applied were rarely very severe. So why did these married women reveal what would probably become their shame, if they could not expect some retribution or compensation? I believe that their words reveal their motivations, but only indirectly. They took action because they believed that they had honor; if they did not report this type of act, they would be acquiescing in the intimation that they did not. They believed themselves to be virtuous and thus honorable, and so they defended their status within their local communities by accusing their rapists. In effect they were reasserting their honor and trying to recover that which the rape had temporarily negated. In their petitions the word *honor* is not a synonym of virginity but rather means virtue. The act of rape potentially put them in the category of women who were not modest or circumspect and thus succumbed to seductions and attacks, so to report the rape was to remove themselves from this group and reaffirm their virtue and honor.

This construct perhaps becomes clearer in the case of married women who only very reluctantly reported rape. María Antonia, a mestiza from the city of Puebla, did not report the fact that she was gang-raped and beaten severely on the night of September 19, 1784. She did not want her husband to know, because the circumstances did not cast her in a virtuous light. Her husband sent her out on an errand at six o'clock in the evening; she was already a little drunk. On her return she met a male friend who invited her to drink some pulque. They went to a tavern on the outskirts of town and drank a little. Three men then arrived who chased away her male friend and grabbed her, took away the knife she was carrying, dragged her some distance away, and then both beat her and raped her many times. Yet if her rapists had not then proceeded to kill another man, María Antonia would never have told this tale; the authorities approached her as a witness to murder, not as a victim of rape. She was in fact a most reluctant witness, more worried about the impression her conduct previous to the rape would make on her husband and the community.[35] In contrast María Gertrudis, an Indian from Tlayacapa, made the report without the support, the consent, or even the knowledge of her husband. She stated "so that my husband does not suffer any more than already, I have not told him of the infamies that they committed with me," but she was clear as to the crime: "the theft of her honor, her goods, with the additional crime of force."[36] María Antonia de Acosta, Spanish and a married woman, described the man who tried to rape her as the "offender of my honor."[37] These women reported the rapes because they believed that their honor was at stake, yet this was not the equivalent of virginity. Thus honor must here be equated with virtue; by succumbing to a rape, they had been placed in the unpleasant category of women who did not enjoy the respect of the community. The only redress they had was to clarify the circumstances of the rape and make sure that their conduct was not considered to be lacking in modesty or circumspection.

WOMEN AND HONOR

The explicit desire to maintain personal and family honor permeated colonial Mexican society. This discourse was neither limited to the upper classes nor solely to men, although class or gender could alter the perceptions of those involved. That women should be concerned with the maintenance of their sexual honor should not come as a surprise, but the direct, active, and very often violent manner in which they engaged in the protection of both their reputations and their chastity must also be recognized. Apart from personal defense, women were also adamant in the preservation of family or household honor. This role is one that traditionally has been associated only with men. Clearly such a limited vision of colonial society must be expanded to accommodate a more active and aggressive role for many women.

The women described in this essay reacted to two different sets of problems.

They acted in response to an insult or a transgression that offended their honor, or they tried to hide situations that would dishonor them or their family. In the first instance, they lashed out at those who showed disrespect by gossip, by physical proximity, by outright insults, or by refusing to recognize their social standing. These confrontations were attempts to guarantee their place in the hierarchy of their particular society and to ensure that their honor was accepted. The second set of problems followed a different logic. Women tried to prevent a loss of honor by concealing illegitimate pregnancies by infanticide, for example. When men seduced or raped them, these women or their families tried to ensure that marriage covered up their lack of virginity.

The strategies elected by these various women depended upon their relative status within the social hierarchy. When confronted by a transgression committed by someone deemed socially inferior, many women used violence. The distinction between two women such as Luciana and Marta María may not have been recognized by the elite, because the gradations within the lower classes were of no concern to them, but they certainly existed in the minds of the participants. Therefore plebeian women acted in ways similar to those of elite women when facing an insult from a social inferior. But the response to this violence by the victim was usually to refer the matter to the courts. In fact for lower status women, recourse to the judicial system was the only acceptable route when confronting a person with greater social standing.

If we return for a moment to the edifying story with which this essay began, we might say that these women were trying to hold Honor very tightly by its hand. They were worried that if they let go, they would never find it again. Yet as seen in this essay and those of Twinam and Nazzari, above, honor was not as fragile a quality as the editors of magazines for elite ladies would have us believe. In fact there were many avenues open to both elite and plebeian women for defending their honor and recovering it, even when it had been challenged. Honor might not have a sign, like Fire and Water, but it most definitely could be found again.

NOTES

Research for this paper was supported by generous grants from the Social Sciences and Humanities Research Council of Canada and the GR-6 fund of Carleton University.

1. Conde Gaspar Gozzi, *La semana de las señoritas mejicanas,* (Mexico City: Imprenta de Juan R. Navarro, 1852), 4:28; see also Lee Michael Penyak, "Criminal Sexuality in Central Mexico, 1750–1850" (Ph.D. diss., University of Connecticut, 1993), 39.

2. The concept of honor as derived from Spanish and wider Mediterranean culture is

probably best described by Julian Pitt-Rivers, "Honour and Social Status," in *Honour and Shame: The Values of Mediterranean Society,* ed. J. G. Peristiany (London: Weidenfeld and Nicolson, 1965); for colonial Latin America, some excellent discussions are found in Patricia Seed, *To Love, Honor, and Obey in Colonial Mexico, Conflict over Marriage Choice, 1574–1821* (Stanford, CA: Stanford University Press, 1988); Ramón Gutiérrez, *When Jesus Came, the Corn Mothers Went Away: Marriage, Sexuality, and Power in New Mexico, 1500–1846* (Stanford, CA: Stanford University Press, 1991); Ann Twinam, "Honor, Sexuality, and Illegitimacy in Colonial Spanish America," in *Sexuality and Marriage in Colonial Latin America,* ed. Asunción Lavrin (Lincoln: University of Nebraska Press, 1989), 118–55; and Richard Boyer, *Lives of the Bigamists: Family, Marriage and Community in Colonial Mexico* (Albuquerque: University of New Mexico Press, 1995).

3. Archivo General de la Nación (hereafter AGN), Civil, legajo 23, parte 2, carpeta A, expediente 8, 1801.

4. AGN, Criminal, volumen 27, exp.8, folios 230v–236, Teotihuacán, 1773; AGN, Criminal, vol. 41, exp. 25, fols. 389–389v, 1741, Xochimilco; AGN, Criminal, vol. 27, exp. 14, fols. 495–498v, October 16, 1802, Teotihuacán; AGN, Criminal, vol. 193, exp. 5, fols. 50–55, 1778, Texcoco. See also Gutiérrez, *When Jesus Came,* 222, 223, for comments on the role of gossip in small communities.

5. Gutiérrez, *When Jesus Came,* 203–6, 208; Susan Socolow, "Women and Crime: Buenos Aires, 1757–97," *Journal of Latin American Studies* 12 (1980): 49, says that hair cutting branded women as morally loose.

6. AGN, Criminal, vol. 41, exp. 25, fols. 389–389v.

7. The fact that a woman was assigned to live in her household is also significant, because it means that the authorities considered her home to be an honorable place.

8. AGN, Criminal, vol. 27, exp. 14, fols. 495–498v, October 16, 1802, from the testimony of José de Alfaro, and fols. 497v–498, October 17, 1802, the report of the surgeon.

9. James Scott, *Domination and the Arts of Resistance: Hidden Transcripts* (New Haven, CT: Yale University Press, 1990), might echo this explanation for the strong reaction of doña Teresa and company. Perhaps such vehemence arose because the Spanish women felt threatened by a breaching of what Scott calls the "hidden transcript."

10. AGN, Criminal, vol. 27, exp. 14, fol. 498v, 1802.

11. AGN, Criminal, vol. 27, exp. 14, fol. 499–499v, October 18, 1802.

12. AGN, Criminal, vol. 124, exp. 12, fols. 136–48, 1807.

13. AGN, Criminal, vol. 27, exp. 8, fols. 230–231v, 1773.

14. AGN, Criminal, vol. 206, exp. 4, fols. 36–42.

15. AGN, Criminal, vol. 131, exp. 27, fols. 425–80, 1802.

16. AGN, Criminal, vol. 80, exp. 10, fols. 290–358, 1808.

17. The literature on objections to marriage usually concentrates on racial questions, but the morality especially of lower-class women is mentioned by Susan M. Socolow, "Acceptable Partners: Marriage Choice in Colonial Argentina, 1778–1810," in *Sexuality and Marriage in Colonial Latin America,* ed. by Asunción Lavrin (Lincoln: University of Nebraska, 1990), 220, as a rationale for the opposition of parents to a marriage.

18. Twinam, "Honor, Sexuality, and Illegitimacy"; and Socolow, "Women and Crime,"

226, discuss premarital sex. Seed, *To Honor and Obey;* Verena Martínez-Alier, *Marriage, Class and Colour in Nineteenth-Century Cuba: A Study of Racial Attitudes and Sexual Values in a Slave Society* (Ann Arbor: University of Michigan Press, 1989); and Socolow, "Acceptable Partners," all discuss the opposition of parents to prospective sons-in-law or daughters-in-law.

19. AGN, Criminal, vol. 40, exp. 16, fols. 375–406v, 1809.

20. Ana María Atondo Rodríguez, "De la perversión de la práctica a la perversión del discurso: La fornicación," in *De la santidad a la perversión o de porqué no se cumplía la ley de Dios en la sociedad novohispana* (Mexico City, 1985), 144, states that "[i]t is important to emphasize that in this period, the word *soltera* had a particular connotation, and it meant that the woman was not a virgin and engaged in (or was likely to engage in) illicit relationships" (my translation).

21. Testimony of José Castro, AGN, Criminal, vol. 40, exp. 16, fols. 40–89, 1809.

22. AGN, Criminal, vol. 40, exp. 16, fols. 402–4v., 1809.

23. AGN, Criminal, vol. 40, exp. 16, fols 375–78v, 1809.

24. Twinam, "Honor, Sexuality, and Illegitimacy"; Seed, *To Honor, and Obey.*

25. I have not been able to locate many cases dealing with infanticide, but my impressions as a whole are based upon the following documentation: AGN, Criminal, vol. 68, exp. 7, fols. 220–50, 1819; AGN, Criminal, vol. 98, exp. 16, fols. 412–14v, 1796; AGN, Criminal, vol. 98, exp. 9, fols. 230–52, 1807; AGN, Criminal, vol. 52, exp. 12, fols. 478–84v, 1807; AGN, Criminal, vol. 222, exp. 16, fols. 211–22, 1811; and AGN, Criminal, vol. 251, exp. 10, fols. 275–305, 1806.

26. Kristin Ruggiero, "Honor, Maternity, and the Disciplining of Women: Infanticide in Late Nineteenth-Century Buenos Aires," *Hispanic American Historical Review* 72 (3) (1992): 353–73, makes the connection between infanticide and the preservation of female honor.

27. AGN, Criminal, vol. 68, exp. 7, fols. 227–28, 1819.

28. AGN, Criminal vol. 68, exp. 7, fols. 233–37, 1820.

29. AGN, Criminal vol. 98, exp. 9, fols. 243–44v, 1808.

30. Pitt-Rivers, "Honour and Social Status," 47, explains that this logic comes from the Spanish code of honor, in which "the defiled one should be the object of contempt, not the defiler." See also AGN, Criminal, vol. 91, exp. 15 bis, fols. 337–39v, 1801; AGN, Criminal, vol. 123, exp. 29, fols. 360–63v, 1816; AGN, Criminal, vol. 143, exp. 1, fols. 1–26, 1760; AGN, Criminal, vol. 264, exp. 1, fols. 1–37, 1756; AGN, Criminal, vol. 29, exp. 11, fols. 204–49, 1743; AGN, Criminal, vol. 11, exp. 26, fols. 411–413, 1748.

31. Gutiérrez, *When Jesus Came,* 213, discusses this contradiction. He says that men enhanced their honor by sexual conquest of women and the concomitant dishonoring of another man but jealously guarded the sexual purity of their own women.

32. AGN, Criminal, vol. 29, exp. 11, fols. 205–205v, 1743. The rape of Michaela María, ten years old, by her uncle shows some similar overtones. In this case her aunt whipped her when she discovered her husband raping the girl. AGN, Criminal, vol. 672, exp. 8, fols. 158–66, 1740.

33. Patricia Seed, "Narratives of Don Juan: The Language of Seduction in Seventeenth-Century Hispanic Literature and Society," *Journal of Social History* 26 (4) (Summer 1993): 752, makes this connection between honor and virginity. Fatima Mernissi, *Beyond the Veil:*

Male-Female Dynamics in Modern Muslim Society (Bloomington: University of Indiana Press, 1987, 2d ed.), 103, provides an example of the same type of equivalence between honor and virginity in modern Morocco.

34. AGN, Criminal, vol. 480, exp. 4, fol. 186, 1799, petition of doña María Candelaria de Castro; AGN, Criminal, vol. 105, exp. 10, fol. 308–308v, 1792; AGN, Criminal, vol. 105, exp. 15, fols. 335–37, 1775; AGN, Criminal, vol. 141, exp. 7, fols. 191v–192, 1808; AGN, Criminal, vol. 141, exp. 25, fols. 544–544v.

35. AGN, Criminal, vol. 656, exp. 2, fols. 2–51, 1784.

36. AGN, Criminal, vol. 228, exp. 1, fols. 1–2, 1766.

37. AGN, Criminal, vol. 194, exp. 17, fols. 261–62v, 1778.

38. Gutiérrez, *When Jesus Came,* 185, 208, 210, gives a few examples of jealous behavior on the part of men; William B. Taylor, *Drinking, Homicide, and Rebellion in Colonial Mexican Villages* (Stanford, CA: Stanford University Press, 1979), 95, also comments on jealousy as a particularly male reason for attacks.

39. Some examples are: AGN, Criminal, vol. 18, exp. 18, fols. 552–54v, 1807; AGN, Criminal, vol. 180, exp. 12, fols. 302–50, 1806; AGN, Criminal, vol. 80, exp. 14, fols. 466–91, 1815.

40. Ruth Behar, "Sex and Sin, Witchcraft and the Devil in Late-Colonial Mexico," *American Ethnologist* 14 (1) (1987): 47–48, notes that in the use of pacts with the devil, women wished to attack their husband's mistresses but not their husbands. She believes that this corresponds to the presence of "different codes for men and women concerning permissible physical violence."

41. AGN, Criminal, vol. 18, exp. 18, fols. 552–54v, 1807.

CHAPTER EIGHT

HONOR AMONG SLAVES

SANDRA LAUDERDALE GRAHAM

Consider the following story. Henriqueta Maria da Conceição and Rufino Maria Baleta had married in January 1855, in the parish church of Santa Rita. Although they lived in the parish, they were not from there. Both were Africans from the Mina Coast of western Africa, shipped as slaves to Bahia on Brazil's northeastern coast and from there sold south to the imperial capital of Rio de Janeiro. Rufino still wore the facial scars that identified him as belonging to a particular African *nação,* or ethnic and cultural group, although the scribe of the case saw no reason to inquire and record which one. Some eight or nine years earlier, in the mid-1840s, and as slaves belonging to different owners, Rufino and Henriqueta had become lovers. Before marrying they had acquired their freedom, first Henriqueta and then Rufino. Each having been baptized while still in Bahia and then married in the church, these Africans professed at least the externals of the Catholic faith. In June 1856 only a year and half after they married, Henriqueta petitioned for a *divórcio ecclesiástico,* or ecclesiastical divorce. Although in nineteenth-century Brazil the Catholic church formally and routinely used the word *divórcio,* its meaning is more accurately rendered by "church-granted separation." As decreed by the Council of Trent in the sixteenth century, separation did not dissolve a marriage and hence neither partner was permitted to marry again; but a separation approved by the church did allow a couple to proceed to a civil court for division of their property, as in fact Henriqueta and Rufino did.

As Henriqueta and Rufino told their story—or, rather, as they told competing versions of their story—in the course of the proceedings of two court cases, we gain access to their renderings of one another's conduct and their differing reasons for ending a relationship that had lasted more than ten years.[1] As we listen to their accounts, they instruct us about their expectations of—and their perceived disappointments regarding—the conduct of married and domestic life in mid-nineteenth-century Brazil. I suggest that what was at issue for this couple in their domestic dealings reflects the concerns of thousands of others who lived in like circumstances. From their allegations we can begin to elucidate a code of personal ethics or honor as it applied in the lives of slaves and former slaves. How did such people suppose they should act toward one another? What were the elements that can be said to comprise such a code of conduct? Honor can be seen to operate in two domains: a civic domain of political action that is principally the reserve of men and a domestic domain in which family and the relations between women and men are central. Both are public and both have consequences, but of the two only notions of domestic honor fully include women. It is this domestic dimension and particularly the rules of honorable married life accepted by the partners themselves that concern me.

There is nothing that initially directs us to scan the past for demonstrations of honor among slaves or the poor or even centrally among women. Honor, we are led to think, is a matter of contestation among men with at least a credible claim to reputable status. As noted above in chapter three by Ann Twinam, our expectations for what honor might signify derive from work by anthropologists and sociologists on contemporary Mediterranean societies, ranging from Algiers to Greece and the Iberian Peninsula, and especially from what has come to be regarded as the classic formulation by Julian Pitt-Rivers (also discussed by Geoffrey Spurling in chapter two, above).[2] Although Pitt-Rivers himself studied village life in the region of Andalusia in modern Spain and readily acknowledged that the meanings of honor vary from one period or region to another and from one class to another, he nevertheless insisted that honor possesses a "general structure." It is a term of evaluation by which an individual measures himself and is measured by society. Honor, he wrote, "is [a man's] estimation of his own worth, his *claim* to pride, but it is also the acknowledgment of that claim, his excellence recognized by society, his *right* to pride."[3] From that starting point Pitt-Rivers then sketched what he took as the pattern of meanings that comprised a Mediterranean code of honor. Because I want to draw from that proposed pattern in order to discover distinctive Brazilian meanings, it is worth reviewing here.

In societies ordered by status, the well-born are assumed to possess by inheritance the "character and sentiments" appropriate to their rank, which will be seen in their conduct. Thus a man of high position *is* a virtuous man. Honor both reflects and validates one's position in society. But status is never entirely secure, and a person is always measured against those with more and those with less—that is, everyone except king or pope simultaneously occupies a position superior to some and inferior to others. According to Pitt-Rivers status and the honor that attaches to it are always contested and always competed for among those who are near but never exact equals. Their competition results in the ritualized behavior by which one man's honor is affronted and must then be defended, with humiliation imposed or satisfaction gained as the affronted emerges either as victor, his reputation enhanced, or as the vanquished, the superior status of his contender acknowledged. To be effective both challenge and response must be publicly performed, for it is a matter of public judgment to decide the extent of the damage inflicted and whether the avenging action has restored honor. In this way, says Pitt-Rivers, "public opinion forms . . . a tribunal before which claims to honor are brought. . . [4] Matters of honor are public in the further sense that individuals are not autonomous but members of families, lineages, villages, neighborhoods—that is, members of some group larger than themselves whom they represent and whose collective honor they can affirm or impair. Individual action carries weighty public consequences.

In this schema, honor has the further dimension of differing according to gender: male honor differs from female honor and therefore, Pitt-Rivers claimed, implies "quite different modes of conduct." A man is said to have honor and is obliged to defend his honor and that of his family, while a woman must conserve her purity or sexual virtue. She too protects the honor of the family, for by guarding her purity she additionally assures the purity of the family bloodline. A woman is said to have shame, or in Portuguese *vergonha* and in Spanish *vergüenza*, a term with several meanings that shade into one another. Shame is a "concern for repute," the sentiment that "makes a person sensitive to the pressure exerted by public opinion," and thus to have shame is to be honorable and applies equally to men and women; but shame can also denote qualities of modesty or decorum that belong exclusively to women. A shameless woman acts without regard for her honor or that of her family; she is without honor. But either men or women may be shamed or forced to recognize that they have been humiliated by an affront from someone else—in a word, dishonored.[5]

What matters here are the opposing clusters of characteristics ascribed to men and women. While a woman's sexual purity requires restraint, a man's sexual potency requires courage or manliness in the defense not only of his own honor but of that of the women of his family (mother, wife, sister, daughter) whose purity he must defend against the aggressions of other males; although women are thought too frail to defend themselves alone, it should also be noted that a woman must fiercely resist any threatened violation of her body however futile her effort. By insisting on female purity, men render themselves vulnerable to the actions of women. A wife's adultery not only infringes on her husband's rights but demonstrates his failure to protect his family, for the responsibility to prevent sexual violation falls to the protecting male (husband, father, brother, uncle), not to the would-be adulterer. A compromised husband is publicly ridiculed while the adulterer, although he risks being found out and punished, is admired for his success. Honor is largely male business, with men as the contenders and defenders of honor, women the prize. Women's usual field of action is strictly circumscribed, characterized by restraint and passivity.[6]

For their part historians have searched for contests of honor among the high-born, for whom the stakes of marriage, lineage, and inheritance were high. In these histories women figure, but only secondarily, as the contributors of dowries and family connections and as bearers of children. Lusanna, a woman of beauty and cunning but only middling wealth and family name, earned the starring role in one account of "love and marriage in Renaissance Florence" precisely because she nearly succeeded in imposing her marriage on Giovanni, the young nobleman who outranked her by far and who must, for the honor of his family, marry a woman of the nobility. Francisco Nogerol, a Spaniard who sought his fortune in the Peru of the Pizarro brothers, did even better by marrying two women of wealth and honorable reputation, causing Beatriz, the first of the two wives, to pursue relentlessly a suit of bigamy against him. If Nogerol remained the principal figure in the account, the women—his mother, his two religious sisters, the two wives—and especially the second wife, Catalina, emerge as resourceful, competent, and determined, with their own very clear and distinct understandings of honor. Against Beatriz, Catalina defended her marriage to Francisco through the courts all the way to the pope, with the hint that she had perhaps bribed even His Holiness.[7] In matters of honor historians have largely ignored the poor, assuming they had no interest vested in family, property, or reputation.

In hasty strokes these are the lines that describe a model of Mediterranean honor. As a colony of Portugal and thereby belonging broadly within the boundaries of Mediterranean culture, Brazil inherited both Iberian customs and a formal body of law based on Roman law, codified in 1603 as the Codigo Philippino, which at least influenced colonial practices of honor. A woman who married someone of lower social 'condition' without her parents' permission and by so doing brought discredit not only to herself but her family could be disinherited, a severe penalty in a society that by law stipulated equal inheritance for all children, male and female. Or, seduced on promise of marriage, a woman could demand that her seducer provide her with a dowry that would compensate, if not altogether cancel, her nonvirgin status and enable her to seek an alternative husband. But the law further specified that such a woman could only claim a dowry appropriate to her father's status and no greater. To that extent the law protected men against calculating women who might be willing to trade virginity for handsome dowries and the possibility of marrying better than their origins would otherwise permit.[8] The Codigo Philippino, although modified first by Portuguese laws and then by Brazilian laws following the colony's independence, remained the legal basis for regulating marriage, family property, and inheritance during the empire and into the early decades of the republic when, in 1916, a new civil code was promulgated.[9]

Despite these long-persistent ties to an Iberian past, what set Brazil decisively apart was its pervasive reliance on the institution of slavery and on the African men and women forcibly transported across the Atlantic and their descendants, whose labor sustained the vast quantities of sugar, tobacco, gold, and coffee exported to European and North American markets. In the slightly more than three hundred years from the 1530s until the early 1850s, when the slave trade was effectively halted, it is estimated that some three to four million Africans were shipped to Brazil. The presence of slaves was pervasive. Slaves planted and cut cane, they pressed, boiled, and strained the juice; they stood knee-deep in streams panning for gold; they planted, hoed, picked, dried, sacked, and transported coffee in 132-pound bags, permanently damaging hip and knee joints. Through city streets daytime slaves carried parcels, jugs of water, sides of beef, and baskets of bread, or shouldered the curtained sedan chairs that bore privileged women on outings, or pulled the wheeled chairs that moved whites up the steep *ladeiras,* or hillsides, of Salvador; at night they carried barrels of excrement to the beach for dumping. Slave men were stevedores, boatmen, blacksmiths, fishermen, bricklayers; slave women cooked, sewed, cleaned, hauled water, and scrubbed laundry at city fountains, nursed babies not their own, served as ladies' maids, and were sent as prostitutes to market commercial sex. Africans and Brazilian-born blacks also formed families and fought to keep them together; some married but most did not, and some baptized their children and in so doing connected themselves through Catholic ritual to godparents who were themselves frequently slaves. Some were granted freedom, more often women than men, and creoles more than Africans; others managed to buy their freedom. Some rebelled or returned their own variation of violence against their owners, but most did not. Most slaves lived ordinary lives, laced as such lives were with routine practices of violence against them.[10] As human property slaves constituted one distinct and not entirely fixed ranking in a finely ranked society. From their numbers came the freed slaves who combined with free-born Brazilians (whose skins ranged in color from black to white) and with ever-increasing numbers of Portuguese immigrant men and women to comprise the largely illiterate, often unmarried working poor of cities and rural areas.

I want to extend and qualify the standard model of Mediterranean honor to include just such persons. In this variation, slaves and freed persons became their own court of public opinion; they decided who measured up and who did not. Those who say that only the privileged made—or had reason to make—claims to honor will find it odd to search for evidence of such a code of right conduct among the lowly company of slaves and freed persons. We are more accustomed to examine these groups in relation to those who exercised power over them—master, overseer, employer, government official, police. The excuse presumably is that the sources do not exist. I would reply that as historians we have severely limited what we see by our insistence on understanding slaves principally as victims. When instead we look for the rules by which slaves and freed persons governed relations among themselves, we discover that the sources (however fragmented) are many and rich.

The principal sources on which I rely here are the written texts of two court cases. In the first Henriqueta successfully petitioned an ecclesiastical court for permanent separation from her husband, the stated grounds being physical abuse. The second case followed from the first. Having been granted separation from her marriage with Rufino (a separation of "bed and board," as the church worded it), Henriqueta gained the further right to request a division of their conjugal property in a civil court.[11] Such cases are themselves rare, for in the hundreds of ecclesiastical divorce records for the two cities of Salvador and Rio de Janeiro, only a very few concern African freed persons. And because they are rare, the cases are immeasurably valuable for what they can be made to reveal about the lives of persons who otherwise would remain obscure to us. These special texts nevertheless require caution in their use as historical evidence. That such texts were produced at all requires explanation. A trial in Brazil was conducted by the presentation of written testimony and argument by attorneys to a panel of judges. We should not imagine a courtroom confrontation between contending parties. Instead in differently intimidating settings, accuser and accused separately made their statements in response to a prepared roster of questions, as did any witnesses subsequently called. In ecclesiastical cases it was usual for depositions to be taken by the vigário geral do bispado (vicar general of the diocese)at his official residence or, in large cities such as Rio de Janeiro, at the offices of the church court. Either way a scribe (typically more than one even in a single case) recorded testimony as the words spoken directly by the witness, but with the difference that he converted them to third person. I have avoided the awkwardness of referring to Henriqueta and Rufino as "plaintiff" and "defendant," and instead attribute directly to Henriqueta and Rufino the phrases I quote from their statements. Because the attorneys wrote the arguments and counterarguments that were incorporated into the record of the case, authorship of their statements is less problematic. The result of trial by written deposition and brief is a dense text, each case numbering about 30 manuscript sheets written front and back, for a total of some 120 pages. Yet for all the richness that such records contain, much is necessarily lost to us. We cannot recall the nervous or defiant gestures, the false starts and uncompleted sentences, a rush of words finally given a hearing or words spoken so softly as to be barely audible. Some of what we would most like to know is flattened out or tidied up, filtered through scribes and the requirements of legal language. From what remains we piece together as much as we are ever likely to discover of these individuals and their actions.

RUFINO AND HENRIQUETA

The setting for Rufino and Henriqueta's story was the parish of Santa Rita, an older part of Rio de Janeiro that on its northern and eastern edges bordered the wide-spreading Guanabara Bay. The point, capped by São Bento Hill and the Benedictine monastery, with its magnificent views of bay, open ocean, and rain-forested granite hills, belonged to the arsenal of the navy. Conceição Hill separated interior streets from the northern waterfront of Vallongo Beach, with its stretch of docks and warehouses that served not only international ships but also those that brought coffee from the Paraíba Valley across the bay or up the southern coast for marketing and export. The Praça Municipal, near the docks and the customs building, together with the city's central market on the southeastern edge, tied parish life to the sea and to commerce. Among streets and narrow alleyways with such names as the Rua dos Pescadores (Street of the Fishermen) and the Beco das Canoas (Alley of the Canoes), were the Rua do Jogo da Bolla (Street of the Ball Game), the Rua dos Cachorros (Street of the Dogs), and the rowdy Alleyway of the Braganças, famous as a hangout for runaway slaves despite bearing the name of the imperial royal family. The Chapel of Santa Rita, constructed in 1721, became a parish church with five altars in 1753, when Santa Rita separated from Candelária. A fountain, built in front of the church where the bodies of newly arrived slaves had once been buried in the cemetery of the *pretos novos*, or new blacks, brought the first fresh water to the parish beginning in 1840, only a few years before Henriqueta and Rufino began their lives there.[12]

By the nineteenth century Santa Rita was no longer an outlying area of royal land grants and large estates.[13] It had become a place for trade, shipping, and business. Wealthy coffee agents might keep quarters on the upper floors of their warehouses where planters could stay while in the city briefly on business, but most housing in the parish was for working people, at or near their work. Locals, worried about the wholesomeness of their bread, complained that bakers slept shifts in filthy rooms at the back of the bakery. We know that Henriqueta and Rufino did not live in one of the parish's seventeen tenement houses. And it would have been unusual if as Africans they had, for the tenement population was overwhelmingly Portuguese, then Brazilian, and only marginally (about 6 per cent) African.[14] Instead the couple rented a house on the Rua do Fogo, earning part of their own rent of sixteen *mil-réis*, or about nine dollars per month, by subletting rooms to tenants for half that amount.[15]

Densely populated and commercial, Santa Rita could almost be said to belong to the slaves and free and freed blacks—that is, the poor who worked and lived there—together with the merchants who operated large and small houses of commerce. On the "Nominal Roll of the Business Houses of Santa Rita Parish for the Year 1840," among some 758 businesses, appear the names of an English clockmaker, a Spanish tailor, a German wholesaler of dry goods, a Portuguese shoemaker and carpenter, and a Brazilian woman who owned a coffee warehouse. Candles, soap, and cigars were manufactured there. Barrel-makers, bakers, butchers of beef and pork, barbers (including one who sold leeches), a sawyer, sugar refiners, and sellers of flour and pottery—all could be found there. There were taverns, with and without food, cheap eating houses, and confectionery shops. Women were among those who owned and rented out wagons for transporting goods across the city or canoes for use on the bay.[16]

Both Rufino and Henriqueta worked, he selling fish and poultry at the Praça do Mercado, she as a vendor of fruits and vegetables (Brazilians called such produce *quitanda*, and those who sold it *quitandeiras*). Each would have found both company and competition from other Africans and *crioulos*, or Brazilian-born blacks, in pursuit of similar livelihoods. Quitanda sellers, a few more men than women, were scattered throughout Santa Rita; nearly every street listed at least one, and most had several. Some, like Antonio Francisco da Fonseca, a freed African from the Congo, specialized in "greens"; others, like the Brazilian woman Maria Emilia on the Alley of João Baptista, sold only in "small quantities." Of the sixty-three quitandeiros in the parish in 1841 (thirty-five men and twenty-eight women), more than half were either African or locally born blacks. Sixteen of the twenty-seven Africans were women. With an effective end of the African trade in slaves to Brazil in the early 1850s, the Africanness of the city's population would have begun to decline, so that by the time of her separation, Henriqueta might have been able to notice slightly fewer fellow Africans in the parish. The 1841 figures nevertheless provide us with a rough approximation of the presence of women like herself who sold produce. They include only the regular vendors with stalls permanent enough to be assigned a street number, such as Maria Perpetua, an African from Benguella, who sold greens from her place on the Rua do Livramento, number 58.[17] Those more casual sellers who worked the streets selling produce from wide baskets balanced on their heads did not appear in the parish roll.

Neither did men like Rufino, who hawked fish and poultry. A city ordinance required that they sell not from private stalls but at the central market where, local authorities supposed, regular hours and standards of cleanliness could more effectively be imposed. Without a complete census of occupations, we cannot know reliably how Rufino's occupation compared with those of other men. As an imperfect guide we can refer instead to a count of the tenement population made in 1857 and a tally of their occupations. Of the seventeen vendors of fish and chickens counted, thirteen lived in Santa Rita.[18] We have no way to know how many other peddlers there were who, like Rufino, lived outside the tenements, but the parish's proximity to the market suggests that they were numerous. Selling at the central market not only put Rufino among other slaves and freedmen, but also among those men of color who were notorious for being a tough crowd. They earned the name *capoeiras* from the closed baskets they carried on their heads, in which they transported live birds to and from market. The term *capoeira* came to refer to those skilled in the highly disciplined performance of a deadly fighting style that involved the dazzling use of feet and usually a knife. Capoeiras organized into gangs, their skills hired by politicians to deliver the vote in local elections, but they also were known to taunt, brutally beat, and even murder lone and vulnerable slaves. Contemporaries were convinced that market men doubled as dangerous capoeiras, although Rufino himself was not so accused.[19]

Rufino and Henriqueta's occupations were standard among the working poor. It was work requiring experience and some capital but not an apprenticed skill. Of all slum dwellers in the city identified in 1857 with an occupation, 110 men and women were counted as produce vendors; of those, 65 women and men, or 59 percent, came from the Santa Rita tenements. Only 13 men appeared as sellers of fish or poultry. If we consider the total working population of the parish of more than fifteen thousand men and women, the number of vendors would of course increase. In 1857 selling produce ranked third after sewing and washing clothes as occupations listed for tenement women, while most tenement men labored as skilled artisans, worked in manufacturing, or hauled goods.[20] We would expect Rufino as male and husband

Figure 30. A quitandeira *sells goods from a tray, wearing a shawl and turban made from the brightly striped cloth known as* pano da costa, *or cloth from the coast. (Painting,* Platz in Rio de Janeiro, *by Eduard Hildebrandt, 1844.)*

Figure 31. A street vendor in Brazil could work for a master or for himself. Such work, however, was key to respect and to a man's position in his household and local society. (Painting, Platz in Rio de Janeiro, *by Eduard Hildebrandt, 1844.)*

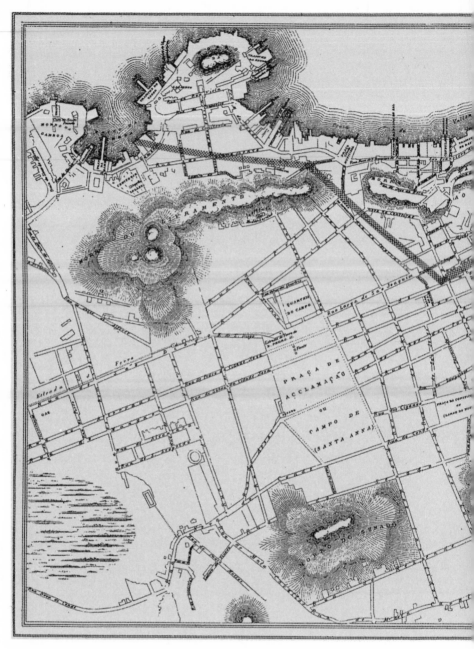

Figure 32. Rio de Janeiro was divided into several parishes. The parish of Santa Rita, where the drama of Henriqueta and Rufino's marriage and subsequent ecclesiastical divorce took place, is to the north of the heavy boundary marked on this map. (Guia e plano do Rio de Janeiro, publicado por A. M. McKinnery, Roberto Leeder, *Rio de Janeiro, 1858.*)

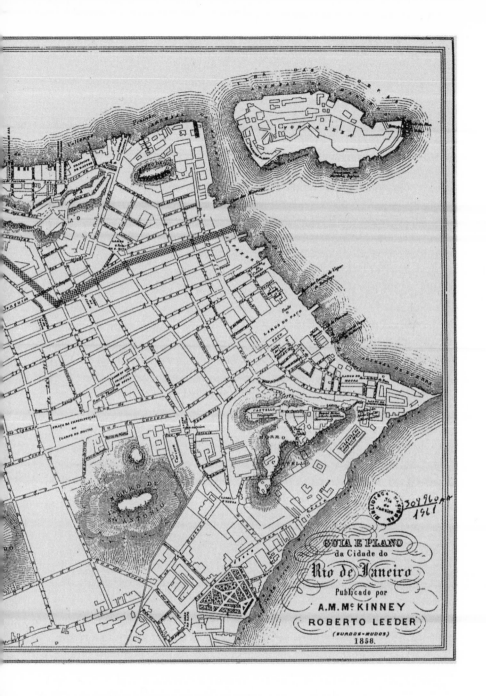

GUIA E PLANO
da Cidade do
Rio de Janeiro
Publicado por
A.M.McKINNEY
ROBERTO LEEDER
(SURDOS-MUDOS)
1858.

to work, but Henriqueta's working should hardly surprise us either. Poor, black, first a slave and then a freed woman, Henriqueta can be counted among the thousands of women in Rio de Janeiro who worked to support themselves and their families. From the census of the city conducted in 1870, some thirteen years after Henriqueta sued for divorce, but the first year in which occupations were counted citywide, 63 percent of free, working-age women fifteen years or older worked for wages. Among slave girls and women, for whom I estimate that working age was eight years and older, the proportion listed with an occupation was predictably higher, 88 percent.[21]

In Santa Rita Henriqueta and Rufino lived among their own kind—the African born. In 1849, about six years before Henriqueta married Rufino and two or three years after they became lovers, and while they were still slaves, Henriqueta would have been one of the 3,082 African women in the parish. African women figured as 63 percent of all slave women and as many as 76 percent of all the *libertas,* or freed, women. That Santa Rita was home to more freed African women than to freed creole—that is, Brazilian-born—women is surprising, because generally more creole slaves than Africans were favored with manumission. But if we consider only African women in the parish, fewer than one-fifth had gained their freedom, a percentage that mirrored almost exactly the figures for the city as a whole. Libertas and slave women accounted for nearly 42 percent of all women in Santa Rita and 44 percent of all women in the city in 1849. Rufino was one of an even larger number of African men in the parish, some 7,135. Among the men Africans made up 79 percent of all slaves and 83 percent of all *libertos.* Among all African men in the parish, even fewer—only 8 percent—were freed men in 1849, similar to the 9 percent for the entire city.[22]

In Santa Rita in 1849 African women accounted for nearly two-thirds of all colored women, and African men 80 percent of all colored men. Combining women and men, Africans represented nearly 75 percent of all persons of color in the parish. The presence of Africans began to taper off, however, as older Africans died and were no longer replaced with newly imported slaves, while at the same time the creole population of locally born slaves gradually increased. By 1872, the year of the first national census in Brazil, only about 2,000 African men and women, slave or freed, lived in Santa Rita, compared with more than 10,000 in 1849. The decrease in the number of African freed persons was much less marked: the 1,124 libertos in 1849 had diminished to 716 in 1872. By 1857 Henriqueta and Rufino would have witnessed the beginnings of that slow shift from African to creole.[23]

As married people, and especially as Africans and former slaves who married, Henriqueta and Rufino were among a definite minority. When they married in the church in 1855, they joined the one-third of Santa Rita's popula-

Figure 33. This scene illustrates the disorder of the plaza in front of the church of Santa Rita in Rio de Janeiro. Women and men collect water from the fountain where perhaps they gossip while a band is playing. The fountain replaced a cross, which previously had marked the location of the old slave cemetery. (Eduard Hildebrandt, The Brazil of Eduard Hildebrandt *. . . [Rio de Janeiro, Distribuidora de Servicios de Imprensa, n.d.].)*

tion of free and freed persons who, according to the census in 1849 and the only one available for the period, were married or, as widows or widowers, had once been married. The census did not bother to include married or widowed slaves, although some slaves did marry: records for the years 1840 through 1847 show that sixty-seven marriages among slaves were registered in the parish churches of Rio de Janeiro.[24] Slaves of course could marry only with their master's permission, and that was not always or readily secured. Beyond that, marrying was a costly business that required both partners to present proof of eligibility—that is, proof that they had not married previously or had any living spouse. Proof consisted of statements from the priests in all parishes in which either partner had previously lived as an adult for longer than six months. If challenged a couple had to prove they were not kin within the prohibited degree, cousins for example. Those were difficult proofs for the poor and illiterate to assemble. The stamps and fees could add up to a burdensome and for some a prohibitive amount. Despite such obstacles, Henriqueta and Rufino had married. That a smaller proportion of Santa Rita's population was married than the 44 percent recorded for the city as a whole perhaps reflects the commercial character of the parish and the general poverty of its working population. From the summary figures presented in the 1849 census, we cannot separate out liberto couples from those couples who had never been slaves— that is, former slaves from persons who were born free. Nevertheless Henriqueta and Rufino were not altogether rare in being former slaves and married. The ordinariness and commonality of the external aspects of their lives gives weight to the conviction that their view of things can be generalized beyond their single case.

THE DIVORCE

Henriqueta initiated the petition that brought her case before priests and lawyers with allegations that Rufino beat her, inflicting wounds and bruises so severe that had the situation continued they would have endangered her life. He beat her "atrociously," she alleged, "sometimes with a stick but mostly with fists and kicks." Once after beating her he threw her out into the street in the rain. Another time she was so battered she had to find someone to "apply *ventozas*" (a therapy by which heated glass cups were applied to the skin, creating a partial vacuum as they cooled to draw blood to the surface) "and other cures" to keep her from dying. In these attacks he gave vent to a "dark, irascible temperament." To escape his "clutches" she sometimes went to the house of her *madrinha*, a term that could mean baptismal godmother or sponsor but here referred to a confidant, a protecting and probably somewhat older woman.

Charges of physical cruelty, however grisly, were nevertheless unexceptional and appear routinely in nineteenth-century requests for church-sanctioned separations. Second only after adultery, the church recognized extreme physical abuse as possible grounds for divorce. The Portuguese word used to describe such maltreatment was *sevícias;* it refers precisely to physical harm or cruel punishment done to a subordinate—a husband to his wife, a father to his child, or a master to his slave. Both canon and civil law permitted the male head of household to castigate moderately all those who lived under his roof and authority, including family, servants, dependents, and in the case of Brazil, slaves. But sevícias was seen to exceed the physical chastisement of usual and legitimate "domestic correction" and permitted, even required, intervention.[25]

Rufino predictably denied that he had injured his wife either physically or verbally, a formulaic denial that offered no details by way of explanation or any justification of the kind presented in some cases in which injury was witnessed or acknowledged. Although Rufino's denial recognized implicitly that injury was unacceptable, no one found his statement persuasive. A neighborhood inspector testified that several times neighbors complained of the "disorders" caused by Rufino; his conduct was vile and he maltreated his wife, the inspector reported. By finally refusing to tolerate his beatings and separating herself from him, Henriqueta made clear that such treatment was not a part of married life that she must silently endure. Relief from domestic violence would have had particular resonance for a former slave who might well have known and certainly had reason to fear the casual or calculated violence delivered by an owner. As with other nineteenth-century women who brought charges of physical cruelty, the court arranged for Henriqueta to be "deposited"—that is, in order to ensure a woman's safety during the proceedings, she was sent to live with a respectable guardian, usually a family member or married couple but sometimes a single female relative. The practice was additionally intended to protect a woman's virtue and guard against possible pregnancy and the accusation of bearing an illegitimate child just when questions of property and inheritance were to be settled. Henriqueta was assigned to her madrinha, Joaquina Matildes do Espirito Santo, and her husband, Venancio Francisco dos Santos.

If Henriqueta's case was built formally on allegations of physical harm, both she and Rufino also spoke more passionately about other grievances. Through his defense and counteraccusations and her elaborated replies, we can piece together their revealed understandings of how married life ought to be conducted and their perceived violations of that conduct.

Fundamental to any characterization of the poor as respectable was work. By the fact of working, blacks, immigrants, or former slaves could present themselves as disciplined and reliable persons, distinguishable from the disorderly, from those seen as lazy, the sick and broken people who "lived by their wits," and from the mendicant beggars who were permitted to receive alms from a specified parish church. Those who acquired the valued skills of stonemason, cook, laundress, boat caulker, tailor or seamstress, shoemaker, or stevedore, for example, became the privileged among laboring people. With work came association with an identifiable employer, someone with authority who could ensure a worker's good habits and vouch for her or his trustworthiness. Those who like Rufino and Henriqueta worked only for themselves were more vulnerable to charges of vagrancy. But even they dealt with suppliers, making good on credit received, in turn extending credit to their clients, perhaps renting a stall from which to sell—relationships that were seen to stitch them

Figure 34. Behind the church of Santa Rita the streets are quieter. Some vendors have set up a makeshift stall. The closed basket is of the kind used to transport live birds to market. (Eduard Hildebrandt, The Brazil of Eduard Hildebrandt . . . [Rio de Janeiro, Distribuidora de Servicios de Imprensa, n.d.].)

securely into society. Through work the poor could establish themselves as responsible and respectable, a reputation that had to be earned and demonstrated and did not attach automatically to their status as honor is said to attach to the well-born by virtue of their birth.

Work further enabled both men and women to support their families. As head of the household, a man was obliged to provide for his family, but that did not mean that other family members did not also work and often at a similar trade, which made the household also an economic unit. A man's occupation defined the social place of his household within neighborhood and city, within civil society.

These prescriptions belonged to the larger culture, and Henriqueta took them seriously. According to her Rufino fulfilled none of them. By her account she alone earned the money that sustained them, even the rent for their house, while he "lay around or wandered the streets." When she complained he told her she was "out of line as a woman to want to rule her husband and dare to rebuke him." According to what he called the *lei de brancos*, or law of the whites, by which he meant the rules of common property, half of everything she had belonged to him. And when she replied that he too should work and half of his earnings should go to her, "so that the lei de branco could be justly observed," he hit her. Whenever she came home with money, he immediately seized half, and from the remainder she was left to pay all their expenses. He gave her none of the rent money collected from their subtenants, but neither did he spend it on anything of mutual use. And from a drawer that she kept locked, he took her gold chain. As for his supporting her, that was "laughable," she said, because he refused to work and had nothing that was his.

Against her accusations Rufino tried to defend himself. He claimed that from his earnings he fulfilled his obligation as provider and offered as proof of his "devotion and love" the care he took of his wife's needs. Beyond the necessities he gave her all that would make her "life pleasant" (all this it was added, and probably at the lawyer's dictation, was "in relation to their status as a poor couple and their condition as blacks"). Even while still a slave, he bought her "jewelry, clothes, everything within his power." When she was sick, he called the doctor to bleed her and "to apply leeches and treat her." Being regularly employed hawking fish, he supported them. Henriqueta worked, he said, because she was accustomed to selling quitanda, and when they married, not wanting to cross her—a reference to her strong will—he allowed her to continue, but what she earned was hers for clothes and diversions, never to maintain the household or pay rent. When she lost money, it was he who paid her produce suppliers. He denied piling up debts that she then was forced to pay off. As a parting shot Rufino reminded the judges that Henriqueta had landed in jail—probably the women's section of the fetid Aljube jail, built into the side of Conceição Hill in Santa Rita[26]—and would have been flogged for fighting with "a white man on the Rua Direita . . . in broad daylight and in full view of everybody" had he not gotten her off by explaining that she was his wife and a liberta. That is she was not a black vagabond without family or address, nor was she a slave but a freed woman. Having a husband made her a plausibly respectable woman. A husband could also save the state the trouble of taking charge of an out-of-line wife.

Although the evidence thoroughly discredited Rufino's defense, what matters for us is that he sought to portray himself as a reputable provider. We might say, of course, that he was merely led to that portrayal by a lawyer's adroit questioning, or that prescriptions of hard work and familial care were more imposed on the poor than embraced by them. But from both Henriqueta and Rufino, the language of accusation and counteraccusation is precise and vivid enough to persuade us that each took seriously the scripted roles of steady worker and provider, however imperfectly they fulfilled them. Less believable is Rufino's claim that Henriqueta's earnings were merely frivolous. The domestic economies of the poor required household members to combine their meager incomes. Even if Rufino had acted as provider, it is unlikely that alone he could have maintained them both. Henriqueta expected to work and to contribute her share but vigorously resented bearing the burden alone. Nor did she disguise her contempt for his failings.

If work and family responsibility concerned all the poor of whatever color or condition, only slave women and men shared the particular preoccupation of achieving their legal freedom from bondage. An owner might freely manumit a favored slave to celebrate a grand family occasion, a wedding or baptism, or to reward her for tender care given a child during a prolonged illness, or might specify a slave's release in a last will and testament. More often an owner expected payment, either in cash paid all at once or under an agreement of conditional freedom, by which the slave continued to work at a standard rate for a fixed period, until the purchase price was worked off. A former slave and even someone still a slave might buy another slave's freedom, usually but not always a family member—parent, child, spouse. Whatever rules regulated the buying of freedom by a slave or former slave, they operated informally as accepted customs arrived at over time and understood among themselves, outside the formal jurisdictions of white society.[27]

The record does not explain how Henriqueta came to be freed from her owner, Rosa Maria de Jesus, although the woman's name, not a family name but a chosen association with Christ that was common among poor women, indicates that she herself was scarcely more than poor and almost certainly demanded payment for freeing a slave. By whatever means, Henriqueta became free before Rufino. Over Rufino's freedom they differed bitterly. Rufino insisted he had saved the money for his own manumission. He had turned everything he earned over to the already freed Henriqueta, so that she would make the payment to his owner because, being a slave, he feared having money in his possession. The implication is that he would be suspected of having stolen the money.

Henriqueta put it differently. As a slave Rufino worked *ao ganho*—that is, he was sent by his owner, and licensed by the city, to earn cash by hiring out his labor, returning an agreed amount to his owner.[28] Not only had she paid for his manumission, but she frequently made up the *jornal,* or daily earnings, of eight hundred *réis* Rufino owed his owner, Jozé Maria Marleta, when Rufino failed to earn that much. Eight hundred réis was a good wage for a hired male slave in the 1850s and a substantial amount for her to pay from her earnings. But rather than see him whipped, she paid the balance, sometimes an entire week's worth. And if he could not earn even that much, how, she asked, could he have bought his own freedom?

Freedom did not come cheap. She had paid one *conto* and 400 mil-réis, or about $784, the going rate for a healthy, working-age male slave. It would have drained her resources. For the same amount she could have bought herself a working slave, hired him out, and lived from the income! Evidently she considered the price worth paying; she had bought his freedom, she explained, in obedience to "the impulses of her heart" and so they might be married "in legitimate nuptials." Marriage and freedom were linked in her mind: marriage mattered deeply, but she wanted them to marry only as free persons. That she had to bail him out with his owner and pay for his freedom put him in a bad light as the failed partner in an exchange that belonged—and could only belong—distinctly and particularly to slaves and slave culture.

If the case focuses largely on male failures, Rufino nevertheless had telling things to say about expectations of female conduct. Rufino blamed the "disorder" in their lives on the Mina black woman, Joaquina Matildes do Espirito Santo (because she was an African, we know that she was once enslaved and had become a freed woman), who was Henriqueta's sponsor at their marriage and then assumed the role of madrinha toward Henriqueta. In Rufino's view Joaquina gradually came to dominate Henriqueta's life. Joaquina would come by their house and after whispering with Henriqueta, Henriqueta would dress and together she and Joaquina would go out "on the street even at night," returning only at ten o'clock as the bells tolled the Ave Maria or sometimes as late as eleven o'clock. Joaquina took Henriqueta, Rufino said, to "dances, diversions" and did so "without asking [his] permission." It was Joaquina, he insisted, who, on finding that he opposed what he described as "outings and debaucheries," persuaded Henriqueta to leave him. And worse, Joaquina encouraged Henriqueta to "live where and how she wished, delivering herself to a dissolute life with the aim, being a beautiful black woman of elegant build, of earning a fortune at the cost of his honor and hers." Faced with such conduct from his wife, he had no choice, he said, but to "reprimand her and give her a piece of advice," warning her that such behavior was "ugly and inappropriate from a woman as *honesta* as she." For nineteenth-century Brazilians, honesta meant honorable or modest. In reprimanding her he sought only to protect her "honor." This account is the closest he came to explaining why he had beaten her. From Rufino we discover what he, a poor black man once a slave, thought a wife's proper behavior should be.

But the story has another twist. Rufino's manly and husbandly honor was challenged, but not by the standard contest in which another man attempted to bed his wife. Rufino might have handled that by direct action—a fist or knife fight with the male interloper and a salutary roughing up of the inconstant wife.[29] But in this case the competitor was a woman, married and apparently somewhat older than Henriqueta and who, in Rufino's understanding, urged Henriqueta to a life apart from her husband. Rufino repeatedly used the word *seduce* to describe Joaquina's hold over Henriqueta. But we would be mistaken to read into the friendship a sexual relationship. In Portuguese *seduction* does not have the English meaning of enticing someone into a sexual liaison, but only the broader sense of leading someone astray or persuading a person to bad or rebellious behavior. And Rufino's hint at Henriqueta's selling herself as a prostitute was a charge he never made explicit, one to which Henriqueta never replied, and which the court ignored. Or perhaps Joaquina's influence was merely prosaic, a domineering temperament. In either case Rufino could not rely on standard forms of male force to deal with her. What is puzzling is that Rufino did not challenge Joaquina's husband to keep his own wife at home, making of the conflict a matter between men, at once more familiar and manageable.

But neither could he ignore behavior that compromised more than Henriqueta's good name as an honesta or honorable woman. Out at night after the church bells rang the curfew to call slaves off the street and decent people home, without her husband and against his wishes, she put not only her own reputation at risk but also his. Through her he was made vulnerable to public humiliation as a man who could not govern his own wife. Feeling compelled to demonstrate male authority over household and wife, but constrained by having to face a female contender, Rufino turned on Henriqueta.

THE PROPERTY CASE

Rufino finished badly. After two days in jail in October 1855 for theft (only months after they were married), he spent another two days in jail in September 1856 for fraud. In November he was again jailed, this time for robbery, and was still prisoner in February 1857 as Henriqueta's case against him proceeded. He thoroughly undercut his own case in the judgment of the court; even his lawyer quit. Rufino allowed the case to run without taking further action. In April 1857 an ecclesiastical court granted Henriqueta a sentence of divorce, by which she could live permanently separated from her husband and was entitled to a legal settlement of half their property.

In one sense property was not and could not have been Henriqueta's motive for seeking a divorce, not because property did not matter for her, but because in the end there was none. In the inventory of their goods, Henriqueta declared that she possessed, besides the "clothes of her use," a gold chain, a bed, a cane-seated sofa, and six chairs, "all very old and in bad condition," which she sold for 144 mil-réis, or the equivalent of about $81. Concern over property did enter into Henriqueta's calculations, however, in the form of money owed. She found it necessary to apply the income from the sale of their goods to her husband's debts, "seeing that he did not pay them and the creditors constantly importuned her for payment." The debts totaled 550 mil-réis, or about $308, a staggering amount for a poor woman in 1858. She lived from her own daily labor, she said, and possessed no goods to divide. Although an order to sequester Rufino's property was made in March 1858, he declared none except the 100 mil-réis he had borrowed at 3 percent monthly interest from another Mina black. By the rules governing common property, debts as much as assets were owned jointly, regardless of which partner contracted them. The settlement of their property made Rufino liable to Henriqueta for half the debts she had already paid, together with court costs. As late as July 1859, when the civil case for a property settlement ended, Henriqueta was still trying to cite Rufino for not complying with the court's ruling. She continued to live on the Rua do Fogo, but had moved to a different house.

On the surface about all Henriqueta gained was an end to further debts and release from a marriage that for her had soured. But I think there was something more. Pitt-Rivers argues that honor or reputation once humiliated can be restored only by direct and usually violent action and never by recourse to law or the courts, for court action merely publicizes the damage without repairing it. For those with name, position, and wealth, perhaps. For an illiterate black woman, born in Africa, who could barely escape her status as slave, the courts offered a persuasive solution. Henriqueta's petition brought together the oral culture of the poor and the written culture of those with a corner on official power. In Henriqueta's experience money was lent on trust and recalled by words spoken person-to-person. Rent receipts, if there were rent receipts, were filled in by a third party, notaries read aloud to a client the contents of a needed legal document, and the illiterate dictated their wills. In order to stop the physical harm Rufino inflicted and restore her good name as a person who earned an honest living and paid her debts—keeping in mind that a good name was her only credit—Henriqueta required some convincing and public way by which to distance herself from her husband. Throughout the nineteenth century suits by the poor notoriously filled the dockets of Rio de Janeiro courts. But who was audience for these thick bundles of paper written in language remote from the everyday vernacular of the street? Who would have known of Henriqueta's success at securing the approving signatures of ecclesiastical judges or the careful assigning of property rights by a civil judge? I suspect the answer is: everybody. Everybody, that is, who was relevant in the exchanges of her life: Joaquina her friend and madrinha, her landlord, and certainly those who made the loans to her husband that she repaid—Guilherme, also a black from Mina, Custódio Gomes, João Luiz Morâes, Antonio José Barreto, and Bendicta Joaquina da Silva, among others. Those who supplied Henriqueta with produce or bought regularly from her would soon hear of her divorce. On the street where not much went unnoticed, her success in the courts would be remarked on and her status as an independent woman who conducted herself honestly and honorably would be noted. If Rufino had been stripped of his "right to pride," Henriqueta had claimed hers.

HONOR AMONG SLAVES

Through Henriqueta's and Rufino's accusations and counteraccusations, their case becomes instructive in the particularities of a slave code of domestic and marital honor. It is necessarily incomplete. There was no mention of sexual fidelity, for example, or loyalty to fellow slaves or freed persons; no mention of physical courage appeared here or concern over the care of children. We do discover, however, what was at issue for one couple. Work, savings, the purchase of freedom, marriage in the church, modesty and obedience to a husband, bodily injury—these were the disputed areas of married life that separated Henriqueta and Rufino. Henriqueta expected to work, save, pay for her own freedom, contribute to their household expenses; she expected the same from her husband. She resented it when the burden of reimbursing Rufino's owner for his wages, buying his freedom, or paying his debts fell to her. If in attempting to file a successful petition before an ecclesiastical court, Henriqueta's lawyer emphasized the physical harm done her, Henriqueta spoke most often and always hotly about money. Money was hard-earned. She wanted something to show for her effort, and instead she thought herself ill-paid for her sacrifices. Rufino wanted a wife who obeyed, one he could govern, not one who compromised both his reputation and hers by unseemly and defiant behavior. Henriqueta refused to believe that she should merely endure the beatings and wounds to her body that Rufino inflicted. She went first to the safety of her friend's house and then to an ecclesiastical court to end a damaging relationship. Such were the rules by which they had expected to live, a code more acknowledged in the breach than in the observance, but a code nevertheless. In broad outline it was derived from the wider culture in which all slaves and the working poor participated and altered to fit their particular circumstances. These were concerns that would have been familiar to others like Henriqueta and Rufino in the managing of their married lives.

NOTES

1. All details are from the two cases, Juizo da 2ª Vara Civel, Divórcio, defendant, Rufino José Maria Baleta, Rio de Janeiro, 1857, Arquivo Nacional, Rio de Janeiro, Seção do Poder Judiciário, maço 877, no. 686 [unnumbered]; and Juizo Municipal da 3ª Vara Civel, Inventário, Rufino José Maria Baleta and Henriqueta Maria da Conceição, Rio de Janeiro, 1858, Arquivo Nacional, Rio de Janeiro, Seção do Poder Judiciário, caixa 300, no. 828.

2. Julian Pitt-Rivers, "Honour and Social Status," in *Honour and Shame: The Values of Mediterranean Society,* ed. J. G. Peristiany (Chicago: University of Chicago Press, 1966), 19–77.

3. Ibid., 21.

4. Ibid., 27.

5. Ibid., 41–43.

6. For useful and suggestive summaries of the qualities of honor, see Maria Pia Di Bella, "Name, Blood, and Miracles: The Claims to Renown in Traditional Sicily," in *Honor and Grace in Anthropology,* ed. J. G. Peristiany and Julian Pitt-Rivers (Cambridge: Cambridge University Press, 1992), 151–65; and Pierre Bourdieu, "The Sentiment of Honour in Kabyle Society," in *Honour and Shame: The Values of Mediterranean Society,* ed. J. G. Peristiany (Chicago: University of Chicago Press, 1966), 191–241.

7. Gene Brucker, Giovanni and Lusanna: Love and Marriage in Renaissance Florence (Berkeley: University of California Press, 1986); Alexandra Parma Cook and Noble David Cook, Good Faith and Truthful Ignorance: A Case of Transatlantic Bigamy (Durham: Duke University Press, 1991). On honor in non-Mediterranean societies, see E. P. Thomp-

son, "The Sale of Wives," and "Rough Music," both in *Customs in Common: Studies in Traditional Popular Culture* (New York: The New Press, 1993), 404–66 and 467–538, respectively; and Bertram Wyatt-Brown, *Southern Honor: Ethics and Behavior in the Old South* (New York: Oxford University Press, 1982).

8. Candido Mendes de Almeida, comp. and ed., *Código Philippino; ou Ordenações e leis do reino de Portugal, recopilados por mandado d'el-rey D. Philippe I. 14 ed. segunda a primeira de 1603 e a nona de Coimbra de 1824. Addicionada com diversas notas* . . . (Rio de Janeiro: Typ. do Instituto Philomathico, 1870), liv. 4, tit. 88, tit. 82, tit. 96, and liv. 5, tit. 21–22. I cite the 1870 edition because Almeida's notes explain or qualify Portuguese law as practiced in Brazil; this edition further includes many of the Portuguese and Brazilian laws that over time gradually modified the 1603 code.

9. *The Civil Code of Brazil [1916]*, trans. Joseph Wheless (St. Louis: Thomas Law Book Co., 1920), Special Part, book 4, tit. 1, art. 1576, and tit. 2, art. 1603.

10. From a vast literature, see Stuart Schwartz, *Sugar and the Formation of Brazilian Society: Bahia, 1550–1835* (Cambridge: Cambridge University Press, 1985); João José Reis, *Slave Rebellion in Brazil: The Muslim Uprising of 1835 in Bahia*, trans. Arthur Brakel (Baltimore: Johns Hopkins University Press, 1993); Stanley Stein, *Vassouras: A Brazilian Coffee County, 1850–1900: The Roles of Planter and Slave in a Plantation Society* (Princeton, NJ: Princeton University Press, 1985; first published 1958); and Mary Karasch, *Slave Life in Rio de Janeiro, 1808–1850* (Princeton, NJ: Princeton University Press, 1987). On slave prostitutes, see Sandra Lauderdale Graham, "Slavery's Impasse: Slave Prostitutes, Small-Time Mistresses, and the Brazilian Law of 1871," *Comparative Studies in Society and History* 33 (4) (October 1991): 669–94.

11. For the complete transcription of the original ecclesiastical case included in the civil court case, see Juizo da 2ª Vara Civel, Divórcio, defendant, Rufino José Maria Baleta, Rio de Janeiro, 1857, Arquivo Nacional, Rio de Janeiro, Seção do Poder Judiciário, maço 877, no. 686 [unnumbered]; for the settlement of their property, see Juizo Municipal da 3ª Vara Civel, Inventário, Rufino José Maria Baleta and Henriqueta Maria da Conceição, Rio de Janeiro, 1858, Arquivo Nacional, Rio de Janeiro, Seção do Poder Judiciário, caixa 300, no. 828.

12. For information on the history of Rio de Janeiro's streets and public squares, the best source remains Noronha Santos, "Anotações de Noronha Santos a Introdução das 'Memórias,'" in Luiz Gonçalves dos Santos (Padre Perereca), *Memórias para servir à história do Reino do Brasil* (Belo Horizonte: Editora Itatiaia, 1981; first published 1825) 1:66–165, and for Santa Rita, 135–36; Rellação Nominal das Cazas de Negocios da Freguesia de Santa Rita pertencente a o anno de 1841, Arquivo da Cidade do Rio de Janeiro, "Estatística da Freguesia de Santa Rita," Codice 43–1-42 [n.p.].

13. Noronha Santos, "Anotações," 101.

14. Mappa no. 12, "Relação dos cortiços existentes na Côrte, com designação de seu numero e população, por sexos, estados, nacionalidades e profissões," in Relatório do Chefe de Policia da Côrte, Annexo D, Brazil, Ministério da Justiça, *Relatório . . .[1856]* (Rio de Janeiro: Typ. Nacional, 1857) [n.p.].

15. During the nineteenth century, the Brazilian unit of currency was the *mil-réis*, or one thousand réis, written 1$000. The smaller unit was réis. The larger unit was the *conto*, equal to one thousand mil-réis and written 1:000$000. The average equivalent of the mil-réis in United States dollars during the 1850s was $0.56—that is, 1 mil-réis was worth $0.56.

16. Rellação Nominal . . . 1841, "Estatística da Freguesia de Santa Rita," Arquivo Geral da Cidade do Rio de Janeiro, Códice 43–1-42 [n.p.].

17. Ibid.

18. "Relação dos cortiços," in *Relatório . . . [1856]* [n.p.].

19. The best history of capoeiras is Thomas H. Holloway, "'A Healthy Terror': Police Repression of *Capoeiras* in Nineteenth-Century Rio de Janeiro," *Hispanic American Historical Review* 69 (4) (November 1989): 637–76. For contemporary accounts, see Alexandre José Melo Morais Filho, *Festas e tradições populares do Brasil*, 3d ed., rev. and notes by Luis da Camara Cascudo (Rio de Janeiro: F. Briguiet & Cia., 1946; first published 1888), 443–55; and A. P. D. G., *Sketches of Portuguese Life, Manners, Costume, and Character* (London: George B. Whittaker, 1828), 304–6.

20. "Relação dos cortiços," in *Relatório . . . [1856]* [n.p.]; "Mappa demonstrativo da população da Cidade do Rio de Janeiro no anno de 1856," in *Relatório do Chefe de Policia da Côrte, Annexo D, Brazil, Ministério da Justiça, . . .[1856]* (Rio de Janeiro: Typ. Nacional, 1857) [n.p.].

21. Brazil, Directoria Geral de Estatística, *Relatório apresentado ao Ministro e Secretário d'Estado dos Negocios o Imperio pela Commissão encarregada da direcçao dos trabalhos do arrolamento da população do Municipio da Côrte a que se procedeu em abril de 1870* (Rio de Janeiro: Typ. Perseverança, 1871), mappas A–K [n.p.].

22. *Recenseamento do Rio de Janeiro, 1849*, 4° mapa, Santa Rita, and 9° mapa, Freguesias da Cidade. I am profoundly grateful to Thomas Holloway for so generously sharing with me his copied version of the original 1849 census, which he located in 1988 at the Arquivo Nacional, Rio de Janeiro, GIFI [uncatalogued manuscript collection] 5B 447.

23. Brazil, Directoria Geral de Estatística, *Recenseamento da população do Imperio do Brazil a que se procedeu no dia 10 de agosto de 1872* (Rio de Janeiro: Typ. Leuzinger & Filhos, 1873–1876), Muncipio Neutro, Parochia de Santa Rita, 10–12.

24. Karash, *Slave Life*, 290. Parish registers cannot tell us about all those women and men who, although not married in the church, nonetheless lived as conventionally married couples; we must discover them through other sources, such as household census lists, wills, and property inventories.

25. See entry for *sevícias* in *Diccionario da Lingua Portugueza*, comp. Antonio de Moraes Silva, 8th rev. ed. (Rio de Janeiro: Empreza Litteraria Fluminense, 1891), and in *Diccionario da Lingua Portugueza*, comp. Rafael Bluteau and rev. Antonio de Moraes Silva (Lisboa: Simão Thaddeo Ferreira, 1789).

26. On the jail, see Noronha Santos, "Anotações," 96; and Thomas H. Holloway, *Policing Rio de Janeiro: Repression and Resistance in a Nineteenth-Century City* (Stanford, CA: Stanford University Press, 1993), 56–57.

27. On slaves and their understandings of freedom, see Sidney Chalhoub, *Visões da*

Liberdade: Uma história das últimas décadas da escravidão na Corte (São Paulo: Companhia das Letras, 1990); and Hebe Maria Mattos de Castro, *Das cores do silêncio: Os significados da liberdade no sudeste escravista, Brasil século XIX* (Rio de Janeiro: Arquivo Nacional, 1995).

28. João José Reis, "'The Revolution of the *Ganhadores*': Urban Labor, Ethnicity and the African Strike of 1857 in Bahia, Brazil," *Journal of Latin American Studies* 29(2) (May 1997): 355–93, examines the political organization and actions of such streets workers—slaves, freed and free blacks—who mounted a strike in protest against a proposed licensing fee in Bahia.

29. Relying on criminal case records, Sidney Chalhoub examines the challenges and responses to male honor among the poor in Rio de Janeiro in the early years of the twentieth century, *Trabalho, lar e botequim: O cotidiano dos trabalhadores no Rio de Janeiro da Belle Époque* (São Paulo: Brasiliense, 1986).

GLOSSARY

alcalde—district magistrate

audiencia—high court at the level of the colony, also a governing body; usually composed of a president and four judges (*oidores*)

cacica/cacique—hereditary leader among the indigenous population

cathedral canon—clergyman who is part of a group with duties in a cathedral

casta(s)—various people of mixed racial heritage in colonial Latin America; see *régimen de castas*

cédula—order, usually issued by the king

comedias—plays

corregidor—royal district governor

criollo (creole)—person of Spanish descent born in the Americas

desembargo do paço—Portuguese royal high court

encomienda—grant of labor initially awarded to the participants of the wars of conquest in the sixteenth century

encomendero—person who received and administered an *encomienda*; allowed to collect tribute from the indigenous population under his jurisdiction as well as to use their labor

escribano—scribe or public notary

fuero—corporate legal rights and privileges; in many cases included an exemption from prosecution in certain courts

gañan jornal—permanent worker resident on an *hacienda*

gente decente—respectable people

gracias al sacar—petition to the king to cancel or make invalid a dishonoring condition such as illegitimacy or mixed racial background

hacienda—colonial estate

hidalguía—nobility, either the quality or the group

hidalgos—Spanish nobles

justicia mayor—official to whom royal judicial authority was delegated

ladeiras—steep slopes or streets that connected lower and upper parts of a city

limpieza de oficios—absence of any ancestors who had engaged in professions or trade considered dishonorable

limpieza de sangre—quality of having no "impure" blood, that is, Jewish or Muslim ancestors; in the Americas, also included lack of any relatives of other races than Caucasian; also a legal proceeding that proved this quality

mestizo—in common usage a person of mixed heritage, usually Indian/Spanish

ministro de vara—official who carried a staff of office

moreno—usual Spanish word for person of dark skin, usually of African heritage

pardo—of mixed race, with African ancestry in both Spanish-American and Brazilian usage.

pecheros—commoners, plebeians

pulpería—general store and tavern

obraje—workshop, usually for textiles

régimen de castas—system of racial ranking

repartimiento—forced labor draft

subdelegado—local official who in the eighteenth century replaced the *corregidor* and *alcalde mayor*

vigário geral do bispado—vicar general of the diocese, priest who acted as the bishop's deputy in the administration of the diocese

visita general—general inspection of government or church practices, undertaken in a particular jurisdiction to examine or evaluate the performance of secular or religious officials

INDEX

stratification, 122; superiority and class position, 179–80, 181; use of word *honor*, 128, 148

Social discrimination, 14

Social mobility, 14, 37, 94; *gracias al sacar*, 37; membership in noble orders, 27

Social ostracism, 90

Social position/place, 13–14, 187

Sodomy, 45–64; male and female roles, 54; nature of crime, 45, 47; significance, 62

Spain: compared to New World, 18; cult of pure lineage, 155; honor in, 19–20; honors, 33; *limpieza de sangre*, 74, 75; manual labor, 41; municipal councils, 31–32; noble lifestyle, 22; nobles, 19, 24; sale of noble titles, 24; stereotypes in literature, 71; titles of nobility, 27–28; universities, 37, 74; Vizcaya, 24

Spousal abuse, 163–64

Spurious offspring, 118

Status, 71–72; honor and rank, 202–3; women, 186–87

Street vendors, 218 *fig.*

Subterfuges, 119–22

Sumptuary legislation, 22

Sword fights, 34

Thompson, E.P., 165

Titles of nobility, 27–28

Titles and prebends, 4–5

Tradition, 69

Transmission of honor, 81

Transport, 104

Tribute, 23, 165

United States, 14–15

Universities, 29; entrance requirements, 40, 74, 88, 155; New Christians in Spain, 20; professors, 33; social advancement, 37, 38

Urban populations, hierarchy, 29

Value systems, researching, 2

Vega, Lope de, 153, 154

Venezuela, 26, 34, 91

Verbal violence, 12

"Vile" occupations, 4, 32, 33

Violence: among women, 182, 185–87, 192; by women over honor, 181; masculine, U.S. South, 15; nature of plebeian, 148; and sexual assault, 146–47; slavery and, 143

Violence against women: Brazil, 106–7, 216; Buenos Aires, 145–46; Indians, 187–89, 190–91; Mexico, 163–64; plebeian, 145–47; *sevícias*, 106–7, 216; spousal abuse, 163–64

Virginity, 82–83, 179, 194–95

Virtue, 3, 71, 195–96

Widows, 116, 120, 179

Witnesses, 57–58, 61

Women, 12; Brazilian honor system, 104; as defenders of honor, 180–81; dishonoring conduct, 4; free blacks, 214; *honra* and, 4; Indian, 187–89, 190–91; marital choices, 90–91; market sellers, 188, 189 *fig.*, 190; Native American, 164–75; occupations in Brazil, 214; ostracism, 90; physical danger, 106–7; plebeian, 130, 145, 160 *fig.*; public shaming or humiliation, 145–46; rancho, 170; role in elite culture, 204; sexual fidelity, 145; slaves, 161–64; stereotypes in literature, 71. *See also* Violence against women

Women, elite: constructions of honor, 96; dress, 92 *fig.*; opportunity for insult, 82 *fig.*; physical attack by, 185–86; public roles, 80–81

Work, 217, 219

Working class, 149

Worth, concept of, 156, 161

CONTRIBUTORS

RICHARD BOYER, chair and professor of history at Simon Fraser University, earned his Ph.D. at the University of Connecticut. He is the author of *La gran inundación: Vida y sociedad en la ciudad de México, 1629–1639* (Mexico City: Secretaría de Educación Pública, 1975) and *Lives of the Bigamists: Marriage, Family, and Community in Colonial Mexico* (Albuquerque: University of New Mexico Press, 1995), as well as many articles. He coedited (with Keith Davies) *Urbanization in Nineteenth-Century Latin America: Statistics and Sources* (Los Angeles: UCLA Latin American Center, 1973).

MARK BURKHOLDER, professor of history at the University of Missouri–St. Louis, received his doctorate from Duke University. He co-authored (with D. S. Chandler) *From Impotence to Authority: The Spanish Crown and the American Audiencias, 1687–1808* (Columbia: University of Missouri Press, 1977) and *Biographical Dictionary of Councilors of the Indies, 1717–1808* (Westport, CT: Greenwood Press, 1986) and (with Lyman Johnson) *Colonial Latin America* (Oxford: Oxford University Press, 3d ed., 1998). He is the author of *Politics of a Colonial Career: José de Baquíjano and the Audiencia of Lima* (Albuquerque: University of New Mexico Press, 1980), as well as many articles.

SANDRA LAUDERDALE GRAHAM, professor of history at the University of Texas at Austin, did her doctoral work at the University of Texas at Austin. She is the author of *House and Street: The Domestic World of Servants and Masters in Nineteenth-Century Rio de Janeiro* (Austin: University of Texas Press, 1992). She is working on a manuscript entitled *When Family Failed: Gender and Culture in Nineteenth-Century Brazil* and a book of slave stories from nineteenth-century Brazil.

LYMAN JOHNSON, professor of history at the University of North Carolina–Charlotte, received his doctorate from the University of Connecticut. He is the author of *The Political*

Economy of Spanish America in the Age of Revolution, 1750–1850 (Albuquerque: University of New Mexico Press, 1994) and the co-author (with Mark Burkholder) of *Colonial Latin America* (Oxford: Oxford University Press, 3d ed., 1998). He edited *The Problem of Order in Changing Societies: Essays on Crime and Policing in Argentina and Uruguay* (Albuquerque: University of New Mexico Press, 1990) and *Essays on the Price History of Eighteenth-Century Latin America* (Albuquerque: University of New Mexico Press, 1990).

SONYA LIPSETT-RIVERA, associate professor of history at Carleton University, received her Ph.D. at Tulane University. She is the author of many articles on water rights in colonial Puebla and won the Tibesar award for "Indigenous Communities and Water Rights in Colonial Puebla: Patterns of Resistance," *The Americas* (1992). She is also the author of *To Defend Our Water: The Struggle for Resources in Colonial Puebla* (forthcoming).

MURIEL NAZZARI, retired professor of history at Indiana University, earned her doctorate at Yale University. She is the author of *Disappearance of the Dowry: Women, Families and Social Change in São Paulo, 1600–1900* (Stanford, CA: Stanford University Press, 1991) and many articles.

GEOFFREY SPURLING, assistant professor of Latin American Studies at Simon Fraser University, received his doctorate from Cornell University. He is the coeditor (with Richard Boyer) of *Colonial Lives: Documents on Latin American History, 1550–1850* (Oxford: Oxford University Press, forthcoming).

ANN TWINAM, professor of history at the University of Cincinnati, earned her Ph.D. at Yale University. She is the author of *Miners, Merchants, and Farmers in Colonial Colombia* (Austin: University of Texas Press, 1982) and *Public Lives, Private Secrets: Gender, Honor, Sexuality, and Illegitimacy in Colonial Spanish America* (Stanford, CA: Stanford University Press, forthcoming) as well as many articles.